David Waite is a Master's degree qualified Senior counsellor and supervisor serving adults, children, couples and families in private practice. He is experienced with cancer patients and with those on the margins of society. He found his vocation after a very practical career in professional design and project engineering. He brought his flair for innovation and problem-solving into a sector which has suffered from stagnation for far too long and consequently underperforms. His unique approach to psychological issues has been derived from doing what a counsellor does best - listening. His work has been published in professional journals. His area mental health provider refers patients into his public meditation programmes. He supports rehabilitation programmes in prisons. He campaigns for the reform of counselling practice.

I hope you enjoy this book immensely Mary.

David Waite

David Waite

So Now I Get It

Circle Diagram

Perfect Core   Conscious

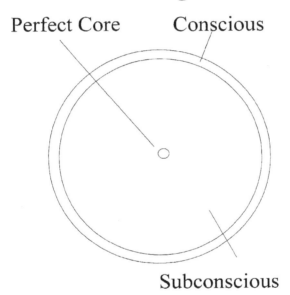

Subconscious

**The Miracle of
Soul-Centred Counselling**

Table of Contents

This Book Is for You

I am sure you will enjoy this book. There is something in it for everyone. It touches all aspects of life, but most importantly, those which trouble you and me, your children and the guy down the street. It's a refreshingly new way of looking at how we think and feel and work - and how others tick too. I call it 'So Now I Get It' because that is what my clients say. The subtitle is 'The Miracle of Soul-Centred Counselling'. I need to explain that. It's not actually the method that is the miracle. The miracle is the healing process that resides in all of us. The method just helps you find that healing for yourself.

I have written the book sequentially. The logic builds up on itself as it progresses. If you tend to sample read, you may get a bit lost at first. I start off with the basics. And why not? I hope you will agree that the ideas I offer just make simple sense. Psychology just has not grasped some of them yet, not least because its foundations are the beliefs of yesteryear. I use a very simple diagram which develops throughout the book. That is how I work with my clients. They say a picture is worth a thousand words. I can get a lot of meaning into quite a small space this way.

I express frustration with a mental health world which struggles to explain the basics. I came from a profession which defined things to three decimal places and then we all knew what we were talking about and could progress our understanding systemically.

In the absence of this level of precision, I have decided to define the psychological features I deal with, at least for myself, but more importantly for my clients. If you disagree with my definitions, at least we can have a debate and discuss how to find better ones. We have then made a start in creating a real profession with a sound vocabulary which will enable us all to build on each other's knowledge effectively and confidently.

I start this process here with trauma. Its understanding is crucial to our well-being because it drives our sicknesses. I describe the healing systems we generally use. I home in on one in particular, meditation. It is an acceptance of the concept of spirituality which opens up this most powerful healing process. Conventional psychology is only just coming to grasp this in the form of something it calls mindfulness - another somewhat imprecise term. In contrast, I offer a very precise meditation method and direct you to a video so you can try it yourself.

I look at how things can go wrong. I avoid all the various psychological behavioural listings apart from the autistic spectrum which I found I needed to readdress in order to help my clients safely. I investigate a feature which I call dysempathy. That approach has enabled me to understand the more challenging elements of human behaviour. I spend some time on this topic as it is so little understood.

Some readers may find the less pleasant features difficult to address. Non-professionals who have never been subject to abuse may find the latter part of the book less relevant. However, talking therapy professionals like their medical counterparts, will need to get to grips with the ground rules operating in pathological concepts. By pathology, I mean anything which afflicts an individual.

If you are on the autistic spectrum yourself, you may find some of the concepts challenging. I would encourage you to persist, as you will get something out of the narrative. So many of my clients have been immensely grateful for the ideas I have offered in this area. They have suddenly seen their partner or child or boss in a completely new and very clear light. It is so empowering for them.

Finally, I apply the pathology concept to the bigger picture and find that if we could work out who the bad guys were before we gave them a wedding ring or our vote, we could stop them before they became uncontrollable and gave us a whole load of trouble.

All professionals need to continue to develop their expertise through life and address old methods which are not so successful. I know the Soul-Centred Counselling method is effective. I invite practitioners to consider it and clients to seek it. That way, it may eventually become available to everyone. I hope that both trainees and qualified counsellors and psychotherapists will embrace this learning: and the psychologists and psychiatrists too.

Section 1
My Journey

1: Where This All Started

I am a counsellor and I have a single objective in my life - to enjoy it. That might just qualify me to help you enjoy yours. What I do works for the clients I see in my practice, so it could also work for you through the written word. Let's see!

So how is it that a selfish pursuit of my own enjoyment can help you? The answer is simple. I get a kick out of seeing people get healthier and happier, most especially if I have been the instrument of their recovery.

I came into counselling by an unusual route, so I have an unusual approach to it. By the time I got into formal training, I had been using my own life experience to develop methods of helping others. Or so I thought. I came to realise that in reality, it was they who were teaching me.

Nevertheless, I felt I needed to take some formal training to ensure my methods were sound and also to give myself a recognised pedigree in the profession. I was disappointed to discover that the particular formal training I took was below the level I had been working at.

It lacked substance, seeming to be politically correct to the point of becoming its own religion, more concerned with avoiding criticism from the few than attending to the needs of the many. It refused to either face the negative power of obvious pathologies or embrace the positive power of a simple spirituality. It was reluctant to consider that a client's ills may be caused by others. I took the view that if I could not concur with what I was being taught, I could not offer that to my clients. I persevered regardless and achieved the required institutional success, but have continued to develop my own methods since.

This book is about what I have learnt in the journeys my clients have taken me on. What I have developed works for them whether they are young or old, suicidal or just upset with life. I practice in the community and not in a hospital or secure setting, but my client base includes some horrendous abuse and even torture. Many have been in the British National Health Service (NHS) system which has often failed to resolve their issues. My methods work best with those who choose to come for help, but can also help the reluctant but reflective client.

In 2017, BMC Psychiatry published a report on counsellor performance using the NHS's Improving Access to Psychological Therapies (IAPT) scheme data. The research was commissioned to discover if the counselling profession delivered results at least as good as the NHS's favoured method, Cognitive Behavioural Therapy (CBT).[1]

It discovered that each was as bad as the other, stating 'It is of concern that half of all patients, regardless of the type of intervention, did not show reliable improvement.' That's the toss of a coin. A previous study in 2014 had found that 5% were actually damaged by the process.[2] And it did not end there. A meta-study in 2008 had already shown that the 'advantages of counselling in the short term were not sustained over a longer time period'.[3]

More recent research published in the Lancet in 2021 was similarly disappointing. PRaCTICED sought again to compare CBT with Person-Centred counselling within the NHS's IAPT scheme.[4] It chose the NHS 'Counselling for Depression' method, describing it as Person-Centred Experiential Therapy (PCET).

The ratio of incoming and outgoing client scores using a nationally recognised CORE system indicated around a 30% improvement in client condition for both methods at 6 months from the start. Therapy durations ranged from 4 to 20 sessions. One of the 508 participants took their own life in that time. I would not regard this outcome as effective.

The process I use reduces CORE scores by a factor of 2.5 on average for adults, with some results for longer therapy being much higher. This represents a 150% improvement. I have had no suicides, although one client returned some years after therapy to thank me for saving his life. I regard that as effective. I will continue to use my own system. It is not prescriptive. It seeks to use any method or information which is likely to help my clients, provided it is ethical and is based on person-centred principles.

Another trial called ETHOS sought to assess the effectiveness of adding counselling to pastoral care in schools using a method it described as School-based Humanistic Counselling (SBHC), which appears to be a basic method. [5] The ratio of incoming and outgoing scores indicated around a 27% improvement in the combined intervention. Even though those at risk of serious harm to self or others were excluded from the study, five of the 329 subjects attempted drug overdoses, three of whom were hospitalised.

I would not regard this outcome as effective either. The process I use reduces the CORE score by a factor of 4.5 on average for young people. This represents a 350% improvement. I know of only one serious incident and that occurred 4 years after my work had ended.

Anecdotal experience in other spheres indicated an overall malaise in therapy. I maintain that talking about the experiences and the emotions which trouble us is essential and fundamental to resolving them and living a healthy life.

In the light of this research, I decided to write this book to tell you about my methods. I owe the very best I can find to help my distressed clients. I see adults, couples and young people on their own or in family groups. What I do works because it is simple. Everyone can understand it because it's designed that way. It is very rare that clients do not appreciate the therapy I offer. Indeed, it is unusual that any individual session does not yield some benefit for them. They pay me for it, so they need to get something from it.

My challenge now is to convey what I give to my clients to both professionals who want to improve the success of mental health care from statistical chance to reliable provision and to laypeople so they can understand themselves and their problems better. I want you, my reader, to enjoy your life more. That is my objective in my counselling work and my objective in this book too.

I have spent most of my life unravelling who I am. I found that the attempts others have made in all sorts of ways - religion, philosophy, psychology, etc - have done as much to mislead as to inform. I needed to understand how I functioned so I could, at least, manage the 'me' inside. So this book is not an academic treatise. It is the result of a lifetime's untangling of my own soul, distilled into a psychological theory and developed in the context of the myriad of my clients' personalities and the issues they have faced.

My professional background is in design. I was given objectives to meet. I designed solutions and then made plans to achieve them. In the same way as I approached my work projects, I see my clients as projects too, albeit very human and often very vulnerable ones. They have a problem. They have come to me for help in resolving that problem. I don't know how we will achieve that or when they will arrive there, but I will employ any and every process I know to help them get to their goal. And we find that the solution is inside them, just waiting to be discovered.

So this book is not so much about new information as about a new way of looking at the information we already have. It is my method which is novel.

Section 2
Basic and Absolutes

2: What Doesn't Change

I start with some basic principles about how we function as human beings. Firstly, none of us even chose to exist. That was the decision (or accident) of our biological parents, regardless of whether they became our carers or not. Whether our conceptions and births were good for them or for us is not too relevant now. Regardless of any of their history, they committed us to lifetime sentences on Planet Earth. We are now here till we die and have to manage our existences in that time as best we can, however long that may be. There will be joys and there will be sorrows. The aim is to maximise the joys.

Just as the decision of my existence was not mine, my physical body is not mine either. It was the result of a random combination of the DNA of my parents. I just have to take care of it if I want to enjoy my life's journey. Interestingly, my mind is not mine either. At the point of birth, I carried sufficient information to survive as a baby of a caring mother; suckling, crying to tell my carer I needed something, along with the multitude of bodily functions we take for granted; breathing, blood circulation, digestion, responding to senses, etc.

By the time I was born, I might even have acquired a taste for music from the safety of the womb if that had been present in the house. I describe all this initial programming as firmware like the basic setup in my computer when I buy it. Part of that firmware is a programme to learn from our environment too and to develop our software throughout our lives. This faculty is bigger in humans than in any other living being.

Learning is very fast in our early years. A baby does not look like it's doing much mentally, but it is starting from a low information base in comparison to the complex society it is entering. It is far less able at this point than any other species. It learns from what is around it. I speak English because those I saw every day did that. There was no concept of any other language. I learnt to smile by watching and copying my carers. That was not a deliberate decision. My firmware programmed me to do that.

I learnt mannerisms from those I saw around me. How else would I learn? What else would I learn? So the dataset of my being is my basic birth firmware plus the software I subsequently absorbed from others in my growing world. I have spent the rest of my life soaking up information from my physical and emotional environment. In a healthy life, that never stops.

Because early years learning forms the child's mind, and that is the foundation of the adult mind, everything we ever do will be very much defined by that initial information base. What we learn subsequently will be formed on those basic building blocks. We can't take in everything that we see, hear, feel, taste and smell, so we filter out lots of what we sense as less important information. The filters we use are the ones we have subconsciously learnt in childhood, as if by osmosis.

So, not only is our accumulated information defined by what we experience in childhood, the selection and therefore direction of our later and more independent learning is predetermined by that too. If racial prejudice was a part of the family script we grew up with, we will express such sentiments unless and until we learn differently from a wider experience. If caring for others was in the script, we will do that in life until we get hurt in the process.

So, the content of the mind is not only formed by the information we are exposed to but is subsequently tailored by the filters we have involuntarily absorbed. It focuses on the topics which were in the air in our early lives. Not much free will here, it seems.

The amount of joy in my life will be very much determined by others, especially those influencing me in my earliest months and years. If the foundation of everything I am and know tells me I am safe and secure and all my needs will be met, then I can always find in the base of my being a place of security in the hard times. It is a memory with a good feeling inside. I am not chasing the basics all the time. I can spend time on higher and more enjoyable things.

That memory and the confidence of ultimate security will serve me until I come out of the hard times. It will encourage and enable me to face life's challenges without being overwhelmed because I know I will get to a peaceful place again. I know that because, deep down in me, right at the beginning, that is what happened and that is what my foundations are made of. It is what I generally feel as I go to sleep at night.

If, however, I did not feel secure in my early weeks, months and years, then the fear that engendered will always be lurking in my subconsciousness. When a new fear arises, it will tap into that basic insecurity and can take over my thought processes. Again, that feeling is the default for when I go to sleep at night or wake up in the morning. Those baby and infant experiences massively determined my security and my demeanour in adult life and how difficult it is for me.

While memory recall only goes back to around three years old, the memories themselves are actually being laid even in utero.

When a young teenager arrived with Obsessive Compulsive Disorder (OCD) issues and the family gave all the indications of love and care, I enquired further. I was told he was born very prematurely and needed resuscitation at one point. We treat these neonatal events as medical issues and all are relieved when they end well, but this little human being actually died for a while and that memory will be in there somewhere, so survival was not the end of that event.

That aspect was understandably overlooked by the parents. It is recognised that OCD is anxiety driven and death ranks high in the fear stakes. I have no way of knowing if it had any relevance to his current condition, but at least there was now a possible cause. That idea engendered some sympathy for him when times got a bit fraught, so this was not so much a teenager being deliberately disruptive, but a young person with an emotional legacy in need of some attention.

A more obvious source of distress is in the adult whose life is turbulent and who reports routine sexual abuse in their childhood years. Psychologists have now formulated such potentially traumatic incidents as Adverse Childhood Experiences (ACE) to enable us to find perspectives on the various types of stresses children incur.

British people woke up to the concept of sexual deviation with the Jimmy Savile case and it's been heartening to see how the now international Me Too movement has challenged that abuse for adults. Violation of a child's personal security leaves lifelong damage which all too frequently leads the victim to make poor decisions in the choice of sexual partners and in managing subsequent relationships. The abuser's actions cast a shadow over the victim's entire life.

It is easy to see that there are ways to bring up a child which can augment it and there are ways which will diminish it, although it can be a little harder to differentiate these in practice sometimes. Regrettably, child-rearing is a skill which few people are trained in.

This is a major issue because everything anyone does and feels is massively influenced by the quality of their upbringing. I resist using the words 'right' and 'wrong' to describe how children are treated because they can become moral judgements which can be mutated to suit the powerful rather than the vulnerable, and this topic is nothing if not about the vulnerable. Everyone 'knows' what right and wrong is - when it suits them. That does not necessarily ask the relevant question.

I prefer to say that a child is augmented if the parent respects it, cares for it and seeks to support its development. A child is diminished if the parent neglects it or abuses it sexually, emotionally or in any other way. The line between occasional parental lapses and outright abuse can be more difficult to draw, but those concepts of augmenting or diminishing will provide simple guidelines.

Similarly, there are ways to treat a partner which either augments them or diminishes them. Relationships can never be equal across all aspects of life, so each has to respect the other at all times. Beating a partner routinely clearly diminishes them. The occasional flaring up of anger is different if it is managed and controlled between partners. None of us is perfect.

As a counsellor, I am normally focussing on one person, my client. The world suddenly becomes a lot easier. I ask what is good for them and what is bad for them; what will augment their life and what will diminish it; what will bring them peace and what will bring them fear.

I don't need to ask what is the right thing for anyone else in their world because that can be far too complicated. I just need to help this one person right now. If they can identify what actually augments or diminishes them, as opposed to what others might be telling them, they can pursue their true needs and their relationships with others will become clearer. If they cannot, their relationships will remain confused and that will be to no-one's genuine advantage. My job is to help them discover their true needs. That will never be to the ultimate detriment of others.

If a person is truly augmented, then those around them can be too. They will be more self-sufficient and able to offer help to others. If a person is truly diminished, they will be less self-sufficient and more needy and therefore want to take from others. We all know people who make net contributions to society. We know those who are a drain on our society too. We try and put some of these into prisons, although there are many more who do lots of harm without ever infringing statutes. Both of these types are down the street and at the school. They are managing companies and countries too.

On the individual level, I see that when one person succumbs to any form of addiction, their whole family seems to deteriorate. They have diminished their family members. I also find that well-delivered authentic meditation always enhances life. I observe that when one of my clients starts to meditate, very often the mood in their whole family seems to improve. My client has augmented their family members.

There is clarity to be had in the idea of augmenting or diminishing others when the words right and wrong might be contestable. Some religions still promote life views which may have made sense back in the culture of the time, but which now actually diminish adherents and those connected to them. Attitudes towards gay communities are a prime example. We have to be mature about the beliefs which have been imposed on followers, recognise errors in them and make honest progress. We must be clear in ourselves in absolute terms about what augments and what diminishes our lives and the lives of those we influence.

A historical example of an aberrant view is the seemingly tacit acceptance that the reputed Roman propensity for child sexual molestation. That would have massively diminished children then just as it would today. It would also have diminished the molesters. It always does. Our species has not changed so much. It is not acceptable and that sort of behaviour should never be allowed to continue by our silence, but all too often does.

Immigration can present moral challenges too. Hand in hand with religions and traditions comes diversity. In our well-meaning desire to welcome people from other cultures into ours, we can be led into a blind and valueless political correctness by which we may accept attitudes and activities which diminish not only us but the immigrants too. It is not acceptable to declare that 'they have always done this'. We are not differentiating well between flavour and poison.

For instance, Female Genital Mutilation (FGM) always diminishes, no matter how long a culture has been doing it. The Rochdale scandal, in which a group of men routinely sexually abused vulnerable girls, was ignored for over a decade because none of the authorities involved could face the consequences of convicting the aggressors who were largely from a particular ethnic community. They feared being accused of prejudice against a religion with which these men were seen to be associated.

Treating women as inferior at any time diminishes them and is not acceptable, just as our treating Africans as slaves for over two centuries was not either. A different order of magnitude, but still unacceptable. Yet outright misogyny is very much alive and accepted in many cultures today. Societies seem reluctant to address the absolutes these examples demonstrate and continue to allow violations of the rights of their constituent human beings.

I recall being told about diversity in my training, but not a lot about the absolutes of augmenting or diminishing. The result can be an attitude of bland acceptance of principles by rote which fails when faced with deviant and destructive behaviour. It is important in counselling to have a clear idea of these absolutes, not to instruct or even direct a client, but to have these concepts available in their quest for truth and peace.

We may think that we are very different from each other, but we are all basically animals with animal emotions. Humans share a lot more similarities than differences, so there are absolutes to be found and applied. Acquiescence to domestic violence or addictions, for instance, never augments any clients or indeed those dependent on them in any way.

In his 1987 book, *Motivation and Personality*, Abraham Maslow helped us understand the concept of human absolutes in his Hierarchy of Needs. He described physical and emotional human requirements. They were not optional 'nice to haves'. They were essential to healthy upbringing and healthy living, so deprivation of these would diminish us. Ascent in his hierarchy is augmenting. Being forced into descent is diminishing.

Couples counselling often brings the issue of absolutes into sharp focus. There is frequently abuse, usually significantly more from one side than the other. The counselling challenge is how to address such diminishing behaviour without destroying the therapy process. Dictating values to clients is probably the fastest way to lose them. Then I can do nothing. I have to respect where my clients are and just give them the opportunity to find behaviour that augments and to avoid behaviour that diminishes. Adopting compromises can easily result in behaviour which is half diminishing, which is after all, diminishing and therefore not acceptable.

However, I may have to accept that if they never get to a place which I think would be best for them, that cannot become an issue for me. Providing they are not harming someone vulnerable about which I can actually do something, this is their journey and I will do my best to be with them. I will support them as best as I can towards their own fulfilment in life within the limits they set me.

3: Hardware and Software

I find it useful to liken myself and indeed my clients to a computer. They don't normally mind! It has hardware; the case and the circuit boards, etc. It also has software. This is what I can see on the monitor when it's live, but I cannot touch these images. I can only see them. They are real in terms of information but not in any physical form. I can act on the data it delivers to me, so its impact can be as real in my life as anything physical. I can select and buy a book on my computer or find out where Timbuktu is, but I still can't physically take anything out of my screen and walk away with it.

As a human being, I too have hardware and software. The hardware is my material body, which I might take to my doctor if it's giving me problems. The software is what I think and feel, along with quite a lot more going on beneath my awareness. I should equally be able to take my emotional software to a therapist to help me resolve my mental programme problems. Information is an imperative of life, not an add-on. If my eyes tell me I am about to crash my car into a brick wall, my existence suddenly depends on my processing this information properly. That's real.

When I think of someone, I recall their personality, their software. Their physical body is their hardware. For me, and my profession in particular, their appearance is not much more than a means of identifying them, a memory flag. I used to see myself as a body with a mind in it, but now I prefer to regard myself primarily as a software entity supported by some biological hardware.

What matters to me is how I am experiencing my world today. When asked, "How are you today?" I want to be able to answer honestly, "I am very well, thank you." That is all I care about. It is all I ever want. However complex my life problems are and whatever my hardware looks like, this is a software question. It's about how I feel.

I am aware of most of the major organs in my body and their whereabouts. I am far from an expert in this. The only bit I normally see is my skin, but that is such a small part of my whole physical being. The really clever bits are all the organs underneath, the exact functioning of which I will never understand. For the most part, providing that I treat my body well enough and I am blessed with good health, this phenomenally complex organism ticks along just nicely. I don't have to know very much about it.

The mind is similar. It has a conscious thinking bit, whereby I am aware of what is going on around me and what I am doing, but the vast majority of my software is underneath the surface, doing its own thing. It is the engine management system, silently keeping all my mental and bodily functions running smoothly. We are now recognising it to be massively complex.

When I switch my computer on at home, it takes a few minutes to warm up. I don't know what is going on in there. I am not a computer expert. In actual fact, it is far too complex for any one person to fully understand everything in detail. It has been developed by so many minds over many years.

I too have evolved over time, I am not the result of a one-off design project. The time it takes for my computer to start up is a clue to the fact that there is far more going on behind the scenes than we observe. We just take it for granted. I might 'Google' a query. I am presented with numerous pages of data with a flag telling me that it accessed a million sources in 1.5 seconds. It has been around the world and back, peering into a whole host of other computers in that brief period of time. It's very hard for us to contemplate the enormity of that power, yet there it is.

Then we are told that our brains are even smarter than that. I know mine does not feel that way, but then I don't know what is going on underneath, other than it is quietly running a highly complex organism, my body, for the most part very efficiently. In the same way that my computer warming up gave me an insight into the enormity of its hidden operations, the ability of my own human software to manage my multifarious bodily functions gives some indication of the intricacy of the operations constantly being performed subconsciously.

Anyone who has intimate knowledge of how dementia reduces these functions will testify to the complexity they never realised was there in the fully functioning person they once knew.

4: My Soul

So who are 'we' really, other than a bit of clever software carried around in a highly complex organism? Do we need to study psychology to find out? And would that tell us? I once asked a practising Doctor of Psychology what the word 'psychology' meant. She quoted a dictionary definition: 'The study of mind and behaviour.'

I accepted that the concept of study was adequately expressed in the Greek word 'logos', but the ancient Greek word for mind was actually 'phren' as in schizophrenia. The word 'psyche', from which 'psychology' is derived, means 'spirit' or 'soul', not 'mind' as my psychologist suggested. So, psychologists say they are studying the mind, but they call their profession 'soul study'. I find this so-called social science world I have arrived in to be full of poorly formed vocabulary like this. The materials science I once studied was the exact opposite. It was very accurately defined.

While the psychologists busy themselves with mind study, despite the etymology, the counsellor in me is doing something different. I am not concerned too much about how my clients think. My concern is how they feel; a much broader and much deeper concept. It is the raison d'être of my profession. Once my client feels happy, they can and will leave me. My job is then done. I may never find out how they think. Am I the 'true psychologist' because my study is of souls?

I like the Greek concept of 'Soul'. "How are you?" is quite different from "What are you thinking?" As a counsellor, my interest in my client's soul, their whole sensory being, has led me to use Person-Centred Counselling as my basis. It is the talking therapy method most taught and used in Britain outside the National Health Service. I have since developed it into a much more powerful 'Soul-Centred Counselling', in which I regard my 'soul' as the software of my being.

The concept of Person-Centred Counselling is to give clients space to express themselves more fully than they might with their current confidantes. They feel the need to talk, but their relationships might be damaged if they make scary revelations to family or friends. The counsellor will offer to walk with them into their emotionally disturbing places so they can find some understanding and thereby relief from the pain which has been arising from them.

Counsellors do not diagnose their clients in order to 'treat' them for a psychological illness, as do psychologists or psychiatrists. We are primarily interested in the person underneath the woes and not in a pathology label some professionals might apply to their behaviour.

The Soul-Centred Counselling method goes beyond Person-Centred Counselling. It uses a visual aid to help clients look objectively at the issues which are troubling them, at whatever level that may be. It also offers a specific form of meditation which the client can utilise between sessions to sense the deeper parts of themselves better. Through the meditation, the client receives seven-day self-care on the back of their one-hour counselling sessions and a lifetime practice on top of whatever duration of counselling they choose. A good bargain I would say!

5: The Evolution Mismatch

I would not have a job if everyone was happy. So when people are not happy and they come to me, I need to work out what it is that is ailing them. There is no denying that we humans are actually animals, albeit social ones with a more powerful cognitive capability than any other, but the animal in us still calls the shots. I recall a trailer for a television series on Chester Zoo in England in which a keeper said that the more she worked with animals, the more she understood humans.

We humans are able to present a caricature of ourselves to others. We prefer to hide the less savoury parts of our animal functioning. Whilst a dog will happily pee and poo publicly, we close the bathroom door for such bodily functions. Dogs are equally uninhibited in their sexual advances. Homo sapiens is discreet. And we hide a lot of software issues too.

There are people who would not understand what we might do and why we do it. They might even take advantage of some of our secrets if they knew them. I am a fool if I trust everyone with everything, so like everyone else, I keep my counsel until I can trust someone. I present a persona which says, "Fine" when asked, "How are you?" even if I am suffering inside. And there is a lot more going on underneath my hat, of which I truly understand very little.

I think of Darwin at this point. Like every other creature we see around us, we exist because our predecessors have continued to survive and reproduce over the ages. Whatever other reasons, philosophical, religious or otherwise, that we may imagine for our existence, this view of life is at a level we cannot deny. Evolutionary science is likely to give us some useful answers, in the first instance at least.

Humanity carries the most unattractive accolade of being the only species which is not only stupidly and selfishly rendering the planet progressively less and less habitable for all life going forward but has developed the capability of wiping out its own species and probably all others too in a very short time, even before it has finished degrading it. The myth of humanity being the superior species is well shot in the foot. Clever we may be. Wise we are certainly not.

We have communally and mistakenly flattered our tiny consciousness into believing it is wiser than the subconscious within us. That inner subconscious is as amazing as the nature we so much admire around us, but we repeatedly ignore its wisdom because we are blinded by the consciousness which surrounds it. We would be best to resort to reviewing some reasonably plausible facts of life and refrain from indulging in a somewhat arrogant misplaced faith in our own pre-eminence on the planet.

Our cognitive minds are observably evolving in an age of rapid information development, and the technology exists to observe those mental changes. Our bodies have been evolving too, but at a far slower rate. None of us can ever achieve perfection because we are simply the latest model that has been able to survive and reproduce. We are equipped with enough faculties to get by and procreate. Just like all other living matter, we are not built for perfection or for complete self-satisfaction. Accordingly, we just have to do our best with the bodies we have been given in the context of the environments we are part of.

If being born with an imperfect body/mind system was not enough, my upbringing was not perfect either. My parents didn't go to parenting classes and it showed. For myself, I have several esteemed academic qualifications, but none were directed toward the most important thing I would ever do, bring up children. I look back in regret at the many mistakes I made for which my children are paying. They are generally progressing well in life, but there is always pain too and some of that is because I was an amateur parent - like most of the rest of us.

At one time, generations of families lived together or near each other and the younger members would learn child rearing from their related families. Now many leave to study or work away from home so the on-the-spot childcare training under supervision they might have received is less available. They are more on their own in their new parental roles.

That is the nurture element of change. But nature also continually drops in mutations in reproduction which, if they survive, shape the next generation and all the ones after that too. We have evolved into the shape we are, not because it is perfect or even efficient for the lives we lead, but simply because this edition is capable of surviving. We are not therefore nature's perfection. So, despite some people's beliefs, our intentions and our actions are not inherently right. It can be just the opposite in fact. We do what we do because we are what we are. Nothing much grander than that, it seems.

Amongst many other physical differences, gigantism keeps appearing. If our species finds that beneficial to its survival, its prevalence will expand. If not, it will simply keep reappearing at a relatively low level as long as its reproduction can and will continue. There may also be some cognitive influences on our own physical evolution. There has been considerable debate on why human skull shapes vary across the world.

One of the latest theories suggests it was mainly our own selections of what we saw as most attractive in a particular part of the planet, evolving in the same way as dog breeds have been developed, albeit with less conscious deliberation. But despite that possibility, I often wonder that we haven't been built more efficiently as I have to roll over in bed when my arm is hurting because I have lain on it too long.

Reproduction is essential to species survival. We carry the necessary physical and emotional elements for reproduction every day for much of our lives, but in our very efficient and overcrowded world, we only need to reproduce a few times to maintain the species. These physical and emotional aspects can become inconvenient for the rest of our living. They can even become diseased. The most prevalent forms of cancer are breast and prostate.

The emotional aspects of menstrual cycles can affect mood, sometimes severely. Persistent sexual desires can be massively disruptive to families and even to societies if not curtailed. It is arguable that the protracted religious conflict starting in Tudor Britain was partly the result of one man's sexual proclivity. There was carnage in the harems of the Ottoman Empire when the rulers' sexual desires were not matched with their responsibilities for the outcomes. Unwanted offspring were a threat to the upcoming monarchy and so were slaughtered en masse.

Our sexual desires are there for much of our lives because without them our species would not have prevailed, but they can also be the cause of enormous conflict and distress. We have to live with and manage what we have, physically and emotionally, convenient or not. There will always be a challenge to control our inner selves.

Our rational processing capability in the higher part of our brains is developing at an extraordinary rate, generation after generation. We now find ourselves referring to our children for assistance with the latest technology. But the vast majority of who we are is still the basic animal underneath we were a hundred thousand years ago. We carry the same emotional drivers now as we had then.

Let's imagine a cave-dwelling scene. While Mum is at home nurturing the children, Dad is out with his mates on the prairies hunting down the bison. At some point, the bison may decide that they are not going to be had for lunch today and choose to attack Dad and company instead.

In-built into every animal is a device which transforms the body's chemistry for survival. The moment danger is perceived, even before it is cognitively processed, glands above the kidneys secrete adrenaline and hormones come into the bloodstream gearing up the muscles for action. Vision becomes highly focussed and any existing pain sensations are suppressed. Those whose alert systems worked best in this scenario survived to reproduce another day. Those with weaker alerts tended to fall and their genes disappeared from the earth.

Thus, as evolutionary survivors, most of us have our adrenalin systems intact. We call the resultant impulse the Fight-Flight response. Whether we like it or not, we are geared up to either stand and defend ourselves physically or run very fast indeed when we are faced with danger - of any sort.

While this response to perceived danger was an essential component for survival in a predominantly life-threatening existence, it is a bit of a nuisance in our contemporary office and school lives. Society has evolved in a way which is incompatible with such responses. Our bodies remain thousands of years behind in evolutionary terms.

So, when we are given terrible marks in our exams or are treated unjustly at work, we should not be surprised if our initial instinct is to give the messenger a black eye. The problem comes when we do. We think of violence as an extreme expression of anger, but physical expression is quite literally our first instinctive line of defence. It comes straight from the primeval limbic system at the base of our brains before our more sophisticated higher brain gets a look in. This system has prevailed because if it hadn't, we would not have survived as a species.

Homo sapiens developed its thinking capacity and responded to the pressures of survival in a changing world by converting from relatively solitary hunter-gatherers to villages of cooperative farmers. Those who failed to manage their emotions in their new and tighter environment would be cast out to survive or die outside the communities. Their genes would tend to disappear. Those who prevailed in communities were those who could manage their animal impulses in favour of higher-level thought processing and effective communication.

That allowed the more intuitive process of decision making to flourish. We could now contemplate the consequences of today's actions on our lives tomorrow. Evolution created another layer of behaviour. There have been suggestions that the reason the stronger Neanderthal man died out was because he could not form the same community bonds as Homo sapiens. The benefits of community living such as division of labour and collaborative working enabled Homo sapiens to survive tough times when a more solitary species might fail.

However, our European genes are still some 5% Neanderthal, so there must have been some interbreeding.[1] Perhaps this is the source of the impulsive aggression which is still there in our species, although now more subdued in favour of a non-contact physical expression of anger. Anger is principally aggressive communication mainly limited to gesticulation and vocal expression. The damaging impact is psychological rather than physical. That response to stress is less likely to land us in prison these days, but it can still result in us being ejected from our place of work or learning.

A higher level of stress management is suppression. Here, we manage the attack internally. There is a certain amount of emotion we can absorb. The ability to do that is a measure of our maturity in the circumstances we find ourselves. That is key to our happiness in life.

After that, the anger is converted into frustration in an internal battle between our impulsive limbic system and the higher functions, where we consider the longer-term consequences of failing to curb our natural and immediate instincts. Our frustration will need to be resolved at a later time. Physical exercise is a useful outlet. Generally, successful societies have developed ways of expressing and communicating difficult issues and, for the most part, that keeps its members safe. Our legal systems are but one example of that.

Within a species hard-wired to be social, individuals have to learn how to use their abilities and talents to manage their internal animals in the social and physical environments they find themselves in. The better they do that, the more successful they will be and the happier they will be. And I want to go for 'happy' every time. What is the point if I am not happy, apart from the hope to get there?

My own personal mission is to work out what I have got to survive with and make the best of that; to use the best of my conscious being to maintain the balance of my soul, my subconscious being.

And, as a word of encouragement to those who feel they need a special raison d'être in life, I have usually found one and right now this book is part of it. Working with and helping other people is a major part of that too. If we have not done so already, finding out for ourselves our specific calling in life is crucial to our happiness. The famous psychologist Maslow called the outcome of this search self-actualisation.

6: Circle Diagram

Soul-Centred Counselling's primary visual aid is the Circle Diagram.[1] It is a template for the 'soul '. I find it really useful that my client and I can sit down and look at the things which are troubling them in the same way that we might look at a project we are doing together - except that this project is a really important one; 'How to enjoy life'.

Quite literally, we put their problems on the table and that depersonalises them. That way I can avoid being critical about the person of my client and what they are doing or thinking. A doctor will focus on a patient's physiological issues. Their like or dislike of the person is irrelevant in their professional capacity. Similarly, I focus on my client's psychological issues. My like or dislike of the person is professionally irrelevant too. We are just a little team with a common goal called Client Happiness.

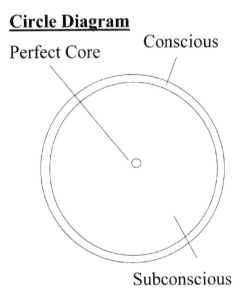

Circle Diagram

Perfect Core

Conscious

Subconscious

The Circle Diagram consists of a simple circle with an annulus around it and a centre. The whole circle is my client's soul, the software of their being. The annulus around its circumference represents the conscious part of their being: what I am aware of right now. To resort to the computer analogy, the consciousness is much like a computer monitor but with some limited data processing.

The rest of the circle is my subconscious, i.e., everything that we are not conscious of and there is a lot of that. It's the CPU which processes data, the Random Access Memory and the Hard Drive, the memory.

But in comparison to my home computer, it is absolutely massive. Its input is all the data I take in through my senses in my life, whether I am conscious of that or not. Much of this data is then processed at levels we can hardly imagine and compiles a whole library over my entire lifetime. Only a small fraction of that is retrievable at any one time, reflecting the limited capability of my relatively tiny conscious mind, a fact of which I am acutely aware when I can't remember the right word for something I think I know well.

I can, however, vividly recall a five-minute event from the age of three. The rest of my life will probably be in there somewhere, but may never surface as most of it does not matter much now anyway. That pattern of recall is most obviously evident in dementia sufferers who might forget the names and possibly faces of the closest relatives around them now, but are lucid when drawn into singing the songs of their youth: a remarkable feat of memory when we consider the sum total of all the other data in there! But also a salutary reminder of how early information, good and bad, can influence us throughout our lives. We are all formed in our early years.

All my bodily functions are managed in this subconscious zone too and if I am healthy, I won't know a thing about them. There are vast amounts of mental processes on the go which, thanks to modern electronic scanning equipment, neuroscience is only just discovering.

So, if we find ourselves not fully in control of our actions and thoughts all the time, we can perhaps forgive ourselves for that. We cannot possibly contain all this vast complexity in our tiny consciousness all at once, let alone manage it. In comparison, my internet search engine looking at those millions of keyword entries across the planet in a second or so might seem quite modest.

My scientific background made me wonder what might be at the centre of this Circle Diagram. It's not just any circle, but the one which defines my very being, so it could be quite important. I call it the Perfect Core. My clients agree it has some very interesting properties. There seems to be a consensus amongst them:

- The person I was meant to be before all the bad stuff happened.
- A place of perfect peace.
- The source of all the strength I will ever need.

This is the essence of Soul-Centred Counselling practice; for my client to find their fully functional inner being. The Perfect Core is in everyone, albeit well hidden in some. This is also the aim of the meditation practice I offer. The focus is finding inner peace.

These are healthy objectives we humans have always sought. They are the basis of those world religions that claim a source of great goodness at the centre of our beings. Christians, for instance, will recognise their 'Holy Spirit' in this. I too would consider this central zone as being 'spiritual' in nature.

Regardless of their cultural upbringing, my clients are greatly encouraged to be told that the secular practice of counselling can help them connect with something so powerful. All religions claim to espouse peace, even if they often fail in their attempts. The idea of 'the person I was meant to be' corresponds to that of rebirth. Christians use the term 'born again' to describe the discovery of one's own soul within the faith.

So, there is nothing new in Soul-Centred Counselling other than the methods employed to achieve the age-old objective of peace. The meditation I offer as part of my practice goes back to the Vedic tradition, predating Buddhism and modern Hinduism. A main difference is that it avoids belief systems which can cause so much damage when left unchecked. Further, its secular nature means it does not conflict with normal religious codes.

So far, so good. But what is happening with this soul I have depicted? If it was as clean as I have drawn it and remained that way, we would all be very happy, but it never is. Life is dynamic. It comes into existence, not of its own accord, sustains itself for as long as it can and then expires despite its efforts otherwise. It is the long middle bit I am interested in and indeed, so are my clients.

Healthy happiness is the goal of my life and why ever not? That means ensuring everything inside is ticking over smoothly, keeping the plethora of functions of my hardware and software finely balanced. Clearly a task far beyond my conscious mind which takes me upstairs sometimes and then forgets why it sent me there.

This is the domain of that wonderment we observe so readily outside ourselves. We call it nature when we are awestruck by the cosmos or by a beautiful delicate flower, but we seem to suspend our awe when we think of ourselves. We are just as amazing. And because we don't appreciate our internal complexity, we entertain a belief that we can control ourselves from our meagre surface-level consciousness.

We are conditioned as children to believe we should be able to 'behave' ourselves because that is what we are told to do and expected to do. We need some humility in this I feel. What I call 'me' is merely the conscious observer in the tiny fraction of the vast complexity of the whole me, albeit with a little bit of a control capability thrown in. What we like to call Free Will is simply the extent to which the conscious me is able to manage the subconscious me.

The subconscious me can be quite a handful for reasons more to do with my upbringing than anything I have decided to do or be. Controlling my inner self can be a challenge sometimes and I have to be humble to accept I may not always succeed.

We may find some of that humility when we consider that the amoeba, a single-cell being, functions like us too. It may not be conscious of itself in the same way that we are, but it has the same objective; keeping itself healthy and balanced. The Simple Balance Diagram shows it taking what it needs from the world it finds itself in and rejecting what it does not want. It continually seeks its physical balance by absorbing nutrients and rejecting waste across its interface with its own world.

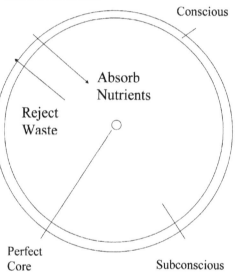

Simple Balance

Its surface is its mechanism of exchange and therefore of survival. And that is what we do too. My subconscious being strives to maintain balance by sending messages about its needs to my interface with the world, my conscious being. If my conscious being can interpret them and act upon them effectively, then the process of fulfilling those needs has succeeded and I will be happy.

However, if it is unable to interpret them or meet their requirements, then my subconscious being will be unbalanced and I will be unhappy. This subconsciousness is the vast majority of who I am and unhappiness is the message my consciousness will be getting. It will remain unhappy until my needs are met or I expire. We don't have to look around much to see that there are a lot of people, both in distant lands and at home, not having their needs met for much of their lives and being chronically out of balance as a result. There is a lot of human misery around and the counsellor in me believes it is mostly unnecessary.

The Feedback Process diagram shows the mechanism of how my inner needs are met to maintain my life balance. I might get partly through the morning and have a sensation coming from inside me which impels me to interpret it. Is it heartburn? Is there something seriously wrong with me?

After a second or so, I realise that I am just a bit hungry. I've interpreted a message and can now act on it. The source of emotion was an empty stomach as recognised in my blood chemistry. My body sensed low sugar levels and demanded a food top-up. My nervous system sent signals which permeated my consciousness and I tried to interpret those feelings. I recognised them as hunger and made plans to resolve the imbalance my subconscious had identified.

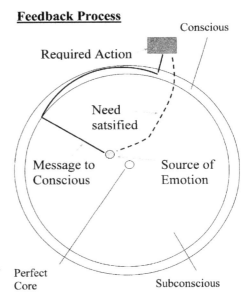

Feedback Process

I might not be able to satisfy the need right away, nor want to, but I can decide to get a sandwich at lunchtime and that will hopefully do the trick. If I have understood my subconsciousness' message well and made the right plan, I will fulfil my body's needs, the balance will resume and the message will be extinguished.

This feedback loop system shown in the diagram is a primary device my body utilises to maintain its balance and its success determines the level of happiness experienced by its consciousness. The mechanism works in all its areas of functioning: for food, drink, sleep, body temperature and all our other physical needs. It also seeks to resolve our emotional needs, even if we don't read them very well sometimes.

We sense these 'out of balance' messages as feelings or emotions, often related to a part of the body. We just need to interpret them accurately enough to respond to them well and thereby alleviate the discomfort they bring before it gets too serious. We can then regain our balance.

The subconscious flagged up a disparity between what it needed and what it had. The conscious me interpreted that need, devised a plan and got the body to execute that plan. Without that conscious processing, things will only get more imbalanced and more uncomfortable.

7: Our Amazing Subconscious

I am often aware of my brain doing some logical processing using information I am absorbing, but the processing I can be conscious of is trivial compared to what is going on underneath. When I ride my bike, I am only interested in where I am trying to go and how to negotiate the various obstacles en route like traffic lights, cars, junctions, etc.

A whole host of other functions are operating underneath, including those which I originally learnt to keep a dynamic balance so I don't fall off. That involves sight, ears for balance and lots of split-second processing. These subroutines are now firmly established in my invisible operating system and I give them no further thought. Much of our processing becomes subsumed into our subconscious over time because our conscious mind does not have the capacity to rethink them every time.

In addition to that, there is a vast array of other processes chugging alongside these elective activities, supporting all the body systems which comprise the entity called me. Our scientists suggest our minds are the most complex items in the universe. They may be right, but we just don't really appreciate on a day-to-day basis how immensely intricate the subconsciousness is. Our tiny consciousness simply does not have the capacity to understand it. However, if we at least give it a try, we may be amazed by it.

I was admiring a goldfinch in the garden recently and wondered at the magnificence of its colouring. The very construction of its body is part of its nature. It did not plan to look like that. It did not think it all out and create its own plumage. Its species just evolved and now is what it is. And we are the same. Beautifully complex, if we could only admit it.

We don't generally flatter ourselves much about our own physical appearances, partly because we often live much longer than our original reproductive sell by date. Our bodies start to age and are not so beautiful anymore. But we can allow ourselves to be impressed by the cognitive sophistication we exhibit in the collective human actions and achievements which come from our innate ability to construct and process complex thoughts.

That innate ability is not of our making. We just have it, like the bird's plumage. It is a gift for us to exercise, not for our own aggrandisement. It is not for us. It is for each other in our communities.

In that expression of our talents, we have imagined and then created amazing feats like going to the moon and countless breathtaking works of art and architecture across the planet. Many millions of years of evolved animal intelligence have produced this marvel of complexity and all that intelligence has been powered by the remarkable, ever-developing subconscious in each of us.

These wondrous feats of human endeavour, not to speak of all the other menial activities we undertake down to planning a car journey or even 'do I make a cup of tea' decisions, are all sourced in the subconscious as I describe it. However, as much as I might think that a certain action is a good idea, I am not going to do it or indeed anything else, unless I am actually motivated to do it.

Ultimately, we act on our emotions rather than on our thoughts, even if it was our thoughts which may have led to our emotions. Indeed, the word 'emotion' is derived from the word 'motion'. It is the desire to do something, to move. I won't be doing anything just because I think it's a good idea. The government in Britain decided that motorists should drive on the left-hand side of the road; an apparently arbitrary cognitive choice.

However, when I drive on the designated side, I am actually making an emotive choice. I choose to conform, not because I think that left is the correct choice, but because if I do not, I will have a short driving career or a short life. I once drove down the wrong side of a long but thankfully quiet road in America. When I found myself careering headlong towards another car, my conscious being worked out that he was right and I was wrong, but it was my emotions which actually responded and emphatically too.

This is why I am interested in what my clients feel more than what they think. That comes from our subconscious. Our 'motions' are driven by our emotions - always and only.

The Emotions Surfacing diagram depicts sensations emanating from the subconscious and arriving in the conscious zone to be recognised and acted upon. They seek to maintain the balance of the soul and find its peace.

There may be angry emotions coming from my traumas. Peaceful ones may come from somewhere near my Perfect Core. There will be physiological ones too, like simple body messages identifying needs for food, drink and body warmth which might be easily resolved. Neuroscience has made great inroads into identifying parts of the brain which correspond to some of our more basic emotions, but it has a very long way to go yet.

However, counsellors and clients alike can't wait for neuroscience to locate and

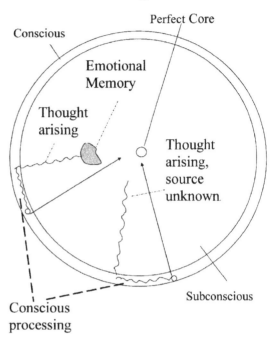

Emotions Surfacing

analyse everything before they address the problems we face in life. Brain mapping may be interesting, but to my suffering client, it is not so important. They don't need a cognitively verified proof. They just need a simple model they can relate to. Our problems are here and now, so we need to work at a different level; not a level which definitively identifies the physical positions of each process, but one which packages experiences into functional black boxes so we can draw some empirical conclusions now.

The Circle Diagram is a tool which enables clients to conceptualise their emotions without having to wait for technical research to identify which part of the physical brain relates to what thought process. It allows clients to express themselves and understand themselves more clearly. The counsellor can then identify common responses between different clients and derive some general rules of thumb to help other clients. This is Empirical Analysis in action. This process is what has driven my own learning and ultimately this book.

8: Selfish Me

The majority of the individuals who come to counselling are people who reflect on themselves and what they do, sometimes excessively so. Those who don't do reflection would not normally see counselling as useful. It's usually someone else's fault. I often find my clients are not valuing themselves well. I usually indulge them in a dose of 'Selfish Me'.

Many of us seem to have been imbued with the idea that other people are more important than we are - parents, bosses, spouses, clergy, etc. and that we have a duty to them above ourselves. This is a myth which needs breaking and that requires effort, not least when we have been brought up with an imperative of having to conform to those who would wish to control us.

I have a routine with my younger clients. I sometimes ask them who the most important person in the room is. They usually get the right answer because I have done some homework with them at the beginning, but it's worth reminding them so they have a good benchmark to measure themselves against when they leave the session.

I don't want them doing or even thinking anything because they are giving credence to me as an authority figure. I am merely helping them to review themselves in a broader light so they give their inner selves a voice in a world which might be dominated by more powerful but maybe not always caring people.

People who had power over us in our childhood may still be in our heads as adults and actively so. They were our parents and our teachers and they needed to have some control over us, primarily for our own good but also for the good of our communities, be that family, school or indeed any group we might have been part of. Much of our learning from them has gone into our minds, programming us to conform to their rules often before our discernment screens were built well enough to sift out the beneficial ones from the damaging ones.

We do need to conform to reasonable rules if we are to live healthy lives in the societies in which we find ourselves, but some of the rules imposed may not have been so helpful. As we mature and move away from the home and classroom, we need to take time out to examine these to check if we still agree with them and can work with them.

We may have misunderstood some or have over-applied them. An unreasonable carer or teacher may have imposed unreasonable rules. Even some rules which were beneficial at the time might no longer apply, but no-one has told us we could stop. If life was frugal in the childhood home, we might retain a frugal attitude even if we become wealthy. Whoever imposed the frugality will be in our heads, influencing what we do, often for the duration of our lives.

That figure and their rules are built into our psyche and if we have had no reason to rewrite that script, it will remain there. The frugal programme would be a relatively innocuous carry-over, but dysfunctional families will bequeath rather more sinister ones. Regardless of our upbringing, there will always be some level of injustice to weed out. Our souls can be infected with malware which comes from obligations to those who may not have our best interests at heart.

Like the malware that gets into my computer, it arrives by stealth rather than in overtly declared rules. We need to identify where these come from and make some decisions about who put them there. Given some good direction and support, most of us can sort out the helpful wheat from the damaging chaff within our normal lives.

Everyone we are connected with has a unique array of facets and features. Some of those features will affect us and some won't, depending on what our relationship with them is. Whether they are an interest in a particular sport or a certain job aptitude may not be so important to us.

However, there are some features which matter a lot to us. If for instance, we wish to decide whether we want a particular person intimately in our lives for a long time and that can effectively mean forever, there is one basic question to be asked: Will this person care for me? That may generate further questions like: Do they possess the capacity for love? Do they really respect me? These are very basic questions couples revisit when they come for counselling. It is also a question that adults may find themselves asking about a parent at some point in their lives.

The 'People in My Heart' Diagram demonstrates how we can't avoid some people being in our lives, and at an intimate and influential level too. We were brought up with them, we married them or they are our children. We all have to satisfy our basic needs in order to keep our own souls balanced and happy. These other people may help us or they may hinder us.

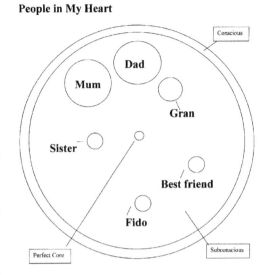

People in My Heart

They are voices in our heads along with our own and we may not be able to work out whose voice we are really attending to at any one time. Many people coming for counselling carry this issue. Some of the voices (and I am not referring to psychotic experiences here) may tell us we are not worth other people's time or love. Or that we always get things wrong. How do they all fit into our life's balancing trick?

The diagram shows a number of people inside me. I may feel a measure of care or concern for them. That care or concern may not be my choice. I care for other people because, whether I like it or not, I was born with a firmware feature called empathy and that motivates me to feel for other people. I can't help it. It can be an especially deep care which psychologists call Attachment. It's just there and the recipients may not respect it. That can become a problem for us.

Homo sapiens is a social creature. Empathy is the emotion which binds society emotionally. It is fundamental to our personal fulfilment as social individuals within our communities. There is evidence that it may be a genetic feature driven by the 'love hormone', oxytocin. The US National Academy of Sciences reports 'Our results provide evidence of how a naturally occurring genetic variation of the oxytocin receptor relates to both empathy and stress profiles.'[1]

The development of brain scanning has enabled neuroscientists to observe empathy actually functioning. They have discovered that when we see someone doing something with emotional content, our brains are stimulated in the same

49

areas as the person we are observing. They have proposed that this involves special neurons they called Mirror Neurons, although there is some doubt as to whether these exist as separate entities.

I always knew that when I was enjoying time with someone, we were both feeling and usually thinking alike and when I was sympathising with someone, I felt what they felt. It is encouraging that science has caught up with human experience and accepts that emotions are real and they can be studied and discussed in the scientific context. This research in empathy may form a basis for further scientific investigation based on clinical rather than on subjective observations which can be subject to interpretation.

The very existence of empathy in me means that when some people come into my life in certain circumstances, they create a bond inside me and impel me to feel compassionate towards them in some way. My in-built empathy is predisposing me to feel for them. If people in my family love me, I will probably feel love for them too. I don't really choose to. They are inside me and that was not my conscious decision. It just happened. They got in under the radar. And there is a vulnerability in this if I don't recognise what has happened and how it works.

It means that if there are people in my life who are unhappy, then I will also be to some extent. Their presence in me is only a prism of them, rather than the whole of them, but I am still affected by them to some degree. If my wife is out and has a car accident, I will not know until someone tells me. Until then, that is her life, but when I find out, I will be concerned for her. Because part of her is embedded in me, I will feel less balanced and therefore less happy. I will want to rectify the situation as much as I can for her and I will not feel fully happy in myself until I think she is happy.

While I am not affected by everything in her life, some aspects impact me emotionally through my empathic mirror neurons. I may not be fully aware of what these aspects are because this is not a conscious process. It derives from our subconscious, so is initially beneath my observations and beyond my control.

Clients with low self-esteem often struggle with the idea that they should be primarily concerned for their own welfare and balance. They think that is selfish and they believe they should not be selfish. They don't realise the distinction between healthy self-care and the greedy acquisition of wealth or power to the detriment of others. They seem programmed to serve others in preference to enjoying their own lives in a wholesome way. They may have been conditioned to comply with a troubled parent and that obligation may remain until the software controlling it is cleaned up in therapy or by other means.

I don't do cup half full or cup half empty in my life. I give when my cup is overflowing. That way, others get the benefits I can genuinely offer but I am never depleted. Mothers with younger children whom they believe they would die for can have difficulty with their obligations. Notwithstanding the essential power of that relationship, there is always room to consider a new perspective. If meeting a young child's needs today means we become too exhausted to do it all again tomorrow, we have to take stock of what we are doing. If a parent does not find a clear understanding of their own boundaries and thereby loses control, the outcome will be confusion for the child and more problems for the parent as the child expects ever-increasing indulgences.

The Selfish Me Model may help the mother put her self-care first and feel a bit less guilty about what she may see as inadequacy. If an adult child has succumbed to an addiction and raids the family home to feed that addiction, this model helps parents make the tough decisions.

A clear perspective of boundaries is essential for a parent's survival and ultimately for the benefit of the offspring. Those decisions are also loving in that they are taken in the best interests of the child, however much that hurts the parent at the time. The parent has taken the courage to take hard actions which can only be justified against the worse consequences of softer ones. Tough love is needed sometimes.

Finding Boundaries

The important message here is that living almost indiscriminately for another, perhaps a young child, an ageing parent or anyone who has influence over us in some way, makes us vulnerable to their needs and wants and to whatever devices they might use to manipulate us without respecting our own needs. We may be allowing them the opportunity to predate on our good nature at their whim. That not only diminishes us, it diminishes them too.

Instead, we are better and safer if our primary objective is our own well-being and balance. We are better placed to assess the situation ourselves than anyone else, so we need to take control of it. Because the people we are bonded or attached to are inside us, we may be driven to care for them beyond the bounds of reason. We must become aware that any care we offer needs to be kept in perspective if we are to keep balanced ourselves.

We need to draw some clear boundaries and define who is allowed to take our time and emotional resource and who we would rather leave outside for others to help instead. We might ask who these people are who have arrived in us and what they are doing there. Did we invite them in at some time and what might we want to do about that now? They may have slipped under our discernment barrier when we were younger and are exercising a power inside us we cannot readily control.

Given the choice, would we invite them in now? Will we ultimately benefit from them being within us in the longer term? These questions often enable clients to reassess their relationships with family and friends. I often ask a client if they met their father/brother/child, not as a relative but as a random person, would they befriend them now. That question can initiate very powerful and sometimes tectonic action from them.

The more we understand the nature of love, the better we will navigate our lives because it's always in there somewhere. The English word 'love' has far too many meanings. Altruism is the love force derived from the basic emotion of peace and it is communicated by virtue of the innate empathy most of us are born with. I describe love as peace on the move. Peace is what those exchanging altruistic love experience.

This type of love is automatically extended to those who have found their way into our hearts, whether by invitation or not. Usually, we don't consciously offer the invitation. My wife acquired our first dog recently, partly so that she would be forced to take daily exercise. I had no desire for one, but it is in my interests that my wife is happy, so the little mutt arrived. Whether either of us liked it or not, we have both become emotionally attached to it.

It is now there, inside our souls. It does not occupy the same space as our children, but it snuck in there and so we love it really. Rightly so you say, but this illustrates the involuntary processes involved. So, in order for me to be happy, I find I have to make sure that the dog is, within reason, happy. I will not die for it, but I will be sure it is fed and cared for properly. It does actually take up quite a lot of my time and that wasn't planned.

Most of us genuinely care for other people (and animals) to the point of making sacrifices for them, forgoing things we might like to do and helping them in preference to that. The Selfish Me Model illustrates that when we care for others, we are really only caring for ourselves as extended by the empathy which is built into us, whether we wanted it or not.

At the end of the day, if our internal residents behave well, it all works out as expected and there is nothing wrong with that. Indeed, they actually contribute to our well-being. Once we become clear about our self-care boundaries, it is easier to see who got inside our souls by consent and who might have invaded them by stealth. Boundaries are crucial concepts in counselling because they are crucial concepts in any and every aspect of emotional life. If I know where my genuine responsibilities begin and end, then I am able to say 'no' without feeling guilty to imposter cuckoos who might try to convince me I should care for them and who then set out to abuse me.

This sort of clarity is often enough for a client to walk away from what seemed to be previous obligations with their head high, making low self-esteem a thing of the past. They are able to take a different view on who they allow in their lives in the future. They are now in control of themselves, possibly for the first time.

Parental Influence

On the grounds that no parent is perfect, especially if they had inadequate role models to follow themselves, then at least some part of every child's upbringing will be deficient. Tragically for some of my clients, that deficiency has overshadowed the positives they have received in childhood, making life a constant struggle and a misery.

Adult clients are often frustrated and confused by a parent who has either not provided well for them or who has actually damaged them. They needed a loving, caring, competent parent. Some got just the opposite but have not yet separated these two conflicting images. A lack of love in childhood is as much an emotional deficiency as a bad diet is a nutritional deficiency. Both can have long-term, potentially lifetime impacts. The difference is that the emotional deficiency does not usually generate illnesses which can kill. Instead, we live on in the pain.

The most powerful memory imprints are the early ones because the infant has no other experiences to measure them against. An infant is totally dependent on its primary carer. It needs it, usually its mother, to care for it entirely, know what it needs and to satisfy those needs. That godlike image prevails even if the child finds out from its friends as it grows older what real caring looks like and that does not fit its own experience.

The growing child is then conflicted between the happy family image the parent may have portrayed and which society envisages and the evolving truth of who its parents really are, with all the problems they are carrying. I help clients differentiate between the parent they have in their lives and the one they really wanted. The one they wanted may not exist and the dawn of that knowledge often can trigger a bereavement process.

However, it also enables them to deal more effectively with the parent they actually have. It may also enable them to understand that it's not all black and white. They may be able to discern the good bits from the bad bits, appreciating the former and understanding that the latter was not really the parent's fault, anyway.

When clients struggle to find enough good in a parent to respect them, they may find a perfect parent model in religion and that can bridge the gap for them. The Christian 'Father God' is often revered as all-powerful, all-loving and all-knowing and that is what we needed our parent to be. Others find perfection in the Perfect Core of their own beings.

The rest of their soul may carry a host of traumas which make life messy and seriously imperfect, but that centre is the solid anchor to work from and return to. The inner strength and inner wisdom emanating from the Perfect Core can give them the courage and ability to understand and accept the imperfections of their inadequate parent too. Counselling must always help the client travel towards truth like this, albeit at the pace they can manage. The Selfish Me Model is a powerful tool in this transition.

I find the Model clarifies the boundaries in couple relationships too. When couples come for counselling, they are often asking whether they should stay together or not. At some time, each believed the other was embedded in their soul, but distress and conflict prevail now. They harboured ideals of each other, but those became tarnished by revelation and reality.

Good counselling will help them consider their life options going forward and discover which route is the best for each of them. If separation is the answer and it frequently is, then hard decisions have to be made to almost surgically remove the other from their empathic boundary of care. The subsequent reprogramming work for each can be substantial and can take some time to reach its resolution. It becomes the counsellor's job to help them deal with this painful process.

By the time they come to counselling, the other's presence in their soul may have already started to die. A prevailing aggression is often the driver which destroys the relationship, especially if it's not managed well. Clear boundaries are the essential foundation upon which to make clear and confident life decisions. The understanding which the Selfish Me Model offers can give them the courage to discover if the presence of the other in their soul is of long-term benefit to them and indeed to those who depend on them too.

I often use a Venn Diagram to help clients assess the worth of their relationships. This one shows two people of opposite genders with significant emotional sharing. The diagram can work for any emotional relationship. The sharing delivers benefits and challenges to each, shown as +ves and −ves in the overlapping parts of their lives. In a free society, the benefits to each is the raison d'être for the relationship.

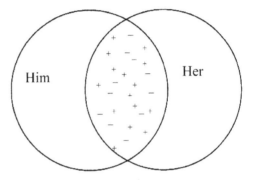

Benefits and Challenges within a Relationship

At the time they got together, each decided that the benefits to them outweighed any challenges that might have been lurking. Otherwise, it would not have happened. As time has passed on, circumstances or perceptions or both have changed and the challenges may have started to outweigh the benefits, for one of them at least. There comes a point where that becomes intolerable and they seek ways of resolving that, either by seeking out the original magic or finding a new way forward. The former rarely works, although sometimes the damage from the past can be addressed successfully and a new honesty can be found.

A fifteen-year-old relationship had been damaged at the start by infidelity. As the children were growing up, that pain had been resurrected, threatening the marriage. Counselling helped identify the source of the pain and enabled the guilty party to offer remorse and assure his wife of faithfulness in the future.

I usually recommend that the area of emotional interaction between a couple in conflict be consciously reduced to a level which decreases the challenges in the overlap, while at the same time, maintaining enough of the benefits to remain functional. If each tries to contain and manage their own emotions responsibly, then a new and clearer climate can evolve and that may enable a refreshing reconstruction of their relationship.

That conscious assessment of the benefits of their interactions is important in itself because they may have forgotten those good things in the ensuing confusion. They can decide between them which areas they want to retain for now and which they need to let go.

That decision process exercises their relationship, but in a controlled way. It can be guided by the counsellor or it may just arrive spontaneously from that eternal source of goodness at the centre of the soul. It may identify and address some of the false assumptions each has made about the other and which each may have inadvertently brought into the relationship. If these often societal stereotypes of the other's roles can be weeded out, some real and lasting features can be revealed. If a level of interaction can be found which is stable and acceptable, the couple may want to first consolidate that to reaffirm foundations before rebuilding further.

A marriage had met the test of time, but each partner still held a higher ideal of the role they expected of the other beyond their underlying personality. Each had made assumptions about the other in the early whirlwind of romance derived from their several preconceived concepts of marital life and these can stick forever. Like many couples, they took each other for granted a lot. When they started to understand each other, their relationship transformed from one of unmet expectations to mutual respect and support for each other in daily life.

Regrettably, around a third of the couples I see find this overlap shrinking to an administrative level of arrangement only, with little hope of recovery. Despite every effort, the better way forward may be separation. It is part of the counsellor's function to support each on that journey, not least because one will inevitably reach that point before the other. In the end, each has to find what is best for them in the whole scheme of things.

The model helps clarify boundaries, even in the context of a dual relationship, but it is often very much complicated by the needs of any children involved.

9: Simple Ways of Thinking

In my original search for peace, I was bewildered by so many options such as herbal remedies, exercise regimes, religions, yoga, new age, medicines and so it goes on. While most of them had some merit in principle, a lot were not so useful in practice for me. Even when I did light upon a process which actually helped me, there were add-ons which did not and that went on for years. How was I to discern? We can try things, but that trying may get us into an even worse place and we have to get out of that first before committing to another painful experimental adventure.

Even when we make a simple decision to rely on the medical profession, we can still become subject to experimentation as psychiatrists try out varying prescriptions on us which may or may not produce success. Even if they work for now, over time that may degrade as side effects surface. While many people benefit from responsible psychiatry, some who could so easily have been helped have actually been damaged. The social and medical anthropologist, James Davies, illustrates this well in his book *Cracked*.

If we can find a single set of principles to live our lives by, we will not be so confused by the multiplicity of choices which our candy shop world offers, particularly through the mediums of television and the internet. Confusion generates fear. Commercialism skews what should be professional wisdom with potentially devastating effect. Lives can be damaged long-term when a wrong decision is made. If we are presented with too many choices, we may spend a lot of time and effort in differentiating and analysing them all to ensure we have the right answer.

Trial and error can be hard work and there is not enough time in a life to do this thoroughly, so we often end up making a guess. The more options we have to reject, the more risk there is of rejecting the right one by a mistake. Our choices are very important and we could regret them for the rest of our lives.

I have always believed that if I could find confidence in a few basic concepts, they could lead me quickly and easily to make sound decisions in complex situations. There was a debate in my school days about how to teach a foreign language. Is it best to teach grammar first and build vocabulary on that, so sentences could be constructed on these basic building bricks or to learn a lot of phrases which get us up and running on our holiday trip, but leaves us without the flexibility of saying anything else?

As I have always had a poor memory and good logic processing, the answer was easy. Learn the basic building blocks and create sentences as needed. I have found my favoured premise of working from sound basic material in any circumstance so much easier and so much more reliable in all my roles in life.

My simplistic approach has good pedigree. In mediaeval times, we thought the earth was the centre of our known universe. That premise meant that the motions of celestial bodies could only be assessed by building complex charts of their locations over many years and even that did not lead us to predict planetary movements well. Then Copernicus and shortly afterwards Galileo, discovered that the physical centre of our immediate celestial world was actually the sun, providing a far simpler model.

However, they were faced with considerable resistance to their ideas. The establishment thought we humans were the most important thing in the whole universe. Our egocentricity made us think our world was geocentric. (I find it interesting that these two 'centrics' are anagrams of each other). It was only when humanity found the humility to accept the obviously convincing evidence that it started to understand the cosmos it lived in. Copernicus and Galileo described the model with the sun at the centre as Heliocentric.

They found that planetary motions, which had previously been assessed with the earth as the centre of their universe, suddenly went from baffling to easily comprehensible. It took enormously complex charts to track all the various movements. Once they started to look at their visible universe from its true centre rather than from somewhere in the middle, it became easy to map and predict movements. A few simple equations defined it all adequately.

This solar system model is simple enough to teach to primary schoolchildren. In one easy move of locus, we travelled from the 'virtually impossible to understand' to 'child's play'.

The Circle Diagram illustrates a psychological counterpart to this. I compare the current Medical Model of our minds to the geocentric mediaeval model. Its focus is on pathologies defined by exhibited behaviours. Behaviour

Pathocentric 1

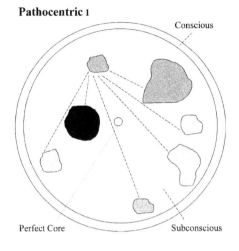

is located in the moving and changing part of the Circle Diagram. The ever-increasing list of symptoms generated by the psychiatric classification models like the American Psychological Association's Diagnostic and Statistical Manual of Mental Disorders (DSM) is trying to map our psychological beings by viewing them from the various pathologies that might be identified at any one time. The two Pathocentric diagrams show views of the same whole being from two different randomly chosen pathological standpoints indicated by the drawn lines of sight. The observer will see quite different views from each other. The nearest pathology in diagram 1 is the large grey trauma, whilst in 2 it is the large black one. This will yield different diagnoses.

Someone may receive one diagnosis on a week they are feeling depressed and another when anxiety may dominate. But these may just be different perspectives of the same illness. That can result in conflicting treatments - and very likely in client disillusionment. That conundrum makes it difficult to establish the real emotional skyscape, especially if the symptoms change over time,

Pathocentric 2

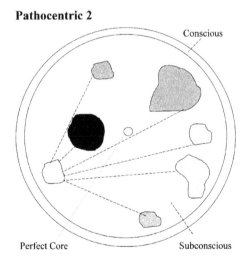

which can happen for various reasons, including the results of any prescribed medication taking effect. Different practitioners focus on different pathologies too, getting different results and applying different interventions.

The client can become defined by their illness in the eyes of the practitioner and if they allow that, the client will define themselves by that too. They may then accept their condition as a permanence even if it is not, leaving no prospect of recovery. I prefer to view my emotional skyscape from the static centre of the Circle Diagram, the Perfect Core. I can have a clear view of all the blemishes and I will always get the same view of them. If they change, I am not confused because I know that my central viewing point which embodies eternal truth will not change. I am defined by that part of me which is healthy and it is that part which will defeat the illness. This Soulcentric Model enables me to address clients' traumas and pathologies with significant clarity too. Sadly, the Pathocentric Model merely serves to confuse.

I suspect that the resistance to an approach which incorporates a perfect

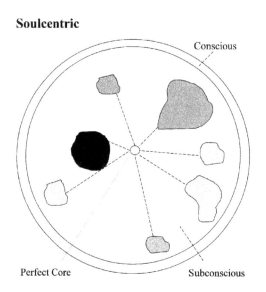

Soulcentric

Conscious

Perfect Core

Subconscious

centre has emanated, at least partially, from an historic aversion to religion. Psychology grew up in a world in which science was questioning Christian tenets through the Enlightenment Movement. It needed to be logical, not mythical. The now discredited geocentric myth was one of many anomalous religious beliefs.

Later, philosophers like Nietzsche wanted to live without the Christian God they grew up with. Nietzsche then struggled to make sense of his spiritually denuded world. It is still a debate as to whether his ultimate insanity was biologically or psychologically precipitated. No-one seemed to be able to separate the concept of a spiritual entity from the prevailing religion.

I see spirituality as a central given and religion as a human construction. Most secular people and indeed many religious people also struggle with a bearded old white man in the sky who is responsible for everything. But Buddhism, in its essence and Christianity, in its Holy Spirit guise, have circumvented the personified deity and found peace in a central spiritual interior which correlates with the Perfect Core of the Circle Diagram.

And indeed, that is where meditation lies too. I see an understanding of spirituality as essential to healthy psychological functioning. Traditional religious dogmas can seriously get in the way if we are not careful.

10: A Binary Concept of Emotion

You will see that I like simplicity in life. The world can easily become far too complicated. I find it useful to boil concepts down into their basic components. Then I can safely build up a logical picture of life's complexities on a simple and reliable foundation of knowledge. That enables easy understanding and easy recall. In contrast, if I cannot understand a concept sufficiently well enough to explain it in simple terms to my client, it is of no use to them.

For that reason, it's not much use to me either. I will not peddle other people's undigested words from any source. So when I am confronted with tomes of psychological literature in obscure language, I know it is not for my practice. I feel academia has a propensity to talk around a subject, sometimes more to generate literature than get to the basic truths. I see it parading round the behavioural periphery of the Circle Diagram and never getting to grips with the all-important Core.

Indeed, the more complicated the words, the less confidence I have in their author. Even if it is sound neuroscience, there is a limit to what I can convey to a client. It's a bit like school maths. Knowing the topic is one thing. Knowing it sufficiently well to explain it is the real test of understanding. I had a maths teacher who knew his stuff so well that he could convey it to almost any pupil. I need to be able to explain my material to my clients well too. It is not so easy to convey emotional concepts through the limitations of the written word as I am doing here, but I am trying my best for you.

I see all basic emotions as being founded on two fundamental elements, peace and fear. A simple binary concept like this, wherein all other emotions except the sexual drive, are derived from these two can provide a sound basis for a client to develop an understanding of their emotional structure. I see joy, love, gratitude and a sense of achievement all emanating from a baseline of peace. Fear manifests itself as anger, violence, fight, flight, freeze, confusion, frustration and much more.

I have never met a client who did not want more peace in their life. My entire personal objective is to continually increase the times and circumstances in which I feel peaceful and at one with myself. The better that gets, the more life just falls into place for me. However elusive that might be in my clients, some semblance of peace will usually be there for me to find and indeed for them to find too. Then they can cultivate it.

I sometimes have to delve into the client's emotional vocabulary to identify the particular feeling they may be trying to articulate, particularly if it's a young child or an autistic 'candidate'. I use the word 'candidate' as a convenient way to describe someone who seems to fit a particular pathology. I don't want to resort to a diagnosis per se, nor indeed am I qualified to do so in the conventional clinical sense.

Waking up may be a time when they might experience peace. The solar plexus is a generally agreed location for a physical sensation of it. I help clients become aware of its presence in quiet situations. If they take up the meditation practice I offer, the experience of peace starts to become more apparent, not only in rest, but in activity too. I help them recognise these times.

Being able to identify peace in a different and specific way enables clients to monitor it more effectively. If they can appreciate that an increased experience of peace in their day is therapeutic and if they can accept that health is their goal for now, they will seek ways to attain that peace and that will help them resolve their issues much faster.

If they have a way of recognising peace, they can start to identify what delivers it and find ways to get more of it. They can also identify what extinguishes it and avoid that where possible. This learning process is classic Cognitive Behavioural Therapy, but applied to the most profound positive emotion we can access.

We sense the emotion of peace in many ways: feeling at one with ourselves. Probably the most apparent manifestation of peace is what happens when it is transmitted from one person to another. I might feel a measure of peace inside when I am thinking of another person, either in their presence or not.

In its purest form, this is altruistic love. Its closeness to the quite different sensation of sexual arousal can confuse and divert the purity of altruistic and unconditional love in romantic relationships.

The sexual drive is hormonal and enhances that 'feel good' experience powerfully. Nature had designed it to be bonding, so it can overwhelm other emotions and their messages. For that reason, it is important to have sound altruistic love experiences before puberty, so sexual emotion, when it arrives, can be differentiated more easily from the more basic and lasting unconditional type of love. This awareness can help people choose romantic partners more wisely. Its absence can result in catastrophic choices of partners who seek sexual gratification at the expense of a genuine underlying altruistic love.

When we feel loving, we feel peace inside and often sense that the other feels the same. I see love as peace on the move. Actions spring from those feelings which can have life-changing consequences. For instance, if a couple feels that their love for each other is sustainable, deep enough and beyond the erotic - and that may not necessarily be expressed verbally - they may believe they will spend their lives together and commit to having a child.

That emotion, sourced in peace, has driven the most important decision any of us can make: to create a new life. Each feels that being with the other will exclusively give them the happiness they seek. A sound family relationship is hopefully formed.

The other primary element, fear, is equally powerful. Peace is born out of a long-term security of knowing we are safe. Fear is an instantaneous emotion designed to prompt immediate response to maintain our safety. It comes from what is often referred to as the reptilian brain, that most basic animal part of us whose actions pre-empt the rational thinking part of our brains. Action can be driven by emotions in that organ without referring to the higher parts of the brain because it is the primeval decision device found in all creatures.

Despite it being emotionally undesirable, fear is essential to life. If we did not experience fear, then we would be unperturbed about crossing the road in front of a bus and our life would be truncated fairly quickly. Fear is the protective system of daily life. Most of us will attempt to construct our lives such that peace is maximised and fear is minimised.

Some of us will have greater success than others in that, very often dependent on the sort of conditioning our childhood brought and on our current circumstances. Those under bombardment in a war zone will have little choice.

However undesirable it is, fear will be a daily reality for them. Fear is not a conscious choice but an animal reaction to prevailing danger.

Sometimes danger happens to us, but sometimes we actually choose activities which entail danger. We will cross busy roads as part of an essential daily routine. Many of us drive. Even in developed countries, driving is one of the more dangerous occupations we undertake regularly.

This and other more optional activities are essential parts of our natural development into new experiences in life. It starts at an early age. A toddler takes steps away from its mother or carer into a busy play area. If it feels secure when it returns to its carer, it will continue to take ever more steps away, going farther and staying away longer each time. It is leaning how to take and manage risk.

By being able to manage its fears of new situations, confident its carer will always be there for it, its mind and consequently its scope of abilities will expand. Because it does not need to be concerned with its own security, it has more thinking space to discover and assimilate new things. This is healthy development.

Indeed, unless it can embrace the fears which come with expanding abilities, it will not progress in life. John Bowlby studied this natural process and what it looks like when things go wrong. He developed his Attachment Theory which enabled us to be more aware of healthy and unhealthy strategies for infant care and what happens in adulthood as a consequence.

We grow up and may leave home to study or work. Scary at the time, but if it's right for us, we must follow our destiny to find our own particular fulfilment. We are always taking risks in our lives with the intention of bettering them by one means or another.

By their very essence, risks generate some level of fear in us. If we did not experience fear in risk taking, we would soon get hurt because we will inevitably misread our challenges. We estimate how much we expect to get from our adventures against the dangers we are placing ourselves in. We will still minimise our fear against the gains we seek. I once did a parachute jump for charity in the days when it was solo. There was no instructor with me. It was very scary, but I satisfied myself that the whole process was sound.

Despite having accepted death as a possible outcome as I stepped out onto the wing at several thousand feet, I absolutely loved it in the end. I measured the risks against the reward and got a good result. Our choices are made in reference to the level of adventure we seek.

Businesses use precise models to replicate this process in a way which can be conveyed to participants in a logical and repeatable manner so that communal agreements can be made. Risk Analyses estimate the probability that an activity will go sour against the impact of such a negative outcome. These risk and impact values are compounded to give a balanced view of the proposed project so it can be compared with the other options.

Cost Benefit Analyses balance the expected advantages with the potential downsides, and decisions are made to proceed or not against a predetermined benchmark. Our own daily decisions are less formalised and cognitive, so more intuitive. We don't have to justify them to the company board, but the principles are the same and the complexities are all there. Committing our thoughts to print can help us process the more complex choices we face as individuals.

Risk taking and the fear that goes with that is therefore an essential component of the development of any animal. We frequently ask how much we want to do something and what happens if it goes wrong? Fear is the main sensation driving the decision. It can often be experienced as excitement, but that is fear based too.

Section 3
Trauma and Its Resolution

11: What Is Trauma?

We experience challenges in our lives every day. We might catch a cold from someone: a biological impact. We might hurt ourselves while doing a manual job: a physical impact. We might be shocked at some bad news: an emotional impact.

Society readily accepts biological and physical impacts as part of life, but can struggle to recognise some emotional impacts, particularly if they are a bit too heavy for us to absorb and process ourselves. If not dealt with, they can become bedded in as trauma. Whilst trauma has commonly been connected with military conflict and more recently with major disasters, it exists in some size and shape somewhere in everyone, only a fraction of whom seek counselling.

Post Traumatic Stress Disorder (PTSD) was first properly recognised in casualties returning from the Great War who appeared to have lost their sanity. It was called Shell Shock at that time. Some victims displayed very bizarre behaviour. A more commonly observed reaction was to a regular phenomenon of the time, the backfiring of cars. Raw fuel got into the exhaust systems in those days and exploded randomly. It turned the eyes of normal people but terrified those veterans who instinctively associated it with shells exploding. They reacted accordingly, dropping to the ground wherever they were, much to the consternation of those around them. A naval veteran of the Falklands War did just that at a subsequent air show when an aeroplane came close to the crowd. Unless dealt with sympathetically, this conditioned reaction, so essential to survival on the battlefront, could develop into a deeper and more debilitating pathology in peacetime.

It is important to differentiate between the word 'trauma' and the medical diagnosis of Post Traumatic Stress Disorder. Counsellors are not trained to diagnose. That is left to the psychologists and psychiatrists, although many people more eminent than I have reservations on the multiplicity of diagnoses available under schemes like the DSM and their usefulness beyond a means of allocating health budgets. However, for the purposes of therapy, I can and need to identify and discuss clients' traumas resulting from unwanted events.

On the one hand, the American Psychological Association (APA) defines Post Traumatic Stress Disorder, as 'an anxiety problem that develops in some people after extremely traumatic events, such as combat, crime, an accident or natural disaster'.[1]

On the other hand, The Australian Psychological Society (APS) says:

'Traumatic events are powerful and upsetting incidents that intrude into daily life - usually defined as experiences which are…significant threats to one's physical or psychological well-being. The same event may have little impact on one person but cause severe distress in another individual. The impact that an event has may be related to the person's mental and physical health, level of available support at the time of the event and past experience and coping skills.'[2]

I constantly meet the feature of trauma in my clients as defined by the APS. I am uncertain as to how many of them would meet the extreme criteria of Post Traumatic Stress Disorder described by the APA. However, as a counsellor, I am not concerned about intensity. I am only interested in whether the issue my client faces is a trauma which is impacting their life significantly or not and how I can help them. I offer the following definition:

Trauma is the lasting negative effect of any emotional impact, regardless of size.

This is useful in my practice because I need to differentiate between client responses to current events and triggered reactions to historic ones.

A client had been brought up in an immigrant family which had focussed on physical survival rather than emotional support. She had been sexually assaulted as a young teenager. Her first marriage had failed. She met a new suitor who was still irrevocably connected to an abusive ex-wife through their children. She wondered how much the difficulties she was experiencing were due to this historic issue. I felt it was relatively small. She was a sensitive person, vicariously involved in her partner's abusive relationship. That would account for much of her emotions. This significantly affected the discourse. To have pursued historic trauma alone could have left her not only defenceless against the current emotional attack, but possibly blaming herself for an abnormal response to it.

I have helped war veterans and torture victims. I have also met children who are upset about bullying in the playground. It's all trauma and in the first instance, I will treat it all the same way. My method is person-centred and not pathology centred, so I will listen to my clients when they are ready to talk about it. I will not force it.

I see trauma as being not so much about the past but about fear of the future. It is a residual and visceral fear that an event which has damaged us in some way previously may recur in some form and damage us again. That is what life is all about at its most basic level; surviving by keeping ourselves safe from the threats which can trigger such emotions. Conversely, if a particular memory, however distasteful, no longer generates fear in us, particularly about the future, we don't call it trauma any more.

Until we have been able to revisit a trauma experientially, and usually cognitively, and maintain our emotional equilibrium with it, our daily emotions will, in part, be defined by that fear of recurrence. I say 'usually cognitively' because the structural memory may not always be available, even though the emotions are. We feel them now regardless of whether we are consciously recalling the offending event or not. I must have remembered how to crawl and walk because I can still do both of those things now. However, I can't recall my learning how to do them. The memory is there but the recall route had not yet been developed. There would have been a lot of parental emotion around my accomplishments at the time, so it's not that it went by unnoticed. A sequel to the last client narrative illustrates this:

A return to therapy a year later yielded something different. As we roamed over her life events in search of traumas, it became apparent that her emotions were most intense as she talked about a year spent with grandparents away from parents from 6 to 18 months. She could have no conscious recall of this time, but her emotional response indicated something very significant. The enormous relief afterwards suggested a great burden had been lifted.

The laying down of memories and recalling them are two different things. That could have been significant for a teenager I saw with Obsessive Compulsive Disorder (OCD) behaviours. She had required resuscitation after a premature birth. There was no conscious access to the memory, but the fear evidenced by the OCD may well have been its emotional residue. All this becomes locked away in our minds. Sooner or later, whether we like it or not, it will come out uninvited in some form or another and take us by surprise.

Whenever a current thought process gets near to a traumatic memory, our reactions can reflect the magnitude and nature of the trauma rather than that of the current event. The original emotion has been triggered. The older we get, the less able we seem to be to hold back the door of the boxes we have consciously or subconsciously locked the traumas in and they can start to haunt us.

12: Processing Emotion

An event generates trauma when it is not processed in the normal manner. It is as though we have emotional indigestion. In 'The Body Keeps the Score', psychiatrist Bessel van der Kolk describes how emotional experiences can get stuck in that very primitive part of the brain common to all animals, the limbic system. It is the entry point for the senses and experiences. If the experiences can't be processed further, they remain there, leaving us feeling anxious.

Matthew Walker is a neuroscientist who has made a life's work of studying the role of sleep and dreaming, particularly in processing information. He tests sleep function propositions, often using modern investigatory techniques such as fMRI scanners.

In a very readable compendium of his research, 'Why We Sleep', he describes how the brain deals with incoming sensory information. He finds it is coordinated and stored in the hippocampus in the limbic area. That provides a limited daily cache from which information is transferred in our sleep to the brain's higher-level processing area.

Like me, he uses computer analogies to describe this. He refers to the hippocampus as a USB stick and the cortex as the hard drive. The transfer process happens in sleep. Walker proved that the non-REM process in sleep stored cognitive memories. He also showed that it was REM sleep which provides the 'emotional convalescence' we need every day.

He points out that sleep is not just a nuisance which gets in the way of doing all the things we think we want to do, but an essential part of body and mind maintenance, which if ignored, will leave us physically sick. Sustained lack of sleep can quickly induce psychosis and worse. In 1983, an Italian man died from a rare pathology in which sleep became unattainable.[1]

That somewhat emphasises the essential nature of this underrated function. Walker bemoans how we tend to undervalue sleep, saying we routinely take less than we need, chronically underperforming during the day and 'under-enjoying' life too. He finds that sports research shows 'that post performance sleep accelerates physical recovery from common inflammation, stimulates muscle repair and helps restock cellular energy.'

'An insomniac client reported that a scar from a physical injury had not healed in years until she started to get the sleep she needed. Then it healed very quickly.'[2]

That healing process applies to all of us in all our activities, not just the physical ones. Sleep heals the normal stresses the body sustains in a day. I might be bruised in an accident. My body will automatically embark on a highly complex set of processes to heal itself. It is remarkably clever. We take that so much for granted. This healing process also applies to our emotional beings.

In his search for methods of helping the stresses his clients carried, Sigmund Freud postulated that dreams were 'day residue', stresses we have been unable to process during our conscious day. There was some truth in his concept, but he could not prove it. He went on to presume that dreams had structural significance and their analysis could identify his client's problems. He linked that into his early schooling of Greek mythology with some bizarre results. A colleague of Walker's, Robert Stickgold, examined Freud's concept of day residue by conducting experiments to identify how much dreams did actually replicate the day's actual events. He found very little correlation.

However, he did discover a totally different result with his participants' emotional recall. He found that 'between 35% and 55% of emotional themes and concerns they were having while they were awake, powerfully and unambiguously resurfaced in the dreams they were having at night.'

In his work, Walker noted that the amygdala, the limbic system's emotional processor, was 30% more active in Rapid Eye Movement (REM) sleep than in waking mode.

In REM sleep, our eyeballs are moving. Other sleep is designated non-REM. Electronic detection systems indicate that REM sleep is the time when we dream. Walker sees dreaming as the subconscious vehicle of emotional maintenance in the same way that sleep generally provides physiological maintenance. By 'dreaming', he meant the brain's activity during REM sleep. We normally think of dreams as what we remember in the morning.

However, REM sleep occurs in a truly unconscious state. If we are disturbed in some way during REM sleep and start to become conscious, then the dreaming sequels during that transition may become available to conscious memory. This sort of dreaming is more an aberration than a normal process, although not necessarily harmful.

Nonetheless, it does provide a window into the more regular dream process. This experience of dreaming is usually absurd in content. It is as though a series of random events have been stitched together to produce a crazy story. While some people believe they can find meaning in this, Freud's idea that therapy can be routinely based on this was discredited as a premise after many years of use or rather misuse. I wonder how much damage has been done to clients by this misdirection. Professionals need to be very wary of the harm they can do.

I liken memory processing to clearing my desk at the end of my working day. There are papers all over it in fairly random order and I need to file them away into segregated folders so I can find them all again at some time in the future. I also need to see the wood of my desk too so I can start all over again the next day. I will file them as I see them, so there is no rationale to the order in which they get into the files. If a passerby were to look at each paper as I filed it and then write a story around the sequence, they would come up with an absurd tale. A great project for a child's creative writing!

This is how those dreams which occur in the transition to the waking state are remembered. As we come to, our barely conscious mind observes and remembers the random sequence of memory filing. Then we try to make sense of it. But there is not a lot of sense to be gleaned from this normally because these are snapshots, randomly sequenced from a number of unrelated events. Clients sometimes talk about their lucid dreams claiming that they offer some insight. I have helped clients work constructively with their remembered dreams.

A client had been seriously beset by some dreadful characters at his place of worship. When they appeared in a dream some years later as his life was changing for the better, they appeared to be subservient to him rather than dominating him as they had. It helped him significantly that we could identify this change. Friends noticed the change in him. We discussed the healing this represented.

Neuroscientists have discovered a mental filing system which works overnight in the subconscious dreaming REM state. Our data input system gets full in the day and the sleep process empties it into a longer term storage facility in an orderly manner so we can retrieve it in the future - for as long as our mind is still working well. We wake up with a fresh mind, ready to deal with whatever the new day brings.

I compare the limbic input function to the RAM part of my computer which is only available when the computer is switched on, (awake) and which processes data and stores it temporarily. I compare the memory in my brain to my computer's Hard Drive which stores everything long-term.

Walker sees REM sleep as a means to 'dissolve the visceral, painful emotional charge that had previously been wrapped around those memories'.[2] The Circle Diagram envisages emotion residing within the shell of a memory, but the principle of fixed memories with resolvable emotions remains the same. Walker looked into the chemical mechanisms involved and found that a 'key stress related hormone, noradrenaline, was completely shut off...when you enter this dreaming sleep state'.

It seems therefore that, during REM sleep, the mind is processing emotional memories which will include stressful ones too, but in the absence of the element of fear because the conscious is turned off. Thus, as the emotional narrative is rerun, re-traumatising cannot take place. The difficult stories are processed in a safe place allowing the emotions within them to be harmlessly resolved. It's worth noting that this is similar to the process of Person-Centred Counselling.

It appears that our brain's software systems are designed to process our daily emotional impacts efficiently. So why do we end up with long-term issues which distress us before we have even started the day sometimes? Like any other system, there can be overloads to the natural process and they can result in residues carried over to the next day. In this, Freud's 'day residue' idea made sense.

If an overload remains after the first night's sleep following a stressful event, then the second night might not be able to resolve it either. If the emotional aspect of this event keeps on carrying over, we can envisage a residue of the impact which will remain for ever unless otherwise treated. This is trauma: an historical experience affecting how we feel today. The result is an emotional memory which is impeding our life going forward because we have a fear of its recurrence. Our normal systems are not resolving it. Everyone has this experience in some degree.

At any one time, most of us are emotionally affected by events which have occurred some time before our last sleep. We might worry we have offended someone yesterday or we are still affected by the death of a relative last year. Our minds are full of all sorts of cognitive and emotional memories, which inform our thoughts and moods continually. Emotions bound into memories of events going back months, years and even decades ago can frequently come to mind.

An anniversary of the Nazi Holocaust reminded me that those who experienced it in childhood are still brought to tears in their twilight years, seven decades later. Because my happiness is all about what is in my head now, the concept of trauma can define my well-being and even overwhelm it. Trauma and its resolution are important to all of us.

13: Impact

Whatever the nature of our traumas, and we all pick them up in some shape or form, they can and will reappear uninvited, sometimes as midlife crises. When nothing seems to be going particularly wrong, we can inexplicably descend into anxiety, depression or both. It is often when the ambient level of our current crises falls, as shown in the Recovery Profile, that the hitherto submerged mounds of our traumas start to appear as islands of anxiety, alerting us to the need to attend to them.

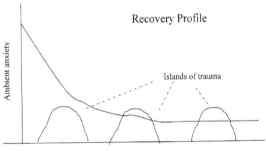

Reducing ambient anxiety over time

In the same way that our bodies demand attention for our physical injuries when the battle is over, our souls will always insist on traumas being attended to after the crisis and until such time as they are healed.

Many people are unaware that they have experienced traumas, especially ones sustained in childhood. They simply ploughed through what was presented to them because they just had to get on and deal with it. They put these experiences behind them or so they thought. Unless we have developed a clear benchmark of healthy living, we may not consciously recognise some events as having being traumatic, even though they were.

If we have been conditioned by our upbringing to accept and absorb abuse because the consequences of retaliation were worse than remaining quiet at that time, then we may continue to accept that sort of abuse for the rest of our lives. That is our norm. We are absorbing the impact, not because we can manage it, but because we saw it as the safest option and still do. Such continued attrition can lead to progressive emotional injury and the trauma will simply accumulate.

While we are dealing with our crises and sustaining emotional damage, the treatment of our wounds remains on hold. When the crisis ends, then it hits. We are distressed for no apparent reason. We find ourselves suffering quite severe emotional conditions of depression and/or anxiety and we can't understand it.

If I have got myself through all that lot, what can be my problem now? Further support is needed, possibly in the form of a talking therapy. If support is not available, these conditions can develop into more serious pathologies, perhaps leading to hospital detainment. Trauma is common in society and can be life restricting for many of us. It follows that an essential component of the therapy process must include attending to traumas.

In the absence of such help, we just have to get on and sort out the rest of our lives. We lock this horrible stuff away somewhere. We firewall it so that we can continue to perform the functions we need to at that time. And that locking away process is far more subconscious than conscious. We don't instigate it.

However, once an emotional memory has been locked away like this, it becomes much more difficult to access. We become blind to its existence and therefore feel able to legitimately deny it, even though it can still affect us. We won't unlock it again unless we are either forced to open it, which will make it worse or we find some extra help to open it safely. I liken emotional forced entry to ripping the bandage off a wound prematurely and doing more damage. We need to be patient and allow it to heal gradually. Otherwise, we can become re-traumatised.

The basic premise of trauma is that the damage is such that it does not go away of its own accord. Rather it festers, and if we trigger it when experiencing another similar event, it will reappear, often in disguise. I constantly meet clients who are surprised at how they feel after the death of a pet or a remote relative.

After some investigation, I often find that they had not properly grieved for a parent because they were too busy dealing with the consequences at the time. This new event triggered that previously suppressed and now dormant grief. We often do not even appreciate the cause of our emotional disturbances. We have lost the cognitive connection to its source, but it still needs attention because it remains in our subconscious. Troubled adult clients will often profess to having had a good upbringing which, on investigation, can turn out to be far from true. Young children are particularly vulnerable to accepting abuse because they have not had time to develop solid benchmarks for acceptable behaviour.

Even when the child grows up, it may still not appreciate the level of abuse it had been subjected to, perhaps not even recognising it as abuse at all. They have become conditioned to it, but when one of the embedded traumas from the abuse is exposed to a trigger event, they might need a trustworthy friend. One who understands the concept of trauma and how to support someone experiencing it. They are compelled to attend to it at some time because the fear is visceral and they can't enjoy their lives because their peace is hidden beneath the accumulation of their traumatic experiences.

There can be so many traumas that they can interfere with the flow of peace and strength from the Perfect Core to the Conscious being, as shown in the diagram, Trauma Blinded. It shows that for this person, few experiences can access the Perfect Core from the Conscious level. All the rest hit traumas and trigger responses more akin to the original event than the present one.

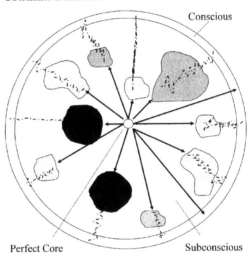

Trauma Blinded

Typically, they might fly into a rage at something others might take in their stride. They fear that the original event may happen again. It may not necessarily be a conscious fear but certainly one residing somewhere in the subconscious soul, and that is where it really matters.

In the absence of any deeper support, our subconscious will avoid the areas of our minds which carry those emotion-soaked memories. Instead of our thought processes going through the normal area, which is now damaged, they will find another route. The Emotional Infarct diagram shows someone's original processing going through an area associated, say with their spouse.

Now she has died, the emotion is too great to go there, so they find a way round it. But until we address the emotion carried within our memories, our brain functioning will be impaired by them and infected with them and our new related memories will be laid with that infection installed in them. It is very easy to see how many of the Great War veterans' minds were damaged for life, often extremely seriously.

This process has parallels with stroke patients. A bleed in the brain causes an infarct, wherein a section of brain dies, taking all its associated functions with it. If the physiotherapists can get the patient working on the affected functions soon enough, the processing can rebuild around the infarct, restoring at least some of the original functions. This brain plasticity is the same process which enables our thoughts to return to normal, except that this is software damage as opposed to the hardware infarct. An emotional infarct.

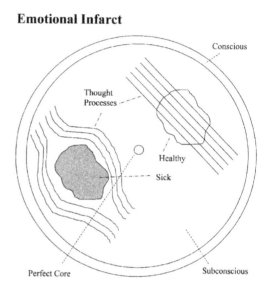

Emotional Infarct

A terrorist detonated a bomb in the MEN arena in Manchester in 2017. 23 people died, 10 under 20 years old and 512 were injured. The 14-year-old boy I counselled was not physically injured himself at the event, nor did he witness any serious injuries, but he was left with a visceral fear of that sort of environment.

No matter how illogical it may seem to all of us, including him, his subconscious being instinctively reacted to any similar situations he went into subsequently and left him feeling afraid for his life. Simply going into the city amidst the traffic and crowds terrified him. The impacts are often multifarious. In his case, it was:

- Experiencing fear in a great number of situations he had previously been happy in.

- Choosing not to go into such situations again.
- Losing opportunities which might be important in his life.
- Generating fears of new situations which might carry danger in them.

This is clearly not a good mindset for someone in his formative years. The damage the bomber caused went far beyond the deaths and physical injuries. There were thousands at the venue that night, most of whom will have been injured psychologically themselves, not to speak of the multiplier effect on relatives and friends.

In his early professional years, Bessel van der Kolk discovered trauma in Vietnam veterans when using informal group therapy. They got together to talk about their war memories. The more they talked, the more they were able to manage the emotions locked into their memories and so normalise their experiences.

In order to relieve ourselves of fear, we have to revisit the offending event in a safe way and discover at an emotional level what we are actually afraid of. We can address this at a conscious level to begin with. Is it structurally impossible for this horrific event to recur? It might have been in a job which we no longer do or with a person we no longer see. Or it might be that the threat is still a potential, as in a car accident or from an aggressive relative.

Either way, the emotions contained within the event memory keep reliving in our mind every time we go near to something similar. They will not be resolved unless we re-experience them somehow from a secure place. Our goal must ultimately be to revisit the memory of the event whenever we want without having to experience the emotion within it. I see it as lightening the emotional darkness within our traumatised memories. Counsellors call this normalisation.

Whatever the intensity of our traumas, we will always prefer to ignore them if we can because they are painful. We lock traumatic memories away by creating diversions whenever our thought processes go near them, both consciously and subconsciously. Indeed, in case of an extreme physical attack, we might have no effective access to the cognitive memory of it at all.

This is not unusual in car crashes. They can become sensitive wounds which won't heal because we can't find them. Diversions away from the hurting zones can be obviously addictive: alcohol, drugs, gambling, self-harm, etc. Otherwise healthy activities such as sport, games or work, can be done to excess too. If the size and intensity of the damage is great enough, these innocuous-looking diversions can start to take on the damaging aspects of addictions too.

Addictions always go on to generate their own traumas, adding to the original ones. It is easy to see how the continual burden of traumatic poison can progressively spill over into daily life as time goes on. It's also easy to see how, with no resolution to this, things just get heavier.

The Trauma Umbra diagram illustrates rather simplistically a few major traumas which might typically reside in anyone's life. In reality, there will be many more traumas than this in my clients. We drag them all around within us, making our lives unpleasant and holding us back from real enjoyment.

They are different sizes, depending on how much of life they impact and different shades for the intensity of the emotion sustained within the memory envelope. Some are depicted nearer to the centre because they happened earlier in life,

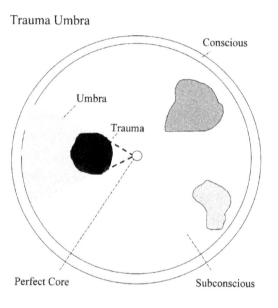

Trauma Umbra

as we might see on a tree stump. Some are more recent and are shown nearer the surface. They all have ongoing impacts down the line. We may react to events and situations in abnormal ways, to our detriment and maybe to others' too. Memories laid down in the umbra or shadow of a trauma are infected with the poison of its impact. Whatever new experiences we have related to that original event will be mutated by its emotional aberration.

As with the client in the crowd in which a terrorist detonated a bomb, even though he was not physically hurt, he became viscerally afraid of being in crowds thereafter, however safe they may be, and that of itself can generate further trauma. He has learnt at a very deep level, far beneath his consciousness, to associate crowded places with bombs and death. The probability of a repeat might be very low but the impact of it would be very high. A whole sector of a life becomes progressively influenced by the fear generated in an original unresolved event. The resultant burden can become debilitating as our ability to contain the emotional memory decreases over time. Time, of itself, is not a healer of trauma.

The resultant emotional indigestion can start to make normal stresses difficult to process too. It is hard to access the life we had before this event and enjoy it. Unless our upsetting emotions are normalised, they will poison otherwise healthy experiences and potentially destroy our enjoyment of them. This can escalate as time passes.

This diminishing ability to contain emotions was evident in a client who had a single traumatic experience in his teens which progressively manifested as panic attacks as he grew older. His level of ambient anxiety became raised by the fear of a panic attack. The Anxiety diagram shows that the higher the ambient anxiety, the smaller the gap to hitting another panic attack and the more frequent they can become. The progression of this pathology is easy to see.

However, as treatment progressed and he became more connected with his

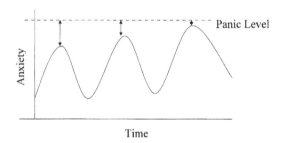

feelings prior to the attacks, he was able to face them down with increasing success. The ambient anxiety reduced and the emotion within the memory started to dissipate.

If he had not sought help after ten years, the panic attacks may have lasted many more. Victims of sexual assault in childhood can still be trying to deal with the resultant emotional load in their 50s and 60s. It is very real and very debilitating for them. When they have gone near to sexual experiences throughout their lives within what otherwise would be ordinary healthy relationships, the original trauma is recalled and fear arrives, dominating all other emotions. Normal sexual functioning can become frightening to the point of relationship breakdown. The soul's solution is to build a wall around the trauma and any emotions connected with it just to make life bearable for now.

In one of her web videos, somatic psychology pioneer Pat Ogden recalls a client who had heard a dog bark while she was being raped, with the consequence of relived trauma every time she heard a dog. That trigger took some teasing out, but then provided a key to the therapy.[1]

If we can get to the point of re-experiencing the original event, but under our control this time, then we will have dissolved the threat in it and need never fear it again. The relived emotional experience will be similar, but now we can manage it without major impact. We have now normalised that type of event. The abnormal damaging memory becomes a normal one because the emotions embedded in it have been dissipated and we can recall it freely without feeling disturbed by them. We can be safely in touch with our Perfect Core while re-experiencing the memory.

The software of our being retells our stories internally in REM sleep where the experience of fear is absent. Counselling seeks to provide a similar environment in the waking state. The client is invited to tell their story in a place where there is no fear of recrimination. They do not have to consider the impact of their story on their relationship with their listener because that exists solely for the purpose of therapy. There will be no consequences outside for their stories and when the client is ready to go, the relationship just ends. It is the skill of the counsellor to ensure that the client feels free to express themselves, not only in narration but also in emotion. Counselling is providing the indigestion medicine for the memories that have become stuck due to the intensity of the emotions residing within them.

The specific meditation I offer in my practice works similarly, but at a deeper level. The process encourages us to routinely assign all arising thoughts to a safe place. That enables the mind to accept any thought or emotion without fear because we can control it by routinely retreating from it in a designated way. That way, we reduce the level of emotion attached to each of our traumas, one by one. By systematically resolving our resident traumas like this, we clear away the internal baggage bit by bit and start to enjoy life to the full without continually triggering unpleasant interruptions.

I find that clients are greatly encouraged by the science and this view of it. They discover that they already have a healing mechanism inside them which will resolve what they thought were intractable problems. They also realise that external help is available and there is a method to that too.

14: Healing Options

Mental sickness is at least as multifarious as physical sickness, but our understanding of it is far less comprehensive. There are cases where the brain suffers physical trauma from a car crash, a tumour or a disease such as Alzheimer's. These are hardware issues calling for physical or chemical interventions beyond the scope of this book and my expertise. But whatever ails us, emotional issues remain to be resolved. The Healing Options diagram shows a variety of approaches aimed at relieving distress.

Pharmaceutical

If we visit a doctor and they identify a pathology such as anxiety or depression, we may be offered an antidepressant. It is quick to administer. General Practitioners in Britain in particular, do not normally have the time to indulge in a counselling function, so this may be the only viable response at the time in this setting.

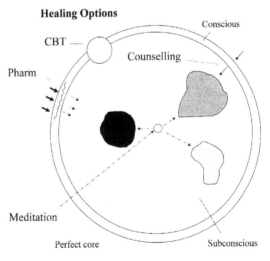

Healing Options

However, while a pharmaceutical answer may help in the short term, it will not generally provide a long-term solution of itself unless the problem is physiological. In his book *Cracked*, James Davies provides ample evidence that the outcome of long-term psychoactive medication can be negative, and sometimes very negative. That can include suicidal thoughts, particularly in younger people, possibly because they find it more difficult to regulate powerful medication reliably.

Antidepressant medication might often provide some insulation in the short term when we are feeling emotionally battered and need some anaesthetic from the prevailing onslaught. The diagram indicates how the external stresses are reduced by the medication before they hit the raw trauma inside.

However, there are a number of downsides to this remedy. If our issues are current and we need to be on the ball to manage them, the prescribed drug may take the edge off our decision making at a very important time, rendering us either incapable of reaching a good decision or being afraid of even addressing the problem.

An early client on my training journey had succumbed to road rage as a result of a previous trauma on a motorway. He was prescribed an antidepressant to deal with a current related incident, but that rendered him unable to address his impending court case properly. That in turn increased his anxiety, so his doctor prescribed a higher dose, making him even less able to cope and, consequently, more anxious. The medication was having precisely the opposite effect to what this client needed. The poor man lost his job, his career and his freedom. Regrettably, I was not in a position at the time to intervene effectively.

There is considerable discussion over the benefits and dangers of psychological medication. James Davies describes massive overprescribing. We know so little about the brain and even less about the effects of chemicals introduced into it. In the USA, infants from two years old can be prescribed psychoactive medication. In Britain, this is avoided for people of school age and below where possible. We are ill advised to interfere with the brain while it is forming lest we do long-term irreversible damage. Brain mass increases up to around the age of five and then stops growing. Thereon, up to our mid-twenties, the physical neuron pathways in the brain, the synapses, continue to form and those not used will expire. It is that formative element which makes the human so adaptable to changing environments. It is also that foundational development that we tamper with when we use medication.

Further development in the twenties tends to be software driven, so any damage sustained then tends not to be hard-wired in. Unlike our physical bodies, our software never stops growing and developing. Adults are not immune to damage, but negative impacts on a well-developed mind can be more easily resolved. I really see this in my inner-city work, which essentially comprises two cohort types: asylum seekers and those whose upbringings have failed them.

Many of the asylum seekers have come from loving families. Whatever their current calamity, they need much less support than those whose foundations are poor. It is clear how important it is to get the foundations solid so we can manage things going wrong later in life. The natural way for this is to provide a child with all the love and guidance they need. There is no substitute.

All psychological drugs have some side effects. For my 'walking wounded' level clients, these can over time defeat the benefits they might offer. Unfortunately, in the all too frequent absence of effective talking therapy, people are left with pharmaceutical responses to psychological problems. Regrettably, once on a psychoactive drug, patients tend not to revisit the doctor when they are feeling better and should be reducing or stopping the medication.

Instead, they can remain with their dosage until the next crisis, when the answer may be to increase it. This can go on until the maximum limit is reached, when a different or stronger drug may be prescribed. When a second drug is added, the amount of unknown effect is compounded. I have seen clients struggling to control themselves on cocktails of four different psychoactive drugs plus ones for physical complaints which may have psychoactive components. I am convinced that their struggle is often rather more to do with their medication than their underlying condition.

After just a few sessions, it became apparent that a client's only malady was the string of medications she had been prescribed for post-natal depression forty years previously. There were simply no significant traumas she could recall and her personality appeared normal. Each change of drug had its own recipe of side effects without reducing the accumulated anxiety they had all generated. As the side effects came to the fore, she was prescribed other drugs until she came round to her original one with all its initial problems. The cost of her private pharmaceutical treatment was such that she could not afford the fractional cost of the talking therapy which may very well have relieved her problems for ever.

Cognitive Behavioural Therapy (CBT)

The most frequent non-pharmacological therapy medically prescribed by the British NHS at the time of writing is CBT. It works on the basis that what we think affects what we feel. In its pure form, it does what it says: it consciously seeks out a behaviour which is unhelpful and devises a way to change that.

A client regularly responded to the greeting 'How are you?' with his medical history. He then wondered why he had few friends. After some discussion, he understood the consequences of his response and changed it to good effect.

The Cognitive part was his understanding the results of his actions. The Behavioural part was the change in his responses and the Therapy part was that he managed to retain some friends. He felt better. That was an essential first step. But while the therapy focussed on his behaviour, it did not address the issues which drove his need to tell everyone about his condition in the first place. The therapy on its own was temporary and he resorted to form when his issues remained unresolved.

CBT is a useful tool in my armoury for addressing the 'now' issues, but something more is almost always needed because the unhelpful behaviour is the result of malware operating beneath the surface. That needs addressing next. Otherwise, the problem only resurfaces in the same or another manifestation later. Group addiction therapy programmes tend to be CBT based. They are often successful initially but addicts tell me the effects don't last without additional personal input.

Indeed, there are specific cases in which, as a counsellor, I would not attempt to change apparently unhelpful behaviour. Younger clients can often use self-harm to help relieve themselves of unbearable anguish. If I try to stop that activity, I will either lose them or, if they do comply, they will simply find another outlet for their pain and possibly a more dangerous one such as an eating disorder. The CBT approach would be addressing a symptom of the problem but not the problem itself. On its own, it may do more harm than good. Another device is required.

Counselling

The majority of the psychological problems afflicting the general population are software in nature and can be addressed by the client simply discovering what is going wrong and why, and then considering what changes might help. This reprogramming may take some time if the problems stem from childhood, but the soul will ultimately gravitate to healthy default thinking once the destructive gremlins have been slain.

The founder of Person-Centred Counselling, Carl Rogers, embodied this concept of natural healing in his Nineteen Propositions, albeit it in the language of his time.[1] Counselling offers a potentially powerful tool for accessing these underlying emotional issues. At its simplest, it is essentially a professional listening service. It is based on a simple premise: If I tell someone something and they understand it, it changes the way I think about it.

I regularly lose my keys, but not infrequently, moments after I have asked my wife to help me find them, I remember where I have put them without her doing anything. My invitation to her input has found and stimulated a part of my memory I was not accessing and that has exposed the dormant information I needed. At a deeper and more significant level, I will seek to share my excess emotions with a friend. The process of communicating my emotions may recalibrate them into a healthier form. That may lighten my load through a realisation of a truth that was there all the time.

A client once told me that her partner was 'great with the kids' until I asked her what that looked like. He did not live with her, but at his mother's house. It turned out that on the few occasions he took them to the park, he spent most of his time on his mobile phone. For her own purposes, his mother had created the rumour that he was 'great with the kids'. The reality just needed exposing. She then got it right away. It changed the way she thought of him and more to the point, the way she dealt with him.

This example demonstrates how someone impartial like a counsellor can challenge established ideas and identify a truth which makes more sense. While we might need someone else to listen to our story to achieve this mental change, our nearest and dearest, however keen they may be to help, might not be the best to help us.

My client had been surrounded by people who had bought into the 'great with the kids' story. She just needed someone to accept what she had subconsciously already suspected. That it was just a story.

Those around us can be too emotionally involved in us to be objective. They may have another agenda for the problem which would influence their response. Their desire to see us happy may translate into offering or even insisting on their solution as if the problem were their own. Their answer might not be our answer. Their ideas will be based on their own experiences which may not concur with our own. If the best solution for us may be uncomfortable for them personally, they may try to persuade us against it.

Even if a mother is trying to be impartial, she may be so concerned about her child's issues that her fear is conveyed to them, adding to the child's worries. Double trouble for the offspring. There may be a solution which might settle mum's anxiety for the moment, but that may not be the best for her child. The young person will need to discover for themselves what has been going wrong.

That could mean them continuing what they are doing for a while until they discover the results of their actions from their own experience. Scary for mum maybe, but essential for the child's own learning, not just for now, but for subsequent occasions.

A mother had wanted her teenage son to maintain a relationship with his father, despite his abusing both mum and him and leaving the family when he was a baby. The boy formed a bond with him later which the father abused in subtle ways, such that any contact would leave him emotionally disturbed for weeks afterwards. Even when the immediate family got to grips with the danger, there was considerable pressure from the extended family to maintain the relationship, despite the damage it was doing.

The obvious solution would be to sever it, but the boy needed to go through a process of understanding it and then leaving it on his own terms, as though it were a bereavement. The journey was arduous for him, but it had to be his way if it was going to be resolved well. It took some time for him to work that out. The father had been at least partly present in his formative years so was embedded in his son's psyche.

The boy needed to unravel the person he was now meeting sufficiently to convince himself once and for all that he was no good for him. Only then could he safely reject him. His solution, and almost certainly a subconscious one, was to maintain the relationship until he gained sufficient understanding to resolve the internal conflict his father had created. He was then able to communicate with him without feeling disturbed.

That way, he could address the history of their relationship and resolve the damage it had done more comprehensively than if he had simply parted company for ever at the time. The outcome was well beyond my expectations and that of his mother. It was a lot of work, but it was his choice of journey. Painful to watch but essential for the ultimate well-being of the young person.

In all cases, it is better to seek out an unbiased opinion. It is useful to have a neutral mind to relate our story to, one which has no agenda other than our well-being and which has no other relationship or connection to care about or to confuse the dialogue. Then we can feel safe that the process will be a clarification of our own thoughts and feelings, with no contamination from elsewhere. Counsellors are trained to withhold their own prejudices and be that unbiased sounding board.

My impartiality in this work is important for the essential truth-seeking mission to discover where my client actually is emotionally at the time and where they might be heading. That emotional journey must be to access their Perfect Core, finding their peace there, taking their strength from there and discovering who they really are underneath. How all that manifests can often be a surprise and indeed a delight, for all. I have often been tempted by clients to affirm their decisions rather than stay neutral.

A young man wondered why I did not congratulate him on the apprenticeship he had just accepted. It seemed just right for him, resolving much of his concerns, but I simply reflected his views, reserving my own thoughts. Four months later, it turned out badly. Because I had not committed myself to his initial plan, I was able to move easily with him to his new plan and stay with him on his continuing, albeit bumpy, life journey.

I regard the counselling process as essential to every psychological recovery. However, like many words in this 'soft' profession, it is not well defined. The most common type offered in Britain outside the NHS is called Classical Person-Centred Counselling. In this simplest form, it is a primary listening tool which can be taught easily and relatively safely. Its power lies in the requirement of the counsellor to walk their client's journey with them. It is a basic and effective method, but has considerable limitations.

It worked for the mother who had allowed herself to be convinced that her child's father was a good parent when her own observation told a different story. The counsellor's role here was to give her space to review the information she already had and reach a more plausible conclusion. She then took action which changed life paths for all involved.

If we liken this to a computer, we can say that she underwent a small bit of self-reprogramming to remove an unhealthy virus which others had planted in there with unpleasant results. This change of mind was completely in the control of the client and produced results she was very happy with.

I believe that all talking therapies should be derived from this listening base but, on its own, the method fails to draw on the experience of the practitioner and of the therapeutic world as a whole. It is effective for clients who are self-aware, who can self-start and who only need an impartial sounding board. But not all are like that. I hear of silences in the counselling room, where neither party has anything to say. Counsellors describe it as being 'stuck'. They even have discussions on how to accept this.

There are indeed silences in my sessions too. I will normally have plenty to say at these times, but I am usually restraining myself because I can see my client is processing some emotions. There is plenty going on and that is what matters. It's just not being said. In contrast to this 'stuckness', these silences are in control and they form an essential part of my work.

Other Therapies

When trainee counsellors practice on each other, they have potentially ideal clients who will oblige by communicating in Classical mode. However, once qualified, they soon find that not all clients conform to this ideal. Some of the better educational establishments will teach a senior version called Integrative Person-Centred Counselling. It embodies the Classical base, but incorporates other modalities such as Psychodynamic, derived from a Freudian base, investigating psychological history and Cognitive Behavioural Therapy, aimed at managing the client's present situation.

Other practices taught independently include Hypnotherapy, Eye Movement Desensitisation and Regulation, (EMDR), Transactional Analysis, Gestalt Therapy and Existential Therapy.

Despite efforts to control it, Talking Therapy in Britain at least, is not well regulated. Some practices are actually unhealthy. For example, the British government is rightly seeking to ban Conversion Therapy, which is based on the misjudged belief that homosexuality can be changed to heterosexuality through talking therapy.

The NHS experiments with a plethora of derived treatments which, like 'online' CBT for instance, do not meet the concepts of 'person-centred'. None are revealing a significant breakthrough in therapy. Many NHS innovations are medical models based on detailed diagnoses which seek to treat the pathology rather than the person. Bessel van der Kolk, amongst many others, decries such blanket approaches.

My strongly held belief is that therapy should always have a person-centred base unless there are serious reasons like physical brain damage for it being otherwise. And even when the issue is a hardware one, there is always the software component which will need to be addressed for recovery. The person-centred method is still likely to be the most effective one. Just as a school teacher needs to reach into their student's place of understanding if they are going to transmit any learning effectively, the therapist needs to find out where their client is, get alongside them and understand how they feel. It is all development of the human software.

I recall a joke in which a holidaying couple got themselves lost in the countryside and stopped to ask a local how to get to a particular town. The reply was: "If I were you, I wouldn't have started from here." Clearly not very helpful, but the message here is that it is important to find out where we are before we try to get to where we want to be. That applies emotionally just as much as it applies geographically. Where is my client just now?

15: Emotional Contract

In the same way that our bodies can sustain a certain amount of physical injury and just get on and repair the damage themselves, so our souls employ mechanisms to heal their emotional damage too. But if my physical injury was not just a bit of bruising but a broken limb, my body will need some help to effect the necessary repair. That might be a plaster cast and the healing will take a little time. Similarly, if I am emotionally injured because I have sustained more stress than my mind can resolve internally, I will need some external help with that too. That process may take a little time.

The psyche or soul will always try and resolve its emotional impacts internally, as shown in the diagram by the arrow going to the Perfect Core. If we are healthy emotionally and well-adjusted to a civilised world, we will be able to absorb most of what we sustain in a day in this way. We tend not to give these impacts second thoughts.

If an impact is more than our soul can absorb easily, we might seek out a caring friend to help us manage the excess emotion. We need to be careful about who we choose and when and how we use them. It will have to be someone we trust. But it may not work well, for instance, if they are currently going through a crisis of their own. We try and sense if they are receptive by broaching the subject with them.

We must be able to trust that they will not misuse our situation either and make it worse by telling their friends. We need to choose the right place too. We won't want to be discussing it on the school playground or in front of others who might interrupt the conversation or observe the emotions. So we may ask a friend if they have some time. If we get an affirmative, they have agreed to accept an emotional package from us. An Emotional Contract is formed.

We tell them our story. It won't be just a factual narrative. We will be expressing some emotions too. Our friend would need to be able to manage these emotions. We need them to feel the same way we feel. While we won't get them to the intensity of our own feelings, the nearer they get, the more we can offload our emotions. Our mirror neurons need to be in synch with theirs for this work. That process will help restore our balance a little and we will feel lighter for that. The diagram shows how the combination of an internal process along with some external support can restore our emotional balance.

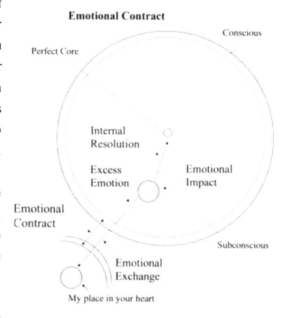

Contracts have two parts to them. While the speaker finds some relief in the process, the listener should get something out of this too. The net result of a healthy Emotional Exchange is that one person is relieved of some of their emotional load and the other feels good about helping. The emotion driving this contract is empathy.

Our physical world functions well by exchanging goods and services between individuals in an agreed and contracted manner for the benefit of all the participants, usually using a monetary currency. Our emotional world functions just as well when we share our emotional loads by mutual agreement, with empathy as the Emotional Currency.

Most of this happens between friends on a daily basis, but counsellors are also partners in Emotional Contracts, albeit in a professional capacity. The exchange is a little more formal in that they are listeners with no other agenda than the client's well-being. But my experience is that I am also rewarded by seeing my client rising out of their stresses and enjoying life for the first time in a long time. My empathy function is alive and well. I am emotionally augmented by providing the listening and supporting part of the Emotional Contract. That is how healthy Homo sapiens functions.

I like to think of the fruitful and fluid exchange of emotions as a currency akin to a commercial one. Healthy ongoing empathic links between people enable Emotional Contracts to form when the inevitable upsets of life throw us off balance. This win-win formula will ensure that both sides are augmented as a result and the emotional balance is restored. If all parties come away with their balances intact, then they will continue to be available to offer Emotional Contracts to others.

Providing all members of a community can maintain empathic links with each other, then individual emotional impacts will not only be resolved, but the whole community will be enhanced by that process. The win-win formula is now not just for the two involved in an individual Emotional Contract, but potentially works for all empathic members.

In just the same way that the healthy use of money enables and enhances the wealth of a community, so altruistic love, which is the currency of the Emotional Contract, enables and enhances the health of a community. However, I maintain that the emotional currency has the edge on commercial currency.

Money of itself will never make us happier.

        Altruistic love will always make us happier.

Love of money will accumulate in the hands of the
powerful to the detriment of the weaker members of society.

        Altruistic love will ensure that all are augmented.

Wealth at any one time is finite and is divided
between us, generally according to the rules of the powerful.

        Altruistic love is limitless and can be generated by
anyone at any time. The rules are universal.

There are smaller communities in which this seems to function well, but it's rarely 100% reliable.

One of the enterprises I have worked for serves those on the margins of society. All there were driven by a desire to enhance the lives of those in need and every success is celebrated there. It might not be utopian, but it exhibits effective Emotional Contracting in a community setting well. They even have paper Emotional Currency. If one person enhances another, the recipient can repay that by writing a compliment note. Notes are reviewed and celebrated at the year end. Primary level stuff, but it effectively encourages spontaneous Emotional Contracts and builds the emotional wealth of the community.

This is the Easter message we all got from the CEO:

Easter, for me, is a time to reflect on the sacrifices you all make with love, for our mission, our work, our people. We remember that, each time someone walks through our doors, it is a chance for a new life for them, to come to this place of hope and opportunity.

Remember how important you are in creating this place and making this.

Thank you for all you do and continue to do.

Even if we do manage to create some loving communities, the world is now too small for us to be happy in just our own corner of it. Global conflict readily spills over into different countries and different continents, with devastating effect for all. It is clear that a lot is going wrong in our world, at both micro and macro levels and a healthy emotional currency system could readily resolve that.

If we are all able to find friends happy to help when we are overloaded, we will maintain a good balance for the community as a whole. It is easy to see how Emotional Contracting can spread between individuals in a community to form a network of responsible empathic relationships which can help manage life's travails throughout that community.

That way, we can all function more happily and manage the emotional impacts we all sustain from time to time. Churches and self-help groups are often models which seek to exemplify this, but we all need to function like this to achieve peace, firstly in our communities and by extension, our countries and our world.

16: Project Client Recovery

While I cannot take credit for the miracles I see in my work, I do have an input to them, so I am constantly seeking ways to improve what I can offer. I see my clients as projects. The concept of a project is that it has a beginning, a middle and an end. The beginning is the level of distress which brought them to me in the first place. The end is them feeling in control and wanting to manage their lives on their own. Our team task it to find out what the middle bit looks like. The aim of my counselling is to equip my client so well that they don't need me anymore. I generate my own redundancy.

The essential mechanism of Classical Person-Centred Counselling is:

- When the client tells their story and they are understood, it changes the way they think about it.

I will invite a client to talk about themselves and how they feel about things. If they feel safe to say absolutely anything to me, they may tell me things which they have never been able to tell anyone else in their entire lives or certainly not to that depth of feeling. It brings an event into another time and space, the counselling room, and inspects it in this new unconditional light. That narration will be the start of reforming and reframing what they think about their life and, therefore, how they feel about it.

It is the feeling element that is the key to the process of normalising their trauma. I am letting my client know I will accompany them into their particular dark wood if they so wish. That is where their trauma lives.

Only when a client is ready to invite me in would I consider going there. I will not break and enter into the defences they have built around it, possibly over many years. I could do more damage by destroying them without providing a remedy for the trauma which may spill out. I must not rush their process. It could wreck the possibility of healing for ever if they rebuild their defences even higher. They have spent a great deal of energy locking the memory away and working around it in order to get on with their rest of their lives. I must absolutely respect the sanctity of their soul in this.

A rape victim came to me after having been through an NHS trauma process in which she was required to revisit the event every week, no doubt with a view to normalising it for her. The prevailing theory at the time seemed good but the practice was that she was re-traumatised every time. The therapist was not listening to her, probably because she was under time pressure to achieve a recovery target. I told her that in my practice we would only talk about it if and when she wanted. That is Person-Centred Counselling. It takes longer, but it works. The other does not.

If and when they are able to take me there, clients usually find that their wood is no longer as dark as they had remembered it all this time. Trauma is the fear of a recurrence of a similar horrible event or feeling sometime in the future. Because they had not been able to face their trauma, they would react badly when current events took them near to where they had subconsciously hidden it.

If they have someone to hold their hand while they take a peek at it, they might find that a recurrence is either not physically feasible or that they can devise strategies, with or without the counsellor, which make them feel safe in future. If they can understand the trauma this time round, they can defend themselves against another similar threat.

When they can see that it is no longer the massive issue that it looked like from their previous 'safe' distance, it is tamed. They got near to it and managed that experience. They are relieved of its long-standing burden and the emotion inside the memory envelope starts to dissolve. They can start to enjoy their lives, maybe for the first time. Once they are free from their undigested traumas, they will find they can control their lives more easily and even find pleasure in that.

I regard my basic practice as Integrative Person-Centred Counselling. It enhances the basic Classical Person-Centred Counselling which is taught in so many British institutions. Like in so much of the helping professions, it is discussed and debated in print and conversation but seldom formally defined. The Counselling Directory offers a general definition: 'Integrative counselling is a combined approach to psychotherapy that brings together different elements of specific therapies.'[1]

The Person-Centred component offers the space for the client to express themselves. This is the principal vehicle of therapy. The Integrative element may include psychodynamic work which considers the impact of the past, typically traumas. It can also include CBT to manage today's issues. I feel I do something broader by using my own life experiences, my learning from other clients and any other method or technique which may support them. I would define Integrative Person-Centred Counselling as:

An extension of Person-Centred Counselling which allows the freedom to use any ethical counselling method which could support improvement while maintaining the basic Person-Centred Counselling concept.

My CBT work with a young victim of a terrorist attack included encouraging him to physically go with mum to places of increasing challenge, continually offering emotional support. In some cases, adult clients have developed enough resistance through therapy to take themselves to the scene of the crime.

One client felt the need to address the rape she had suffered as a teenager, not so much for herself, but to be able to deal with her child who had been sexually predated on the internet. After some weeks of work, she was able to take herself to the place where it happened on her own. She became able to manage her emotions better thereafter. The therapy was then extended to cover other historic issues.

In addition to the essential foundation of Person-Centred Counselling, I normally offer a very specific meditation method to support clients' journeys to emotional health.

This particular meditation type is extremely effective because, unlike so many others I have seen, it is profoundly simple. It enlivens the soul's natural inner healing which is far more powerful than any external cognitive process. The Integrative Person-Centred method then enables the counsellor to guide the client through the changes and developments which are initiated, at least in part, by the healing arising from the meditation process.

I introduce the Circle Diagram to most of my clients early on, not just for them initially, but for us both to keep track of where they are on their journey. It is not intrusive. It is usually on the table, although I may not overtly refer to in a given session.

I find that my regular internal reference to it helps guide the dialogue for me as well as for my client. As we spontaneously build theoretical concepts on it, reflecting our discourse, a record appears of their issues and of the constructs which correspond most closely to their circumstances. That is useful to me too because, while I normally make extensive notes on what my client says, I can't write when I am speaking. By using the Circle Diagram to map out my client's emotional landscape on the table together, their situation appears in graphical form. That additional dimension stimulates different and deeper thought processes.

Thus, the Project Client Recovery takes the client's self-knowledge along with my theoretical and experiential knowledge and applies counselling concepts to all that. If they have taken it up the practice of meditation, that will play a significant part too. That unique combination enables them to look at their own thinking processes in a different light.

Some clients arrive having lost hope of ever feeling good again to the point where a life exit might be preferable. I prefer not to lose clients on my watch and my record is complete in that as far as I know. The life exit problem they might encounter is that we are evolutionarily programmed to resist death, even in the most severe of circumstances, so they live on in their pain. The viscerally emotive barrier to taking one's own life is very powerful. For any suicide, and there are on average 16 every day in Britain alone, the tragedy is not so much the death but the life of abject misery from which they were escaping. The baton of misery often then gets passed on to anyone who cared for them. I believe the more relevant statistic is the much greater one of attempted suicides. The Mental Health Foundation claims that one person in fifteen makes a suicide attempt at some point in their life.[2]

My professional and also my personal concern is the suffering. Life is not worth living for so many people for so much of their lives. No-one should be subjected to this. Death would be a relief for them. When they have gone, they have left behind their pain! That at least is a positive for long-term cases, although if there are any loved ones, they can inherit some of that suffering. I address the issue directly with clients. Some professionals struggle to manage this, possibly due to issues in their own lives.

This pain is so unnecessary for most people for most of the time. It's fixable with the right processes. I see my initial job as instilling in my clients sufficient hope to give life a chance. Because the clients who follow my programme improve, I can offer new ones the confidence that they too will improve. That moves a switch in them from despair to hope, inspiring them to apply effort to now go into Project Client Recovery.

National research statistics reveal poor therapy effectiveness.[3] In contrast, Soul-Centred Counselling is an objective process with clear routines within it and a track record of success. Once I have explained the rudiments of the emotional self on the Circle Diagram, I offer the properties of the Perfect Core:

The person I was meant to be before all the bad stuff happened;
A place of perfect peace
The source of all the strength I will ever need.

These will be the references of their journey. When they are realised, the desired end product is achieved. I tell them that these properties reside in everyone and that even includes them. All my clients recognise these features. The counselling project is to find their internal properties and explore them.

I see this internal resourcing, this self-reliance, as the essence of Person-Centred Counselling. I also see it as the essence of the pure form of meditation I offer, a process which has no reliance on external support. Once a client starts to see an improvement in themselves, resourced from within themselves, they can see that the journey which has eluded them for years has suddenly become possible.

Clients have often been floundering around with a plethora of confusing offerings from friends and the media, trying a bit of this and a bit of that. Because they did not see quick improvement, they have given up, possibly on a journey which may have worked. The confidence I have gained in my process across many clients inspires me, and in turn them, to persist with it. I help them spot signs of progress in themselves. The resultant hope marshals their flagging energies into this exciting new project. They now have a course upon which to focus their efforts. For every little identifiable movement, they gain the hope that they can achieve more.

A group meditation client could see that benefits were to be had, but thought that the experiences from his meditation were inconsequential. However, he mentioned how he kept thinking of the spare bedroom in his house. Even as he was telling me this, he realised that the reason he had not been able to go there till now was because all the paperwork which lead to his current situation was in there. The practice had allowed him to set foot in it and get started on his recovery.

Because the Perfect Core properties are within all of us, once clients can see the method working, they are able to continue to improve for ever, long after the counselling has finished. They now have genuine hope and its long-term too. That assures progress. This is the deeper meaning of Soul-Centred Counselling. Not only is the therapy focussed on the person as opposed to a pathology, but the solution to the client's concern lies at the centre of their own being which they have on tap now and for always.

However difficult a case is, I feel I should not give up even if that means signposting my client to a more specialist therapy. There is a person in their suffering and if I can reduce that suffering, I feel obliged to do so. And I feel challenged to do so. I am always seeking the Perfect Core inside of whoever is in front of me, not least because they want to see it too.

Whatever that person has done to harm themselves or anyone else, it is likely to have been the result of trauma they have been subjected to. My job is to find the good stuff inside and show it to them. They are often amazed at what they discover, not least because they are more used to being criticised than complimented. I am often humbled by the enormous courage some clients have mustered to deal with the massive problems they have faced and I let them know how I feel about that.

The manifestation of their pain has only resulted in condemnation so far. They often tell me that no-one has ever encouraged them like this before. To find themselves praised by a professional they may have been looking up to instantly increases their self-esteem. That also reminds me of my true place; one of supporting a fellow human being in their time of difficulty.

I am no better than the person in front of me, if 'better' makes any sense at all. I just have a different role today. No matter what age a client is and whatever they have done or not done, the task now is to make the future as joyful as possible. That will involve dealing with the past, whatever it is like. It is that relentless pursuit of goodness which will start to transform a client into the person they were meant to be.

They often discover talents that have lain dormant for years because they have been conditioned to deny themselves that aspect of their being. Sometimes those talents arise from the pain they have now conquered. That often occurs in those who have overcome addictions, using their journey experiences to help others who are still imprisoned by them. My counselling has an additional effect beyond the room. Win-win again!

Section 4
Spirituality

17: The Spiritual Zone

The Circle Diagram model shows a Conscious zone, a Subconscious zone and a Perfect Core. I liken it to the planet we are on. The consciousness is like that very thin layer of atmosphere we can see from satellites in space. It is our awareness of ourselves and the world we occupy.

The Spiritual Zone

We can see each other and the things around us through the atmosphere so we are conscious of that part of our world. Our massive subconsciousness is like the rest of the planet beneath our feet. We can penetrate only a little bit and learn something about it, but it is mostly unknown. And what we know of the earth's centre is more conjecture derived from limited evidence than established fact.

We do, however, know that the nature of the tiny zone in which we live is determined by the nature of the vastly greater invisible matter hidden underneath. It is with this in mind that I think of our emotions as emanating from a subconsciousness zone. And I think of the centre as being entirely mysterious but very influential. I ascribe the word 'spiritual' to that deepest possible level and indicate that in the Spiritual Zone Diagram.

Clients are routinely inspired by the concept that inside everyone, and that includes them, is all the peace and strength they will ever need to become the

115

person they were meant to be. They find a realistic hope of better times in this. It does not matter what age they are or what situation they are in. The future is all that matters. Now is the time to start converting anxiety into peace and sadness into joy. It goes further. As they become changed by that inspiration, I feel I can convey the confidence to my next client that their life can change too. And if that sounds a bit like religious zeal, then there may be more to that idea than meets the eye.

I was brought up in a religious environment, indeed a Christian one, but like the majority of my school peers, I asked enough questions to blow a hole in too many of the beliefs I was expected to accept. So, when it came to a counselling career which needed to be secular in order to communicate with the majority of potential clients in a country where less than 6% of the British population regularly attend church services, my thinking process fitted the profession.

So what happened in the gap between the Christian student and the functioning counsellor? A lot of questions and answers and that included a scientific career demanding evidential investigation and practical outcomes. Not the domain of blind belief. And running parallel to my life as an engineer and a family man was the imperative of resolving emotional problems from my own childhood.

I discovered that, despite my confidence in the scientific method, I was not going to succeed by simply thinking through my emotional issues analytically. It needed something deeper. And it was not going to be an unquestioning faith, either.

18: Spiritual Research

Coming into humanities from a technical discipline, I was frustrated to find many words that are freely used but rarely defined. People can argue over a topic simply because each party has a different image in their head of a single word being used. They may not even realise which word is the offending one. Once they discover what they are talking about, they often find themselves agreeing. That is time consuming and emotionally draining.

It is, however, avoidable. If we don't find common meanings for the words we use, we will be unable to communicate ideas to each other and we will not progress our understanding of our world and ourselves. Our knowledge cannot develop until we agree definitions. All the significant advances in our world have been achieved by different people amalgamating their different ideas. They needed a common language to pass on the knowledge baton.

Apart from analytical subjects such as neuroscience, we are making very poor progress in the mental health arena. So a word like 'spiritual', which stands on the edge of mental health, has hardly been investigated. There is limited consensus on its meaning.

Research carried out in December 2016 by Brierley Consultancy in Britain for the UK Faith Survey group seemed to challenge the very existence of spirituality in the public view.[1] It reported that only 48% believed in either a god or a higher spiritual power as against 38% who believed in neither. 14% were unsure.

So, what of the 38%? If we can accept that spirituality is represented by the Perfect Core in the Circle Diagram model, and I find that model to be unvaryingly affirmed, then everyone carries their own spiritual element. It's just that not everyone feels the need to be aware of spirituality or whatever they think it is.

In the same way that those who have been fortunate enough to have had a physically healthy life will normally have little need to find out what goes on inside their bodies, those whose lives have followed manageable emotional paths may have little interest in how the software of their beings, their souls, work.

Thus, emotionally healthy people may have no ready concept of spirituality, perhaps even regarding it as other people's fantasy or a facet of a religion they have rejected. In contrast, those who have experienced emotional difficulties will normally have spent some time seeking out spiritual, religious and philosophical topics in their search for happiness. They may regularly declare they are spiritual, even if not religious. Many others may find solace and success in religious communities too.

My Master's thesis focussed on spirituality in the context of counselling, so I sought a meaning which would work best for me. I investigated mental health sources to see what the experts were saying and found a description which appeared to fit most circumstances. It was not from a mainstream psychology expert, so not even within the normal classification of mental health. Professor Wilfred McSherry lead a British Spirituality Survey for the Royal College of Nursing in 2010. From his experience in nursing and the hospice service, he wrote the following from this research.

'Spirituality is universal, deeply personal and individual; it goes beyond formal notions of ritual or religious practice to encompass the unique capacity of each individual. It is at the core and essence of who we are, that spark which permeates the entire fabric of the person and demands that we are all worthy of dignity and respect. It transcends intellectual capability, elevating the status of all of humanity.'[2,3]

McSherry's vision of spirituality as being at the core of our beings, sits well in the Perfect Core of the Circle Diagram. His idea that it is beyond intellectual capability is also amply demonstrated with it being at the centre of a Subconscious mass, itself covered by a wafer-thin Conscious annulus.

19: The Role of Religion

McSherry believes spirituality is not exclusively a religious property. I find many people who would subscribe to being spiritual, but would not want to be called religious. However, the continual prevalence of religions and cults of various sorts throughout the ages impels us to accept that humanity seems to have a continual fundamental need to see beyond its physical world.

I see the role of religions as attempting to attain the individual and collective peace and happiness which reside within the concept of spirituality. The Role of Belief Systems diagram places the various religions in the context of their imperfect human attempts to aspire to something which is absolutely there but beyond conscious definition. We are all aware of the results of religious imperfections over the centuries and even today.

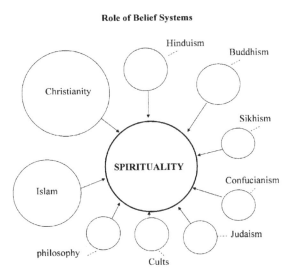

Role of Belief Systems

In contrast, I see the spiritual centre as being perfect in essence. Too often, we forget the natural wonder that is inside us. Not only is it our bodies which are remarkably functioning organisms, but it is our souls in equal measure, too. Our reticence to appreciate this amazing spiritual element ignores its power to hold and to heal. We need to attend to it because that is where our effective resilience really resides in our ever-changing lives.

Religions normally have deities who fulfil the role of providers of security in a world of uncertainty. While Buddhism tries to be an exception to this, at least in the intent of the founder, Siddhārtha Gautama, the prevalence of caricaturistic images of him in and around some temples and in some homes, tells of a need to identify with a potent icon in human form. We seem to need someone and something apparently powerful and successful on our sides. This particular founder would likely be concerned for what our needy humanity has done with his humble acceptance of the wonder of nature.

Our enduring need for deities throughout the ages reflects our realisation that we are not in full control of our lives. We would like to know that we are going to survive in good shape till next week, next year and on into the future. We need enough food and water, but not too much of the latter as we have seen in recent times. We don't want natural disasters, nor manmade disasters like war, even though we relentlessly create them.

We hope so much that we can be in command of these things. We create a deity which can resolve these difficult things for us if we are nice to it. Then we ask it. History tells us that this is not a reliable process. We ensure this unreliability by letting some very fallible national leaders take advantage of our need for a godlike figure and we elevate them to infallible deity status.

That process subjects the destiny of whole populations to the whims of some very suspect examples of human beings with enormous power who feign perfection to the masses in spite of very imperfect actions. There are plenty of examples of this in every age. It is probably safe to say that all the major conflicts and atrocities in history have been generated, at least in part, by this mechanism.

Nonetheless, religions as separate entities do have some success in meeting our needs. They can generate cohesive communities which can bind people together, both structurally and at deeper levels around a shared ethos, expressed or otherwise. They can create common rules for successful living. While many of those rules can be beneficial, some can also be destructive, not just in cults, but in parts of mainstream religion too. They have some spectacular failures, notably in partisan conflict and in appalling behaviour hidden under cassocks. Their dogmas can require irrational behaviour beyond that needed for coherent social functioning.

Once a community is prepared to believe innocuous doctrine without evidence, it becomes vulnerable to accepting malicious propaganda. Their rituals can intimidate other members of society. Historically, at least, the Ku Klux Klan in America is one of many such examples. The creation of an ethos in which the rule makers are beyond scrutiny can also result in unhealthy behaviour such as the paedophilic devastation in a Catholic community called to book by the Boston Globe in 2001.[1]

As a result, many people in developed societies prefer a non-religious spirituality. Unfortunately, those who become disillusioned with formal religion lose the mechanisms religions have built throughout their long traditions. They miss out on the community aspect which is important in the development of an individual's spirituality and for passing that spirituality on. They can also miss out on the ethos of personal reflection embedded in most religions and their rituals.

Secular states generate rules by creating legal systems which define what we must and must not do in order to preserve our social structures. If sound behavioural rules are in place at a day-to-day level, then a state driven legislature will become a safety net for the extreme circumstances only. That has to be a good thing. Religion may inform these rules.

On the other hand, if there are few sound informal rules in place, criminal sanctions will become the norm. Society has become dysfunctional if it relies on legal imperatives for daily behaviour. We see this typically in countries which are unable to control the traffic of illegal drugs. We need to have deep-seated intuitive guidance to live in harmony with each other, well above our legal safety nets. Wholesome versions of religions constrained by democratic secular statute can provide this.

20: The Voice Within

In Chapter 3 of the First Book of Samuel in the Hebrew *Bible*, a prophet called Eli tells the young Samuel what to say when he hears a mysterious voice saying "Speak Lord for your servant is listening." I have a friend who enjoys a parody on the verse. He turns it round: "Listen Lord for your servant is speaking," reflecting the tendency to ask the chosen deity for the things we are desperate for, but failing to pay attention to any wisdom which may be forthcoming. Eli seems to have the idea that the answer is already there for us to act on. We just need to take note of it.

Unlike the story which envisages an external deity, we might be best listening to what is inside us in those quiet moments, the sort of moments which a very simple meditation offers. We are unlikely to get any verbal messages. It will be more the feeling that I am or am not doing the right thing right now. Some religions relate to this. Buddhism is the most obvious candidate, but the world's largest religion, Christianity, also includes this internal reflective facility in its traditions.

Within its Trinitarian deity, the Holy Spirit is a formless powerful entity, which can be thought of as the voice inside. The Catholic denomination offers a very simple service called Adoration in which adherents are free to spend silent time together, listening time. This listening is mainstream practice for Quakers. I see considerable alignment between secular meditation and the spiritual element of the world's largest religion. So, despite its many human failings, Christianity seems to have caught the right basic idea, even if some of its adherents have not quite embraced it yet.

Many of the clients I support are in unimaginably difficult places. My profession does not normally include practical help, so my support for them is at the emotional level. I will walk as close as I can with them in this respect.

They normally accept both my efforts and my limitations in this. It is in these worst of cases that the most effective support tends towards the spiritual.

I recall a middle-aged man from one of the poorest nations in Africa. He was a failed asylum seeker and after fifteen years in Britain still had no national status. I was working for an agency which took care of the practical aspects of his situation, so it was not my place to investigate that. The man had no place to live, being reliant on those he had befriended. He was not permitted to work to earn an income. He had no access to benefits. He had no contact with relatives. My job was to help him emotionally. He said he had been hounded out of his country by his brothers and had lost contact with his wife and children. He had what the psychologists at one time would have described as a persecution complex. He believed that people were after him for an alleged criminal act for which he was never charged over a decade earlier. We worked with that for some time, but the real breakthrough came with his taking up meditation. His demeanour was transformed. This man who had absolutely nothing wore the biggest smile in the centre where he volunteered. He was effusive in his thanks to me for changing his life. He was powered from the very centre of his being. He had discovered the person he was meant to be. He had found his peace and the source of all the strength he needed. I often refer to him when clients think that their situations are doomed. Here is a man with absolutely nothing except the joy and peace effusing from his spiritual core. If he can find this beneath all his problems, we can all find ours.

It is that inner strength which can elude people who are distressed. My client found his through the meditation I taught him. It is too easy to underestimate the power of this particular type of meditation which grows the only thing which really matters in life, our peace. And it is the tangible reality of this power which evidences the existence of spirituality. It is not just a theoretical concept for academic discourse. It is both as invisible and as real as the gravitational pull of the earth.

We take gravity for granted because it is always there and everyone has to work with it. We can forget how powerful it is until we fall down the steps and break an ankle. In the same way, when the emotional chips are down and we get hurt, we can find an inner power and strength which is beyond our understanding. And 'power beyond our understanding', for me, describes the concept of spirituality well.

We can work with this spiritual domain to our benefit or we can fight against it. If we get to understand it, not in a cognitive sense, but in an intuitive, responsive way, then we will be working with it. I liken it to sensing which way the inner wind is blowing. We can choose to sail with it and progress easily. Alternatively, we can predetermine our direction of travel or allow others to do that for us and then find ourselves resisting it.

A client recently told me he felt he was now 'going with flow'. Not in the sense of giving in to whatever impulse arrived in him, but rather intuitively sensing what was going on inside and responding to it. Life becomes not just easier but remarkably easier if we sense our inner direction and follow it.

The Multiple Traumas diagram shows how traumas can restrict access to the Perfect Core which is the source of both peace and power. The arrows show our attempts to access the wisdom of the centre from the various situations we find ourselves in. Sometimes we get through and find the right answer. But if we have too many traumas, we collide with them and get the wrong answers.

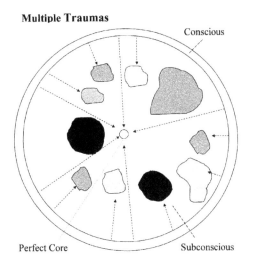

Multiple Traumas

Conscious

Perfect Core

Subconscious

As the traumas are cleared, we can tap into the existing wisdom of our innermost selves more easily, letting it come to the surface and direct our lives in a way which is wholesome for us. We can sense the inner wind. This power, which can be found within us, is the practical and positive aspect of spirituality, and that can bring us the only thing which really matters to us: our own personal peace.

21: Meditation

Some forty years ago I was seeking some help. I came across a mantra type practice called Transcendental Meditation (TM). It probably saved my life at the time and for that reason, I have stayed with it for a very long time. Although the TM movement started to carry some of the unhelpful characteristics of a religion, I am still connected with it and have since developed the practice.

A mantra is simply a sound. Most of us have heard of the Buddhist 'OM.' TM has its own. There are Christian groups who have their versions too. I have found that people can be quite esoteric about mantras, and mystery is precisely what we don't need when we are feeling insecure and in need of help. There are simple unchallenging words we can use, and I offer them during the process of teaching that type of meditation.

TM did a 'black box job' for me at the time. It worked but I did not know why. I have been unravelling that ever since with some measure of success. Now that my career is helping people emotionally, I have a vested interest in finding out more for my clients' sake as well as my own. Writing a book like this obliges me to spell out the logic of my thought processes and indeed, to challenge them.

The Circle Diagram explains some of the mechanics. Having depicted the basic zones of Conscious, Subconscious and Perfect Core, more intuitively than cognitively, I found deeper meaning coming through. It works not only for me, but for my clients and that is important because repeatability is the beginning of theory.

My previous failure to understand myself from a cognitive standpoint became obviously inevitable when I found how trivial my conscious knowledge and capability were compared to the enormous wisdom of the evolved inner being. That being is constantly active within me developing all the time on a vast array of fronts, way beyond anything I could ever understand. I can only tap into it for guidance. I have tried a number of other life enhancing methods, within and without religions, and have achieved a good balance of practice which works well for me. I take the view that I only want to be alive if I enjoy it. And that means enjoying life now, this minute. The meditation I use is designed to achieve just that, so I treat it as an essential part of my life.

Whilst I use a mantra type still, although not the original TM one, the main daily practice I use and offer is the breathing type similar to the Buddhist anapanasati in its simplest possible form. It is an effortless breathing method which can be found in Buddhist Centres, although not all maintain that essential simplicity. It is practiced across the world and has been around for thousands of years as far as we can tell, derived from the Vedic tradition which preceded the Hindu and the later Buddhist cultures.

In that sense, it is not a religious practice so much as a spiritual nourishment which transcends current religious belief systems and indeed, any belief systems.

I originally had doubts as to the universality of its effectiveness, so was cautious about introducing it to my counselling clients for whom I have a professional duty of care. I quickly discovered it to be far more effective than I could have dreamt. Indeed, there are some clients I would struggle with for which this simple breathing meditation seemed pretty much the only answer.

Because I am regularly seeing clients who choose to use the meditation and therefore have in-depth dialogue about their emotional condition, I am able to monitor its impact closer than a group meditation teacher could. It is interesting that the progress of those clients who choose not to use this practice daily is significantly less than those who do. The feedback I get from clients is valuable, both in giving me the confidence to continue with the practice and in providing the learning I need to hold them well on their journey of recovery. It enables me to understand and continue to discover the depths and breadths of this remarkable technique when carefully taught and supported.

Perhaps surprisingly, I have yet to find anyone using a method this simple, but I occasionally come across young people who seem to have developed their own methods very similar to it. It encourages me that what I am teaching seems so close to what comes naturally. It's about feeling right and not just following someone else's prescriptive method. That is why a teacher must be an experienced practitioner too.

Unfortunately, some practitioners want to be clever by adding something on to a perfectly good method and that can then become acceptable practice. It doesn't take many add-ons to reduce its power massively. They can complicate the basic method to the point of practical ineffectiveness for our ordinary day-to-day living, perhaps in an attempt to achieve what some might call higher states of consciousness. This may suit an ascetic but it is not an aim I have for myself or my clients. All I ever wanted was to enjoy my life and that target has been largely met.

Typically, the idea of counting within meditation conflicts with its own objectives because that maintains a level of cognitive thought. The process I use seeks to leave that behind. The same also applies to efforts which require controlling of one's breathing. That demands a conscious engagement we do not want. A main device is the reduction of activity in the clever consciousness, passing control to the wise subconsciousness.

22: The Do Loop

The breathing meditation works on many levels. The vast majority of clients report anxiety in some degree in their lives. Younger clients call it overthinking. A clumsy word for me, but one which aptly describes the process they are experiencing. I learnt computer programming as part of my first degree. Within that was a very basic process to be found in all computer programs called the 'Do Loop'.

Let me give you an example. In my program, I may ask the computer to use an input value; say 5. I ask it to multiply itself until it exceeds a fixed figure, say a million. When it gets there, it stops and sends a final figure to a second programme which goes off into its own Do Loop. A series of such well-designed and sequenced programmes can deliver highly complex algorithms in microseconds to resolve the many complexities we now expect computers to manage.

Unsurprisingly, our brains operate that way too. We have a problem and we keep going at it until we find a solution. All very admirable and stoic, but if the solution is not forthcoming and we keep on at it, worrying and worrying and worrying until our brains are full, we get exhausted. My computer does the same thing. If a virus gets in and slows it down, I can go to Task Manager and find that the CPU is 95% busy but it's not responding. It's just going round in circles, preoccupied with nothing that will help. And that is what my mind is doing.

The moving on answer has not yet been reached and there is hardly any mind capacity left to do anything else. That can result in a panic attack. We are anxious because we believe we need our elusive answer and we are depressed because we are too tired to do all the other things we need to do. The simple breathing meditation process provides an elegant solution to this conundrum. The method seeks to unhook us from that exhausting circular thought process and takes us somewhere reliable and peaceful instead. And when we do that for 20 minutes once or twice a day, we are providing the space for our souls to find the peace and healing they seek.

It is a learning process, so we only get brief periods of relief to begin with. I describe it as emotional physiotherapy. A short exercise aimed at improving our daily life. Once that process is embedded, it starts to permeate our thinking during the day. Because the method is minimally cognitive, our souls gradually learn to convert overthinking into peaceful feeling. That internal wisdom will always gravitate to health and healing once we move the unhealthy inner dross out of the way.

There are some meta-rules about this daily practice, like doing it for a set period each day with no interruptions and sitting comfortably and upright. But within the meditation there is one rule only. I would prefer it if there were none, as the idea is not to dwell in the consciousness, but it's hard to see how to teach with no rule at all. We need some sort of bridge from the conscious to the subconscious.

The whole objective is to be without external stimuli for a set period, normally twenty minutes, giving the conscious me downtime and allowing the subconscious me to get on with the healing process we are so good at thwarting with our habitual hyperactivity.

The rule is very simple. 'When I notice I am thinking, I go to the breathing.' Within this rule, we recognise that we can never stop thinking and we can never keep concentrating on anything, including our breathing. Our minds will always wander and we just accept that. So when we notice our mind wandering, we just become aware of our breathing. And that process can happen a few or many times in our meditation period because our minds will constantly flit from one thought to another.

We delude ourselves if we think we can concentrate on one item for a prolonged period even if we keep practising. Forty years of practice has not changed the experience very much for me. We practise meditation because our minds are not fully under control. While we may experience some level of control quite soon, this is a journey not a destination. Indeed, as long as trauma still needs resolving, what we regard as poor concentration within the practice will not change particularly, even over years of practice, because the mental activity we experience is the process of trauma resolution which is not a conscious process.

I tell my clients it is like daydreaming, but with one difference: when I notice I am daydreaming, I become aware of my breathing. It is that simple and that easy. So in the same way that I eat the same toast every morning for breakfast as I always did and I don't seek to improve it, I do the same meditation process every day and I don't seek to improve that either.

The amazing thing with my toast is not what it is, but what happens to it when it gets inside me. My body converts it into energy and materials for reconstruction of damaged parts of my body. The toast itself is quite boring, really. And the amazing thing with my meditation is not my experience of it but what happens within my soul as a result.

It is like a plaster cast which enables my broken arm to heal. Meditation simply provides a space in which the soul can recover from the damage it has sustained. The practice itself is quite ordinary and seemingly boring too. It is not a relaxation exercise. It is a healing process which may or may not be relaxing. It is merely a method to allow a much smarter thing to happen in our soul's software. That is where the magic takes place.

My toast is food for my body. My meditation is food for my soul. The toast keeps me alive. The meditation resolves my stresses and helps me become happy. As I want both, I do both. Happiness is what I feel or not right now, this minute. That is the essence of the somewhat misdirected and poorly defined notion of mindfulness; misdirected because the practice found outside Buddhist circles generally does not directly address the process of inner healing. It seems to be aimed more at the CBT level with a view to feeling relaxed at the time.

I believe a more accurate translation of the Sanskrit expression for meditation is 'awareness' because that is the active element in the practice of anapanasati. The Anapanasati Sutta, Mindfulness of Breathing, (M118) describes an awareness of one's breathing, whatever it is doing. The method I offer is at a basic level, not inferring conscious control such as counting breaths or trying to change breathing patterns.[1]

23: How It Works

I use the Circle Diagram to depict how the process works. Feelings will continually come from my subconscious and translate into thoughts in the conscious. We can't stop this any more than we can stop our heart beating. If our thoughts come from a deep place, they will tend to be peaceful ones. Others may come from a memory which might be traumatic. They may be a little upsetting. Both are valid. Both are inevitable. Both play their part in the eradication of traumas and the discovery of peace.

I just accept what my soul is doing within the space my meditation gives it. The wisdom of my soul is massively greater than anything I can ever understand with my paltry conscious mind. It will always seek to self-heal just as our bodies do. Rather than trying to fix our minds from the level of consciousness, we should give nature the opportunity of doing the job it is so eminently capable of from deep inside. The Meditation Process diagram indicates the process.

Meditation Process

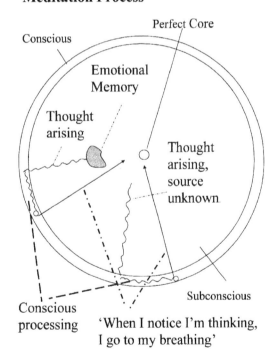

Guided by our experiences, we may use our conscious processes to make our decisions, but the impulse for the action I take comes from the subconscious. Every time we accept a thought coming from a trauma and we go to our breathing, some of the emotion embedded in the trauma memory is resolved. The darkened area gets a little lighter and we get a little lighter with it. This is the normalisation process talked about in therapy training but I was not taught how to achieve it for clients. Meditation is a very powerful answer.

The logic of using our breathing is that it is effectively a 'semi autonomic' process, which means that, apart from some short-term level of conscious control, it will function subconsciously for as long as we live. Not even our conscious selves can stop it, because if we succeed, we die. We might hold our breath for a limited period, but the autonomic process will soon take over.

It has been incredibly reliable to date for me. I trust it totally. And it is the only such body process which is easy to observe; and it is in us and of us. If we spend time every day going to a place of absolute internal reliability like this, we will start to incorporate that internal reference of confidence subconsciously into our rather more unpredictable lives. That progressively delivers a greater feeling of inner security going into the future for as long as we do this exercise.

We find we are increasingly freed of our worry 'do loops', releasing more of our minds for useful and enjoyable activity. And that is just the beginning of the healing process.

I have posted online a video of the theory part of a three session group programme called 'Meditation Can Transform Your Life: - Mental Health'.[1] The theory is unique because it uses the Circle Diagram to explain it. Children often don't even need a theoretical introduction like this. They just get on and do it. But mature and discerning adults rightly need to know why they should adopt a particular practice in the face of all the others on offer out there.

The video gives a basic theory of the emotional person, how we are damaged by the events of our lives and how the process of meditation works on our anxieties in the first instance. Because the real level of experience gained is spiritual and not cognitive, it normally requires the presence of a meditation teacher to actually learn the method. Some clients have achieved the method from the video alone, but that is the exception.

Generally, I see the learning process for meditation as telepathic insofar as its depth is transmitted somehow beyond the normal five senses. To give an example, my wife was struggling to get our one-year-old granddaughter to sleep. Despite the fact that this is normally second nature to her, she was anxious she would fail. I took the baby and meditated. She was asleep in a few minutes. There was no cognitive communication. We held her just the same way, but I suggest there was some mirroring between the peace in my brain and that of the baby's.

Indeed, I suspect the same mechanism was there for my anxious wife in her failed attempt. Her fear of being unable to get the baby to sleep was inadvertently transmitting anxiety to it, defeating her own objective. In each case, our mirror neurons were in tune, it seems, even though there was no observable communication going on.

I see no reason why the more sophisticated signals generated by my brain could not transmit to another person like this and trigger a similar response in it. I often observe this when I teach clients meditation. I usually get a feel of how they are experiencing it, despite closed eyes and silence. I always check afterwards.[2]

Meditation is a self-learning process working at the deepest level of our beings. Once clients understand the theory, they find it easy to see how the repeated use of breathing as a surrogate of peace whenever a thought is noticed, can train their minds to find that inner place, the Perfect Core. They usually discover some of that inner peace first in the daily meditation period, often just as they are coming out of it.

That deep experience can then become more apparent in their daily lives. My job is to help them recognise that process. Because our souls will always try to gravitate towards what is good for us, the subconscious learning from the meditation sessions will constantly and progressively permeate our daily lives more and more.

Unlike our physical food which we continually need to maintain our bodies, our spiritual food, the meditation, not only progressively builds the domain of peace inside every time, but develops our ability to reach it. That daily repetition delivers an increasing prevalence of peace during the day by increasing the size of our Perfect Core and its capacity to hold peace. The bigger it gets, the easier we will find it when we need it.

All of my clients, and they include a broad spectrum within the category of the walking wounded, carry anxiety and/or depression. The continual antidote of peace works hard on those symptoms. The results I see from my work when the client practices a simple meditation far exceed those when they do not. It is not that my counselling practice is not substantial without meditation. But the addition of a meditation which a client does seven days a week greatly enhances the hour I give them in the same week; and the combination is very effective.

The continual practice constantly straightens out our tangled thought processes, a bit like carding in cotton production in which repeated combing of the raw tangled material straightens the strands to produce a useful linear thread that can be woven into garments.

Most Buddhist centres in the UK offer the basic breathing meditation as a stand-alone practice and will not normally proselytise. You don't have to know or even want to know anything about Buddhism to gain the remarkable benefits of this form of meditation. I have found that centres usually suggest a donation and you can go along as many times as you want. They don't normally offer a theory like this, but armed with the cognitive knowledge from this book and the video, the meditation experience at a Buddhist centre should deliver the practice effectively. You just have to pick it up and do it every day. That is the challenge.

24: Spiritual Depth

I call the place deep beneath the subconscious zone in which emotions are sourced the Perfect Core. I liken this to the astrophysicists' black hole. We cannot directly know what is there, but we can arrive at some conclusions from the recognisable emotional results which come out of it.[1] Its three attributes of peace, strength and destiny are all enhanced by the power of the meditation I offer. Clients usually find a new depth of peace in the brief exercise which forms part of the training.

For many, it may be the first time in a very long time they have been able to do nothing for twenty minutes and be at one in it. When I talk to my clients after a session, most report feeling different from usual in some form or another. Some are simply surprisingly tired. Others describe a peace. Occasionally, a client will report euphoria. The deeper experiences are often associated with the centre of their physical body.

When they find they can then replicate that on a daily basis at home, they know that their desperate hope of finding some peace in their lives has just been realised. And it is just the beginning. Whatever language they may use for it, all my clients ultimately seek peace. I regard peace as a spiritual experience because it resides in the greatest depth of our beings. It is the profound internal goodness we need to be in contact with in order to live fulfilling and wholesome lives. If I could live my whole life in permanent peace, I would need nothing more.

That does not imply a static existence, but one in which I am at peace with everything I do. While none of us will ever quite get there, I for one will continue to get nearer to it every time I meditate.

Once clients can see that the meditation is generating peace for them, they have the promise of progress installed within them. Some may have lost hope, but this practice provides a method for dealing with their history as well as their present. However an individual's problems might manifest themselves, they are inspired by the idea that remedial work has started at the very centre of their being so simply, and that its purity and power can tackle issues they have hitherto found impossible to deal with.

An 8-year-old was brought to me for debilitating hypersensitivity. She sat between mum and dad on the sofa. There was a noise outside the counselling room which most of us would hardly notice. Tears poured down her face. The parents had both worked so hard with this girl, but with limited success. Whenever it rained while she was in the car, the tears would come then too. Neither could work out what might have caused this condition. I taught her the meditation. Within 8 sessions she was out, apparently clear of her hypersensitivity. I was not entirely convinced, but did not want to extend sessions and encourage the malady to return. My joy was somewhat deflated a year later when she returned. I asked if she had kept up the meditation. She had not. She then resumed meditation and progress resumed too, steadily working through one issue after another with great success. She finished counselling with me when she realised that she could do all the things her friends could do - and more. She had effectively conquered her affliction. Years later I am still in touch with mum and all is well.

I find that once a meditation routine is established and is working from the inside out, the more conventional counselling can do its work from the outside in. When they meet in the middle, the therapy is complete. The client now has confidence in their continuing improvement to go it alone. Next client please!

It is not unusual that meditating clients describe the changes they are experiencing as miracles. It certainly looks like that to me sometimes too.

However, the regularity with which remarkable transformations have occurred has altered my perception of what is amazing. 'Amazing' is no longer what I see before me. It is the fact that not everyone is doing a practice which can precipitate such remarkable recoveries and make life a joy to live. Ruby Wax cites page upon page of research in her book *Sane New World* on the effectiveness of generic mindfulness, emotionally as well as anatomically.[2]

I would claim that at least for the refined method I teach. The whole world, not just my counselling clients, would be a far better place if everyone practiced a pure form of meditation like this one.[3] It seems almost universal in its applicability, although I occasionally have to adjust my teaching for some clients. Particularly in our new age of mobile media access with our phones, we have become externally obsessed and have lost the art of fluent communication with our internal subconsciousness.

Those who received a religious education at school age will have gained a concept of inner spirituality through the practice of prayer, but as they grew up, the beliefs that go with religions can actually alienate many from their essential spiritual core, making it hard to sustain spiritually powerful practices. Buddhist centres often overcome this with secular poetry. All the participants in my Masters research felt that being outside in nature provided this internal access well, regardless of whether they still held religious beliefs or not. I concurred with that.

I also find that those brought up in a praying culture seem to be more resilient than those who weren't. They seem to be able to navigate themselves through more difficult circumstances. My theory is that whatever the narrative of their religious beliefs now, they have already developed access to their Perfect Cores through time spent alone recognising the existence of an entity beyond the observable human one. It's easier to access our spirituality in adult life if we have a childhood memory of it.

25: The Vedic Tradition

The philosophy underlying the meditation I teach derives from the Vedic Tradition.

The Upanishads are a set of Sanskrit verses dating back three millennia. The Vedic tradition in which they were written predates Hinduism and of course Buddhism. The Mandukya Upanishad seeks to describe the creative energy from which the universe is formed, referring to the sound 'OM'.

It conceptualises four quarters of consciousness: waking, dreaming, deep sleep and the Pure Self. Unlike many other ancient and not so ancient classifications, this one rings true today, not least in the differentiation between dreaming and dreamless sleep, which neuroscience is only just discovering. This extract seeks to describe the Pure Self:

'The fourth, say the wise, is the pure Self alone, dwelling in the heart of all,

It is the lord of all.

The seer of all.

The source and goal of all.

It is not outer awareness.

It is not inner awareness.

Nor is it a suspension of awareness.

It is not knowing.

Nor is it knowingness itself.

It cannot be given boundaries.

It is ineffable and beyond thought.

It is indefinable.

It is the end of all activity, silent and unchanging.

The supreme good, one without a second

It is the real Self.

It, above all, should be known.

It can neither be seen nor understood.

It is known only through becoming it.'

Whilst I tend not to use the Upanishad's 'OM' mantra, this fourth consciousness element resonates with the perception of spirituality I have gained from doing the practice. It does not, however, describe my normal experience within my daily meditation. Most of that seems like daydreaming, but through that simple exercise come deeper peaceful experiences, sometimes but not always during the practice.

The meditation exercise enables peace to permeate in some measure into other times of day. I am aware of a stillness which is quietly and actively nurturing and healing my soul. At the end of a session, I sometimes feel as though my body has stopped, although I know its essential functions remain quietly ticking over. Other people have different experiences, so no practitioner should necessarily aspire to mine.

The purpose of the exercise is one of healing and not of conscious experience, so it's the individual's soul which will control what happens and not a conscious desire for peace or any other experience. My key line in this Upanishad is 'It is ineffable and beyond thought.' It's a bit like tasting an apple. Hard to describe the flavour to someone else in words, but they will know it precisely when they take a bite from it.

Tree of Life

In trying to illustrate the source of the power of this inner zone to a client, I drew the Tree of Life, showing people as individual Circle Diagrams represented as its blossom. Each flower is delicate and beautiful, just as we are if we can admit that. They are grown from the same powerful tree and are sustained by it. That is where they get their form and their strength from. They are nurtured by the tree.

Each is very similar to the other in that all are created and supported by the same tree but each is also unique in its detail. The health of each is dependent on them remaining fixed to the tree. Any blossom which wants to be different and go its own way, will soon find itself dying on the ground. Blossom can also be blown off by the winds of change, as can we. A client named it the Tree of Life. I liked that.

It is this spiritual Tree of Life which created and now sustains my very being, the perfect person I was at the beginning. It provides the strength I need to grow healthily. As long as I appreciate it, I am cared for by the tree until my demise and descent to the ground. And that is the same for all of us. We all emanate from this powerful entity and the more we realise that, the more balanced we will be.

The word 'spiritual' to me describes powers which control us at a very basic level but which are beyond our comprehension and our control. We normally think of the word 'spiritual' in terms of goodness, but the powers which disconnect us from our source of sustenance are also deep. They can hit us unawares. Their destructive quality merits the adjective 'evil' in the sense of their doing harm to us.

In the same way that wholesome food will augment us physically and a virus will diminish us physically, so positive spiritual powers will augment us emotionally and negative spiritual powers will diminish us emotionally. Our best strategy is to understand both types as best we can. We will find peace if we function in tune with the supporting ones and distress if we submit to the destructive ones. We need to be discerning and that wisdom comes from the Perfect Core.

Section 5
When Things Go Wrong

26: My Subconscious in Action

I am frequently delighted by the fruits of my counselling labours. Another human being's life has just changed for the better and I was a part of that process. Lest I get carried away with myself, I do sometimes squirm at the memory of the nasty things I have done to people in my private life from time to time. Both these types of action derive from my subconscious self.

In the former case, it was a talent I happened to possess. I may have consciously cultivated it, but it really was innate in me to begin with and not of my own creation. In the latter case, someone at some time has infected me with unhealthy ideas. They went in, undetected by my conscious self until I acted on them, and I found myself regretting what I had done afterwards. Both these powers are beyond my immediate control.

They emanate from a subconscious I hardly know and they act through the conscious me rather than of the conscious me. I find myself doing something rather than specifically deciding to do it. In one case it was a constructive power and in the other, a destructive power. That does not infer that my conscious mind is not involved in what is happening, but it can't always stop the action in time. My consciousness is a very small part of my psyche, so I can accept it's not all of who I am.

One of the adages posted on boards in the prisons I visit in my work reflects on 'a moment of madness followed by a lifetime of regret'. Most of my personal regrets are not serious enough to merit incarceration, but the same principle applies of an unruly subconscious bursting out from under a well-intended consciousness. I am reluctant to confess my worst misdemeanours in print, but suffice to say that the conscious me has all too frequently allowed impulses from the subconscious me to slip through before I could stop them hurting other people.

Like many of the prisoners I meet in my work, if it's something I have done, I will try to rectify my mistakes and learn from them. While the conscious me may not always be in full control of the rest of my soul, I do have a volume control knob to help me regulate what is passing through. I continually try to improve my grip on it for my sake as well as for everyone else's.

That is the extent of control any of us have. We euphemistically call it Free Will. It exists, but it works in the context of the pain that might lie beneath. It takes a lot of this Free Will to manage the sort of pain I see in some of my clients and essentially, much of that pain is not of their making. We need to remember that when we seek to criticise others. The chaplain I work for has a remarkable bank of profound epithets. One says: 'When I am pointing my accusing finger at someone, I need to remember I have three of my other fingers pointing back at myself.'

The clients I see may have taken someone's life or molested a child. Some counsellors refuse to see these categories of client, possibly because of something in their own past. There are some offenders who are seriously ill and beyond my capacity to help, but those I normally meet do not perturb me because they are people who are able to reflect on themselves, so they are not a danger to me. I will have faith in their inner ability to heal the damage that has been done to them.

Accordingly, I will tell them that at the centre of their being is exactly the same Perfect Core which resides at the centre of me, all my other clients and everyone else too. My process is the same. Why would I change it? A conviction does not necessarily define a person as something so different from the rest of us that the construction of their basic emotional being is somehow unreachable. If they have come for help, and that is the key, they have made a commitment which carries the humility needed to make a start and to create the all-important therapeutic connection. I am not that different from them.

In the 60s Joan Baez sang, "Show me the prison, show me the jail…there but for fortune go you and go I." Some inmates challenged me once when I was supporting a victim awareness course for them. They got the idea that I was just a 'do gooder' coming in for my own egotistical purposes. "If you had been brought up where I was and saw the things I saw, you would be in here like me." I agreed. That threw them.

The truth is that I am very much what my environment has made me and that may well have been, for example, to regard the illicit drug trade as a viable business, just with the added risk component of getting caught and doing time. It was my good fortune that I was not brought up in that sort of environment, but only that. If I can accept that we are all conditioned by our beginnings, and none of us choose that, I may be able to help them. I will need to convince them of my honesty and humility in that. If I can't accept that, I can't help them because I stand aloof from them. I will not be truly with them and they will know that.

27: The Channel Model

I frequently meet clients who find themselves unable to take a compliment. This is often a low self-esteem issue. I tell them how that works for me. I say that it delights me to see a client change in a major way, almost before my very eyes. Insofar as I have been the catalyst in that process, I celebrate the transformation. They may thank me profusely. Their life was miserable and now it is good.

I know that while I played a part, and probably a unique part in that, I am personally not the architect of the change. It happened beyond both our conscious minds, so I am not taking credit for it. When they thank me, I simply tell them it was a pleasure. And indeed it was. I do recognise that can be a rather large understatement. I also recognise that this evidences an enormous power gap. The transformations that I see sometimes are beyond words.

Where did they come from? I absolutely rejoice in these changes and they are the raison d'êtres of my working life. A client comes in one day and is different. Very often they attribute that to the counselling work. Sometimes with young children, it is hard to identify precisely what has effected the change, but it is clearly something I have done and parents are often extremely grateful.

In some sense, something good has passed through me to them. A song derived from words often attributed to the 12th century Italian saint, Francis, starts with, "Make me a channel of your peace." This is precisely what I feel at these times. I am not so much the cause of the change but a channel for it. And some of that goodness which passed to my client has washed off on me on the way through.

In our communication, I too am augmented by the peace which has appeared in them. It's that win-win scenario again. If love is peace on the move, then this love is the Emotional Currency which makes both parties healthy at the same time. And while I would not tell a client I loved them - that English word is far too loose to use - it is unconditional altruistic love which enabled the change and which is the essence of my counselling work.

My lack of understanding for what goes on at these times leads me to ascribe the word 'spiritual' to whatever is in control. That is the rather large gap between the change in my client and my limited abilities to effect that change. Whatever this is, it is powerful, mysterious and blessed. I have tapped into a spiritual energy and it was a good one.

I like to envisage this quiet power beyond our experienced emotions as derived from the Perfect Core in much the same way as immense gravitational power derives from the mass of the Earth. We can't know much about what happens inside in either case, but we know it is there because we experience it. It is immense and it is good news. It is a place where the miracles happen. And if a client is doing a meditation practice too, I will usually check how much that has played a part in the counselling process. That is what they are doing at home and my experience tells me it is the most powerful part of my practice. And it is what they will take away at the end of our time together. If they are conscious of that, then they may carry on with it. It will continue to drive their psychological repair and development work. Indeed, this positive spiritual power could be the source of happiness in our societies as a whole. We just need to learn to let it flow around a bit more. The Channel Model can provide a useful template.

28: The Bad News

I feel very good when my 'channel' is doing the right thing. However, it is not always good. I feel dreadful when it does the wrong thing. I experience both constructive and destructive spiritual powers functioning through the conscious me and I have to take responsibility for all my actions, good and bad.

The ability any of us have to control ourselves is limited. It is therefore very important for those who might officially stand in judgement of others, and indeed for all of us insofar as we have to make judgements, to appreciate that limitation in those we judge. The internal forces at play inside us can be both beyond our control and beyond our comprehension. This may imply the existence of some greater Spiritual Power, whether that be positive or negative. I feel that concept is invaluably practical.

On the one hand, it enables me to take a compliment graciously. It was something residing within me. On the other hand, I can accept there are forces embedded in me which are potentially harmful to others and indeed to me, and I succumb to them sometimes. But they are not the basic me. The concept of a separate actively negative entity enables me to come to terms with my mistakes so I can have the courage to do something practical about them.

The Circle Diagram seeks to show how we have a limited amount of consciousness to try and keep a vastly greater subconscious in control. The size of the conscious annulus on the diagram serves to illustrate its existence, but in reality, its capacity is tiny.

Its ability to maintain control is very small indeed and unhappiness ensues when we lose that control. No-one deliberately loses it. We might take risks and they don't come off, but all creatures will viscerally and ultimately seek to maintain a healthy balance, however misguided their actions are in the pursuit of that.

We humans are no exception, even if it does not look like it sometimes. Circumstances like abuse or the death of a spouse can create stresses which can knock us out of balance for a long time, and if we are not helped, that could be for an entire lifetime. We may then succumb to addictions or harm ourselves in some way. Such self-destructive actions are often cries for help. "I am suffering a lot. I need someone who can understand and help me."

So if we see our consciousness as the part of us which tries to take responsibility for our actions and the rest of us as a subconscious entity which we did not create and do not understand, then we can start to have a realistic view of what we can change in ourselves, and indeed others, and what we cannot. Reinhold Niebuhr's Serenity Prayer, now embedded in the international Twelve Steps programmes for addicts, recognises this duality: "God, grant me the serenity to accept the things I cannot change, the courage to change the things I can and the wisdom to know the difference."

In the prayer, clients appreciate communally what they need to admit to their individual selves that there are forces inside them much bigger than the conscious willpower they can muster on the surface and they need inner strength and external help to get some level of control over them.

Twelve Steps recognises a destructive power and a constructive power beyond normal human endeavour. The wafer-thin conscious self is trying to control a massive body of psychological nature embedded beneath it. I liken the relative size of the conscious self to the earth's atmosphere as viewed from space. It is tiny compared to the massive body of earth beneath. Within it, we can see each other and our activities, but beneath it is the dark of the subconsciousness about which we know almost nothing.

The conscious part of me may not be fully responsible for my harmful actions, but society will declare that the whole of me is responsible. It rarely differentiates between conscious and subconscious causalities, but my misdemeanours do not make all of me a bad person. I learnt that very quickly when I was introduced to prison work. I have met some remarkable people inside prison walls. What got them there was only a part of them and often a very small part.

I now apply that to myself rather than beating myself up when I get things wrong. And I don't allow others to do that to me either. I now appreciate that some part of my inner subconscious has misbehaved and I need to work out how to stop that in future and control it in time. The conscious me needs to discover what ideas have precipitated the destruction and take action to avoid a repetition.

I have supported a victim awareness programme in prisons called Sycamore Tree, run by the British charity, Prison Fellowship. It is a particularly effective programme because it uniquely identifies the prisoner as being a primary victim. It is not soft on the crime, but it accepts the challenge faced by the prisoner in managing their own unruly subconscious.

I call the recognition of positive and negative forces beyond our comprehension the Spiritual Power Model. It works effectively for us to address our own errors as well as our successes.

29: Managing the Aggression

At a deep level, which I think of as spiritual on the grounds that I don't understand it, both constructive and destructive impulses pass from the subconscious through to the conscious in all of us all the time. This is the Spiritual Power Model working in me. We can apply this idea to others too. It allows a victim of any sort of abuse to accept that their aggressor may not be deliberately and maliciously hurting them in the full knowledge of the damage they are doing. It is coming from within them and they may not be able to sense how that would feel for us. The hurt we experience may be from a deeper power, merely enacted by the aggressor.

Relocating this destructive power away from the consciousness of the aggressor helps the victim see this more as an internal emotional sickness arising from the subconscious rather than a personal attack from someone who is fully aware of its impact. They can then reassess themselves independently of this aggressor's actions and criticisms in a more balanced way and hopefully find a sound perception of their own internal goodness to move forward with. That revelation will inspire them towards recovery, separating themselves from the aggressor's attrition.

Clients who are oppressed by a partner or someone else close to them find this approach particularly helpful. It does not absolve the oppressor from their responsibilities to manage their own issues, but it helps the victim understand the mechanics of what is happening so they can anticipate the nature of future attacks and control their own emotions better in the heat of it all. It recognises that bullying may actually be an expression of the aggressor's own insecurity and pain rather than valid criticism of a victim's actions.

Some years before I even embarked upon my counselling career, I felt drawn to help a friend whose husband of 30 years had just left her for another woman. Every time she thought of him, she was massively conflicted between the love she still had of the man still in her heart and the hate for the man who had hurt her so much since. It drained her. I depersonalised it for her using this power construct. While the destruction was created by her husband, he seemed to be a victim himself of a power beyond him. She told me he was indeed unhappy. I did not see her for a year after that, but when I met her again, she said that my concept had relieved her of much of her anguish and she had started out on a healing journey. She could see how he had succumbed to something very unpleasant and his actions and attitude towards her were not a valid picture of who he was.

That approach, which proposed a power beyond our human consciousness, enabled her to observe that her ex-partner was not so much the sole and deliberate perpetrator of her suffering, but part of a bigger force in which he was also suffering. It was as though an emotional disease had arrived unbidden and had infected them both, and their children too. The Spiritual Power Model fitted her situation.

Intense internal conflict coming from violently opposing emotions around another person can be exhausting and can drive people to breakdowns. The better she understood her emotional environment, the better she could manage that conflict and the happier she could be. And that applies to all of us. We all carry disparities of some sort in our heads.

This work constitutes a significant part of my counselling practice. The Spiritual Power Model can dissolve the revenge a victim might feel towards a perpetrator. For someone who is engulfed in hatred for an aggressor, grasping a concept which relocates the source of destruction away from that person can provide massive relief and enable their life to move on.

Indeed, without it they can get stuck in a hateful place which will continue to diminish them, possibly developing an addiction or another unhealthy preoccupation. That could then manifest physically, possibly in the form of a physical disease. The Model does not remove or ignore the damage being done, but reduces the victim's fear and enables them to approach the problems caused by the aggressor more dispassionately. That new logical understanding of the controlling devices employed by the aggressor allows them to reassess themselves in a more realistic light.

30: The Unhealthy Psyche

In the same way that our bodies inevitably get sick and we seek a doctor to help us get better, so our souls get sick too and we should be equally able to access a mental health professional. Just as our doctors are educated in somatic pathology, it is vital too that counsellors have a healthy grasp of emotional pathology. Regrettably that is not very evident in current counselling training. Indeed, it is invaluable for all of us in our daily lives to have enough knowledge of what can go wrong psychologically so that we can manage this sort of malfunction and stop it in its tracks, whether the problem emanates from others or from within ourselves.

Especially with my young clients, I often use the idea of a demon lurking within. I invite them to draw inside a Circle Diagram to depict how they feel. It sometimes turns out to be the traditional devil with horns and a fork. The Demons Lurking.

Demons Lurking

Whatever it is, the act of drawing may enable them to express something more than any words they could muster, and within the concept of Person-Centred Counselling, that will automatically be therapeutic. It is useful and healthy for them to recognise the animal within them as best they can and their need to control it. More often than not, inconvenient behaviour is one of the reasons for the young person's visit. By shifting the blame from little Johnny to the demon inside little Johnny, we can all get on side to try and resolve his issues together, mum and dad included.

It's not adult against child, but counsellor and young client teamed up against the unwanted demon. It is the recognition of the functioning of the subconscious as a separate entity from the conscious person everyone normally sees, which enables me to counsel young people effectively. Without that, they would feel I too was blaming them and they would not want to come back.

We all struggle from time to time with our inner demons and when those demons get too lively and spill out, they can hurt others too. And it's not just children whose demons have spilled out. They spill out of adults too, usually with even greater force. Whilst we all recognise that the image of a demon is a caricature, it is still useful to illustrate the concept of a negative entity or force within ourselves which is beyond our immediate control.

The idea of an evil or malign force attacking the software of our beings is a powerful tool for my clients, both when thinking about themselves, and their oppressors too, if that is relevant to them. It is the malware which got inside and infected the normal functioning of our soul's healthy software.

I think of the Perfect Core as being the healthy spiritual zone. Goodness and peace emanate from there. I see the body of the Circle Diagram as me being born, growing and being nurtured from my Perfect Core, which is in turn rooted in the same spiritual Tree of Life which has produced us all. I perceive the demons as the emotional traumas which affect us all in some degree in our lives.

Trauma Blinded

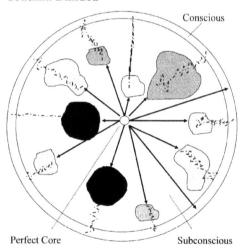

Perfect Core · Conscious · Subconscious

Continuing the horticultural analogy, the petals of the tree's blossom start to rot at these traumas, gradually destroying the whole flower and infecting others around them too. As the number and size of traumas increase, that central goodness finds it harder and harder to reach out into active life in the conscious zone. The Trauma Blinded diagram illustrates how traumas sustained in life can mask the inner voice which speaks from our Perfect Core.

Its way is blocked by trauma damage, so the messages emanating from there are distorted by the emotions living inside the traumas. By the same token, fewer clear lines of sight coming from the Consciousness can reach to the Perfect Core where love and truth can offer wisdom to daily activity and decision making.

Consequently, external voices seem louder and we can become more reliant on them. We lose our sensitivity to our own real deeper needs so we are less able to take care of ourselves. And because we can't sense our own needs, we certainly can't sense anyone else's, so we will hurt those around us and not be aware of the damage we do. That can make us into the unfeeling aggressor. That spiritual deafness will make us unhappy too.

There will be no obvious way out, especially if we are structurally bound into a maladjusted community such as a dysfunctional family which is harbouring too many pathological concepts itself.

31: The Malware

If our medical problems are physical in nature, we seem to be able to talk about them these days, even when they are life-threatening. We might catch a contagious disease or develop a cancer. Pathogens are always around us as a biological threat, so we have to take care of our bodies to avoid them or combat them.

We may inadvertently become infected by a 'hardware' biological disease which had been residing in someone we got physically too close to. We may just as easily become infected by a 'software' emotional disease which has been residing in someone we got emotionally too close to. But because we don't understand much about our internal software and how we can get hurt like this, we are less able to avoid an emotional infection in the first place or cure it when it does take hold.

Sadly, we are treated differently when we have an emotional affliction than when we have a biological one.

Even if our own lack of self-discipline has contributed to a physical ailment, and I think as an example of the progressively more common and often avoidable Type 2 Diabetes, those around us generally take the view that this is not all our fault and we can expect them to be sympathetic towards us. They can see we are ill and they can't help feeling sympathy. It's visceral. They may accept that our physical suffering is part of nature's more unpleasant landscape.

However, the sympathy is not so forthcoming with emotional ailments. They are rather more taboo when it gets beyond well recognised conditions like bereavement or relationship breakdown. We tend to hide them. Emotional imbalances can be even more debilitating than the physical variety, but a general ignorance of these matters and the lack of ready cures leaves most of us not wanting to know about them.

Indeed, sufferers are frequently seen as causes of their own afflictions. "Pull your socks up." "Get a life." "Get your finger out." We know that doesn't really help. If our issues involve an aggressor who is part of our wider community, its members may stand well back for fear of getting infected too. Conversely, they may get drawn in by the aggressor and start blaming the victim.

Whatever the issue is, unless the sufferer carries a recognised diagnosis, relatives, friends and many authorities involved may ignore their struggle. Marital breakdown, for instance, can be very isolating and the process of divorce can do at least as much damage as the original problem. If there is any fallout involving relatives or other possible suitors, those people may find it easier to attack the sufferer rather than help them.

The sad irony is that the person doing the most criticising may often be the cause of the suffering. The chaplain I do work for reminds me of the three fingers I point to myself when I point one at someone else.

The person doing the pointing may very well be a parent. Attacks on a child can range from an absence of love to routine sexual abuse. The child may become unruly or sullen. If the abuser finds this inconvenient, they may sanction the child.

The abuser may deny their actions and denigrate the child, but the child's inevitable anger will eventually come out. The abuser may then blame the child for their disruptive behaviour. Attributing the problem to the child may get it out of the abuser's conscience so they can just ignore what they are doing and carry on as before. This is massively destructive for the child, intially being maltreated for no reason of its own and further abused when it reacts to the maltreatment.

This behaviour happens all the time. As I am writing, my wife and I have refused the dog's entreaties for exercise this morning because we are too busy. The dog gave up and lay down. Later my wife accused it of being lazy. The dog in me would be furious. It was denied what it wanted and its well-behaved response was then used as an excuse for not meeting its needs in the first place. However, we assume the dog does not understand English, so no harm done and my wife took her out soon after. I hasten to add that that did not typify the way we brought up our children and the event would have passed by were I not writing this book! However, it does reflect on how some of my young clients are treated and they are damaged by it.

The professional's job is to seek a reason for disruptive behaviour in children and indeed, sometimes in adults. Their behaviour may be a logical reaction to what is happening to them or to what has happened to them. For adults, it could be due to some historic malware someone had dumped on them before they could discern the nasty stuff and filter it out.

The resulting subconscious psyche with all the rubbish it may be carrying needs to be managed on a daily basis and it may never be fully controlled. Things have gone wrong and it's not always resolvable at the behaviour level. The victim is left to deal with this.

While it is still everyone's responsibility to use their conscious capability to control their own subconscious being as well as they can for themselves and for those around them, some people are not as well equipped at this as others. They need help. Autistic Spectrum Disorder (ASD) is just such a condition. It infers a lifelong condition in which emotional communication with others is impaired.

Typically, someone with ASD may be functioning well enough to attend mainstream school, play sport and get good grades, but might struggle to cope with bullying or even normal authority which they may not understand. A young ASD/Asperger's candidate who is hypersensitive to touch may actually tolerate someone touching them inappropriately longer than most of us because they do not know how to react safely.

Most people would rebuff such an intrusion early on, but the young ASD candidate may hold on in freeze mode until it becomes intolerable and then just lash out. It will be that action which is noticed and it would be them who become the focus of an authority's undesired attention, rather than the true aggressor who slipped out sideways just in time.

In the absence of an understanding of their issues in a school setting, a young person may become accused of having anger issues. Class sizes can preclude the individual attention really needed here for the more serious cases in what is a broad spectrum of conditions. Unless trained properly, decision makers may not give the latitude to understand that ASD candidates may be doing their conscious best with an impaired subconsciousness. Schools in Britain are becoming more aware of such conditions.

Whatever the nature of the subconscious anyone has been given, at the end of the day, the whole person is the only entity which can ultimately be held responsible for their own actions. Society demands that its constituents are kept safe, so has to impose constraints on all individuals within it to achieve that, regardless of their particular psychology. It tends to do that in practical ways rather than empathic ways. In cases where the law has been broken, it can't incarcerate just the subconscious self. The whole person has to go to prison.

In his book, *Incognito*, the neuroscientist David Eagleman considers the harshness of the American legal system, debating the concept of conscious culpability. This so-called developed country has one of the highest incarceration rates per capita in the world, which somewhat begs the question on what the word 'developed' means. As long ago as 1862, Dostoevsky wrote in *The House of the Dead*, 'The degree of civilisation in a society can be judged by entering its prisons.' Some countries have not moved on a lot since, it seems.

One individual was fortunate enough to have residence north of the USA border. In his case, the subconscious appeared to take over the conscious with devastating consequences. Kenneth Parks was married with a young child, but gambling got him into financial trouble. He had good relationships with his wife's parents, but nevertheless, got up in the night, drove over to their house and murdered his mother-in-law and attempted to murder his father-in-law. He then went to a police station covered in blood saying he thought he had killed someone.

The psychological evidence concluded that he had been sleepwalking (and driving) and he was unaware of his actions. He was acquitted, but was required to commit to psychological treatment. The court concluded that the conscious part of him was not functioning so could not be held responsible. It also concluded the subconscious part could be managed safely to avoid a recurrence. It effectively treated his subconscious as an unfortunate vagary of nature like a tsunami or a hurricane or, in legal parlance, an Act of God.[1]

A number of psychologists have informally contested the court decision, but the Parks case illustrates an approach to differentiating the responsibility of the conscious self from the relatively uncontrollable nature of the subconscious self. There had been enough precedence of sleepwalking leading to unfortunate endings to persuade the court to make its lenient decision. My views on this were influenced by my practice:

A client became highly distressed because his nightly sleepwalking left him exhausted and miserable. But most of all he was terrified because he would regularly discover that he had been on the balcony of his 12th floor flat in the night and wondered how soon he would fall over it. He was also concerned about his weight as he would eat extensively in his oblivious state and that even involved cooking.

Crimes of Passion too, in which the subconscious drive has overwhelmed the deliberations of the conscious brain, have been recognised for a long time in England and subsequently in other developed countries.

Typically, a woman may attack and even kill a persistently aggressive partner in a fit of rage. The legal argument is that the emotional circumstances are so specific that it would be highly unlikely that the perpetrator would repeat their misdemeanour and therefore does not constitute a danger to others in the future. The courts have taken this into account in leniency. That does not normally mean acquittal, but it is a clear recognition by the state of the potential power of the subconscious over the conscious. It is not unusual for a perpetrator of a violent crime to say that they did not know what came over them.

The English legal system arrived at a landmark decision in 2018 by accepting an appeal against a murder conviction for the then 65-year-old Sally Challen who had killed her husband. She had suffered continual coercive control all her married life. The original murder conviction was heavily influenced by the fact that she had walked over to her ex-husband's house with a hammer and had bludgeoned him to death as he was sitting at his kitchen table. The retrial showed that she was mentally ill as a result of his coercive control over her since the age of 16. Section 76 of the Serious Crime Act had been passed in England in 2015 to add the domestic abuse concept to the existing domestic violence law. That change made her appeal more likely to succeed. She was eventually freed without a further formal trial, having already served a sentence which equated to a manslaughter charge.[2]

While some malicious actions find 'remedy' in law as society's safety net, most of the harm that is done is at a much less prominent level than Sally's and there is often little we can do about the circumstances. The scenario of humans harming each other plays out every day in homes, workplaces and on the streets in ways which are often so apparently insignificant that they are either passed by or passed off. Passed by because it's not too bad and passed off as seeming so absurd it could not be true.

A mother seen shouting at her child might be passed by as just another unhappy event for the child, with little consideration as to the long-term effects. The casual observer may not perceive this as a reportable incident, but the chronic nature of it might be highly damaging. Most of us don't want to become involved, not least because we fear we may do more harm than good.

A suspicion of sexual abuse of a child of a seemingly nice parent might be passed off as too absurd to believe. The abuse may continue with massive connotations for the child, as society is now progressively learning, but inappropriate intervention can be damaging too.

A client had been sexually abused by her biological father on a nightly basis for most of her young years with strong indications of that having started pre-verbally. It transpired that all her siblings had been similarly abused and later, her own children too. However, he presented as a pillar of the community, which gave him the immunity he needed to continue the damage. He died before he could be brought to justice.

The Jimmy Savile case in Britain triggered a whole new wave of awareness in this area, sometimes going overboard with suspicions being generated about other completely innocent celebrities, demonstrating our ineptitude at detecting abuse effectively. Child abuse, particularly sex abuse, is often concealed well using the child's guilt and shame.

Michael Jackson was alleged to have used his fame and promises of careers to the parents of primary age children to routinely sexually abuse them. His actions caused enormous lifetime damage to the children and all those involved. Insufficient evidence was found at the time and the fans were incensed with such apparently malicious accusations, but the 2019 *Leaving Neverland* documentary showed overwhelming evidence.

He apparently employed great skill in his abuse, such that the children did not fully appreciate the impact of their relationships with him until puberty and adulthood. He genuinely seemed to think there was nothing wrong or harmful with his behaviour. Most of those involved were held in a state of denial of any wrongdoing. One family was so committed to their child's career opportunity that they moved from Australia to the USA to be with Michael. The mother was unable to contemplate the risk involved. The Jackson family denies his wrongdoing.

There are many barriers to such disclosure of sex abuse. Just reporting it could jeopardise the child's existing support system, generally its family. Indeed, the impact of the disclosure on the victims may not end even when they leave home.

As is normal in these cases, my sexually abused client kept it to herself. However, one day as an adult she told her sister who then blurted it all out at a family celebration. The family could not accept it and decided my client was making it up. She was ostracised and even excluded from inheritances.

So it's not safe to speak the truth even when childhood dependence is in the past. Abuse between adults can be entirely hidden too, at least until the victim arrives for counselling.

A vicar in Birmingham, England, employed a young female secretary in the 1980s and had her agree to him walking around the house naked, even when he was sexually aroused. Absurdly it seems, she felt obliged to comply with this behaviour. It was long after that employment had finished that she felt she could make her complaint. She needed to attend to her trauma.

32: Developmental Theory

There has been plenty research seeking to understand how we humans function on the grounds that we obviously get it wrong quite a lot and need to get to grips with ourselves. The original attempts at what we now call psychology were influenced by the Latin and Greek schooling of the time. They produced some obscure results. Sigmund Freud was one such protagonist.

Amongst the many theories he created, and some were better than others, was the personality development model which described the phases of id, ego and superego. I interpret that system for my own working purposes as:

- Id: the toddler saying, "I want."
- Ego: the infant understanding they need to do something like say, "please and thank you" to get what they want.
- Superego: the junior finding pleasure simply from helping others.

Normal transitions through these phases occur first as speech develops and should be well developed coming into junior school at around seven years old. The adult character is essentially formed by this time. In the 15th century, Saint Ignatius is reputed to have identified this saying, "Give me the child for the first seven years and I will give you the man." Psychologists agree.

Within the 'id', the infant initially relies on its carer to interpret its needs and to provide for it. If those needs are routinely met with minimal emotional disruption, the infant starts to differentiate their various issues and how they can be resolved. It is not confused by inconsistent responses to its cries. Parental consistency enables it to interpret its own feelings and convey them more specifically to its carer the next time round.

An emotionally healthy carer will be empathically driven to meet its child's needs, not least because life is much easier if they succeed in this. If the child feels secure enough to respond to its carer predictably, the relationship between the two deepens and it becomes more intuitive and indeed more enjoyable for both. Something beyond the obvious logical transmission of information happens and the carer breathes a sigh of relief as they find out how to satisfy their charge and quell its cries. The Mirror Neuron system is at work.

The normally embedded component of empathy in the carer and infant resonate so that their emotional experiences are similar. A language exists between them beyond the cognitive one. We call this special and deeper relationship 'bonding'. It is visceral. This basic security that the infant finds in its carer provides a stable foundation for all its subsequent learning. It has the ground rules. It has the confidence that, whatever happens, it will be cared for. That frees up brain space to expand its knowledge and abilities in new areas. It has no need to worry where and when it will have its basic needs met.

John Bowlby researched this development stage and produced his theory of Attachment. He was interested in how infant relationships with carers/mothers affected well-being in subsequent life. Essentially, he proposed that from the ages of around 6 months to 3 years, a child fares better when it sees a very limited number of consistent carers.

This has had particular relevance for child care in the decades since his research. Our progressively more efficient homes enable mothers to go back to work sooner after giving birth. Some may be tempted to rely on multiple day carers for their infants, but research indicates there is a limit to this before the child starts to feel insecure. The psychological fraternity has tended to dwell on the detailed pathology of his work, but the simple logic of this theory often proves more useful in the counselling room.

Bowlby's research had carers leave their infants in a room after having spent some time with them. He observed the infant's reactions as the carers left and as they returned. He categorised the relationships he saw in terms of the quality of security the carers appeared to have established with their infants. The natural process of healthy learning for the infant is to find security with their carer, normally the mother, and to venture out a little at a time, returning to base frequently for reassurance.

Notwithstanding that it was the carers who left in the experiment, the research reflected the developing courage of a child leaving its carer for longer periods to do ever more ambitious things from the level of the security they felt. And that is the story throughout childhood. This natural inquisitiveness and ambition ultimately leads children to leave home and make their lives independently. That continues throughout life.

As adults, we often enter new environments and perform new tasks. We return home for reflection and we process the new experiences. I recall how my wife and I progressed from city break holidays to long haul and to backpacking in the increments we could comfortably manage, obviously returning home between and consolidating our experiences.

This aspect of the theory is useful when supporting parents dealing with abnormal behaviour in their child, particularly hypersensitivity which can threaten a child's security. In order to enable the whole family to function, parents may insist on fixed behaviour expectations with sanctions for falling short of that. I usually propose that we assess where the child is up to and lower expectations for a while to that level. Then, in the context of a desired final benchmark, gradually encourage piecemeal advances, accepting some shortfalls as inevitable on the way.

This recognises an iterative learning process as the key to resolving the problem. It may be painstaking in the short term, but patience will reduce the amount of pain overall. Without that empathic treatment, the condition could invite resistance and then develop into a more intractable pathology going into adult life.

In normal circumstances, carers rightly feel the need to socialise their children for their own benefit, for the benefit of those the child will meet and of course, for the child themself. The child needs to learn what they have to do to be accepted in various communities in order to receive the full advantages of those memberships. Parents will normally teach them to do things like say 'please' and 'thank you' as part of the process of getting what they need or want.

That is how I see Freud's ego state. The child learns they have to negotiate for what they want and are normally, but not always, rewarded with their desires being met. A conscious contract. If they develop a healthy relationship with their parents, they will also start to sense and enjoy their parents' pleasure from that. Science now tells us that their brain will be active in the same areas as their parent's at those times of emotional exchange.

They then naturally discover satisfaction in generating that same pleasure in their parent as a stand-alone function without seeking any material gains for themselves. The child instinctively starts doing things to make the parent happy. This is a subconscious contract. I see this as moving into Freud's third state, the superego, in which making others happy spontaneously makes the child happy.

A longer-term reward is that they are more likely to be happy most of the time if their parent is happy most of the time. They have become a social person, actively contributing emotionally to their community, starting with the family, then extending to school and all their other social groups. Most of us recognise people who have acquired that gift.

This empathic being is now tuned into taking care of others in a safe way, regardless of what they are receiving at

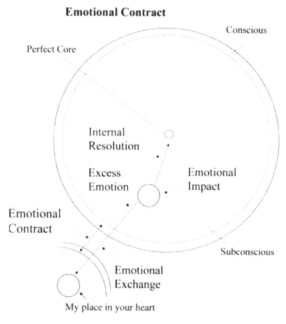

Emotional Contract

that time. They readily form Emotional Contracts, as illustrated in the diagram. They would, of course, expect to be respected for their actions. It is this interactive altruism which is essential to the creation of social groups in which individuals work cohesively and successfully together.

We readily acknowledge that we need healthy legal and commercial relationships to ensure the smooth functioning of our material world. It is even more important to recognise that we need healthy emotional frameworks and relationships to ensure the smooth emotionally functioning of the groups and communities we belong to. The former brings us wealth. The latter brings individual and collective happiness. The former is of little use to us without the latter. My professional world focuses on people's happiness and well-being. After a career in creating material projects, I now realise that none of that, of itself, contributed to the most important thing for all and any of us, our own happiness. The currency of altruism should always be our primary interest in our relationships. Maybe John Lennon was right: "All you need is love."

In very practical terms, any good school will include in its manifesto the altruistic intent to seek and develop the potential of every pupil in its charge. A friend taught at a school whose ethos was mutual respect and care. As a by-product, it was rated highly academically, despite having an unexceptional pupil catchment. The ethical foundations enabled all round success. The security provided left plenty of mind space for pupils' personal development. This is the right start in life.

If we are to become healthy contributing members of society, our parents must be able to read our physical and emotional needs and meet them at all ages, even before we can be aware of the needs ourselves. This is not the same as satisfying wants, of course, so our parents need discernment too. As we grow up, they need to be able to identify our particular latent abilities too so that we have the opportunities to develop them sufficiently well to use them and to be valued in them.

Eventually, we will need to support ourselves and those we care for in our communities and feel confident in our own continued security. Ideally, we will be paid or otherwise supported in those activities we have found we love doing. That's the best job to get. There is a lot of nurturing required in helping a child find their place in the world. In my family sessions, I often offer the following somewhat amusing job specification, (source unknown):

Parent Wanted

- Responsible person, male or female, to undertake a lifelong project.
- Candidates should be totally committed, willing to work up to 24 hours daily, including weekends in the initial 16-year period.
- Occasional holidays possible, but may be cancelled at no notice.
- Knowledge of healthcare, nutrition, psychology, child development, household management and the education system essential.
- Necessary skills: stress management and conflict resolution, negotiation and problem solving, communication and listening, budgeting and time management, decision making, ability to set boundaries and prioritise as well as provide loving support.
- Necessary qualities: energy, tolerance, patience, good self-esteem, self-confidence and a sense of humour.
- No training or experience needed (or provided).
- No salary, but very rewarding work for the right person.

If the parents have performed well in all this, the young person can embark on an independent life with confidence. Maslow considered our ongoing psychological health. His Hierarchy of Needs embodies the following concepts:

- personal happiness is everyone's primary goal.
- we are genetically social creatures and are therefore driven to interact.
- healthy humans are naturally pre-programmed to care for their fellow beings.

He proposed that our baseline needs are our physical ones and that these lower stages need to be satisfied before we attain the higher ones. I summarise this lowest level as food, clothing and shelter. Most of my readers will take these for granted in their lives as I did and may not appreciate how devastating their absence is. Some of my clients do and I learn from those who have had to sleep on cold streets in winter. I often check with my more deprived clients that they have enough food, a place to stay and someone to turn to before I even embark upon anything remotely psychological in nature.

Maslow saw that we then needed a stable environment, the confidence that we would have food, clothing and shelter, not just today, but in the foreseeable future. Once we have this assurance, we will then prioritise our psychological needs of love and intimacy. Love carries the message that someone is committed to ensure our needs will be met today.

Once that is in place, we then need to know that we will be loved in the future. A child who has been fostered may be amply loved at any one time, but if their care has been intermittent, they may feel insecure and their behaviour will reflect that, possibly even resulting in yet another carer breakdown.

Maslow's top level is one of being respected and valued. In simple terms, if we are respected by those around us, we can be confident of our value to our communities and our actions will be generally well received. We fit into our world well. That belonging means our needs are likely to be met in the foreseeable future. We will be loved in some sense by the people who matter to us. My old college motto summarised the essence of our needs: 'We all need to love and be loved', to which I add 'every day'.

This final level reflects a stable environment in which we feel fulfilled in what we do and our efforts are genuinely welcomed. We are able to respond well to the needs of our subconscious self and consistently maintain a good balance for ourselves. This ascension of met needs is the theme of any of our onward journeys. The founder of Person-Centred Counselling, Carl Rogers, tells us in his Core Conditions that we have to be nearer to the higher levels than our clients. I usually am. When that changes, the client is ready to leave therapy.

33: Pathology

The psychiatric world tends to address client pathology with a Medical Model essentially derived from physical medicine. It identifies specific symptoms or behaviours and applies specific 'interventions', usually involving medication. Medication as a psychological treatment is now under some scrutiny, particularly in terms of its long-term effectiveness. Mind-altering drugs can, in relieving stress, also reduce the individual's power to take control over their lives, and that is crucial to psychological recovery. This control is necessary for managing today's problems, let alone resolving the traumas from the past.

In contrast, much of the counselling world, especially the training establishments, focuses on the individual and rightly so, encouraging self-awareness and self-control. However, the training generally avoids pathologies, resulting in a large gap in the understanding of clients' emotional landscapes, both internally and externally. If someone feels bad enough to come and spend time and usually money on counselling, by definition, a pathology exists in some measure.

They are probably anxious or depressed or both. It may not be serious or permanent. Their imbalance can result from life events such as a bereavement, illness, loss of employment and a host of other emotional impacts. Non-relational issues like this are generally covered in general training and in pathology directed therapies such as CBT for anxiety, trauma or depression, however valid they might be. Our vulnerability to these life events is a function of two factors:

- How life is treating us and that very much includes our current relationships.
- How robust our software is to meet life's challenges.

These factors invite questions: How were we brought up? How was our software created in childhood? How the people we are dependent on now are affecting us? Is anyone actually hurting us?

All these infer that our pathology may be a result of someone else's pathology, either a parent/carer or someone who has power over us in some way today. English Law recognises emotional oppression, most interestingly in the very serious case of Sally Challen who killed a husband who had oppressed her all her married life.

Unfortunately, counselling training still shies away from addressing the impact on a client of another person's pathology. While a victim of abuse may seek help, it is unlikely that their aggressor will, so they are usually invisible to the counselling world, until perhaps they arrive in relationship counselling. If we can accept that aggression is unhealthy for victims and therefore pathological in the context of relationships, we are much more likely to perceive a client's suffering as emanating from a pathology residing within another person rather than one within themselves.

This may seem obvious to the layperson, but the world of therapy struggles to address this, seeking compromise in preference to truth. It can infer a failing in the victim rather than in the aggressor, doing yet further damage to them. It seems to be afraid of the repercussions of suggesting third party pathology. The aggressor is not normally going to accept responsibility for their actions, so the counsellor's job is to focus on helping the victim develop resilience. That must include an understanding of the nature of the aggressor's pathology. If the aggressor discovers they are being discussed in this way they may then turn on the therapist. The profession must address this potential issue in a mature and informed manner.

Any profession which sets out to involve itself in people's emotional lives and gains the trust of clients by its claims, must be as rigorous as possible in its training and practice. Proper scientific method insists that all relevant data is considered before any conclusion can be reached, so to ignore pathologies can ignore the very source of a client's distress. Soul-Centred Counselling is able to entertain the possibility of pathology both in the client and in those they interact with.

If an idyllic world of burgeoning empathy in which we all augment and support each other is not the reality we see, then what has gone wrong? The goodness of the Emotional Currency we need in order to interact successfully with each other is altruistic love. Love relies on us all successfully developing empathy in childhood. Freud's process of maturation into the empathic superego is critical to the creation of cohesive societies and therefore of happy individuals within those societies. If the superego is normal and healthy, then the absence of it must be seen as unhealthy or pathological. That pathological absence is what we are seeing in all the conflicts around us, great and small.

If we have all achieved the superego state as I describe it, then we should all have the wherewithal in our communities to manage the vagaries that nature throws at us, reinforcing our connections with each other to all our mutual benefits. I recall a Jew by the name of Jesus who thought this was a good idea two millennia ago. Despite the fact that the religion that stemmed from his teaching is reportedly professed by some third of all human beings, we are still trying to digest his message.

Freud's development process has gone awry in some individuals. We are not all reaching his superego state. The most obvious cause might be inadequate parenting. We are principally what our carers and those around us make us. If we can accept that genuine personal happiness is the main goal of the human endeavour, then ensuring that parenting is done really well must be our primary objective.

Regrettably, it is clear that genuine personal happiness for all is not societies' current main objective. We outstandingly fail to promote the development of our parenting skills well enough. There is very little training for this, even in our wealthiest societies. Our education systems are often more geared towards enabling children to become a part of our production processes, often to generate a wealth which may then rise out of reach of those average citizens who are creating it.

Many societies are less concerned about meeting the emotional needs of the individual than allowing the powerful to gain ever greater power. Meeting emotional needs is what my profession is about and surely all of healthy life is about that too. Our desire to increase our material wealth through monetary currency has somewhat missed the point of living. Given the choice, I would sooner be happy than either clever or wealthy.

All animals tend to be governed initially by basic instinct rather than guided by developed intuition. Cognitive intelligence in the human is bigger than any other animal and we need to learn at an early stage to tune it well into our intuition in order to manage our instincts safely. Within the school system, limited resources mean that significant emotional issues tend to be addressed by pastoral staff more when things go wrong. The quiet but unhappy child may be overlooked.

While training for practical life has now arrived in the British school curriculum, we are not yet teaching practical psychology, so students may finally enter their adult worlds with limited self-care defence systems in place.

One of the first casualties of the 2008 financial crisis, incidentally caused principally by the astronomical greed of a limited number of individuals in the financial sector, was a British national project call Surestart which helped families in difficulty. It reduced the incidence of disadvantaged children becoming maladjusted adults.

The results of the decision to stop its funding would surely be reaped fairly soon afterwards, but the time lag meant that no direct connection would be clearly demonstrable, so the decision makers were not made accountable. The Evaluation of Children's Centres Project in England concluded that Surestart 'can improve the mental health of mothers and functioning of families but that these benefits are being eroded by cuts.'[1]

I suggest that the epidemic of knifing amongst the teenagers around a decade later resulting in deaths most weeks in Britain, was in part a consequence of unsupported parenting and could to some extent be connected to the loss of this programme.

Another casualty in Britain of financial sector avarice was prison staff numbers, with more evident results. Those who missed out on a wholesome upbringing and education are far more likely to appear in the prison system. Many inmates have come through the so-called 'care' system, but because they are effectively disenfranchised, they are seen as less important politically, or at least, not till they get out and re-offend.

They may leave prison without the learning they need to survive well and that is more likely to happen under reduced staff. It is often a learning deficit which got them there in the first place. And that deficit will surely deliver them back again and again unless it is addressed. Over 30% of adults and 40% of juveniles in Britain re-offend within a year of release. This may be effective incarceration but it's not effective correction. Evidence indicates that prisons house significantly more mentally ill people than our mental institutions. An American report in 2016 stated;

Serious mental illness has become so prevalent in the US corrections system that jails and prisons are now commonly called 'the new asylums'. In point of fact, the Los Angeles County Jail, Chicago's Cook County Jail or New York's Riker's Island Jail each hold more mentally ill inmates than any remaining psychiatric hospital in the United States. Overall, approximately 20% of inmates in jails and 15% of inmates in state prisons are now estimated to have a serious mental illness. Based on the total inmate population, this means approximately 383,000 individuals with severe psychiatric disease were behind bars in the United States in 2014 or nearly 10 times the number of patients remaining in the nation's state hospitals.[2]

Given that these figures represent the more extreme tip of a much larger emotionally unhealthy iceberg, we need to learn a lot more about ourselves if we are to find happiness for our societies as a whole and, therefore, for ourselves as individuals. Then we can address the issues which beset us.

While prescribed drugs may have a part to play in some therapies, we always need to attend to the malware which may be embedded in a sufferer's subconscious, usually in circumstances beyond their control and very often at an early age. Their software needs some reprogramming and they will need help in this. Another sympathetic human being, well trained to offer an unconditional relationship, is an essential part of the process.

I observe a distinct difference between clients who have been hit by events in adult life from those whose mental software has been formed badly in early childhood. The Umbra Effect diagram replicates the shadow cast by a planet blocking the sun's rays. The nearer and bigger the obstacle to the centre, the greater is its impact.

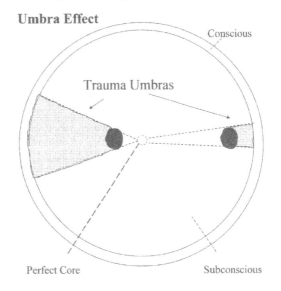

Umbra Effect

Conscious

Trauma Umbras

Perfect Core

Subconscious

It illustrates the difference between the effects of a trauma in adulthood compared to a similar one in childhood. An early trauma impacts a much larger zone of functioning around life's circumference than a more recent one. The affected area is much bigger, requiring a lot more reprogramming to work on all the learning malformed by the trauma since it happened.

Part of my client portfolio has included asylum seekers, many of whom had stable backgrounds but traumatic recent experiences. They progress much faster than those who had inadequate upbringings. An Adverse Childhood Events (ACE) research study in 2014 identified the relatively larger impact that stresses can have on developing minds than on adult ones.[3] I feel somewhat saddened by the fact that we need to deliver research to tell us that a mind in formation will sustain worse damage than a mind which is well formed but similarly afflicted.

When I initially assess adult clients for a counselling programme, regardless of their presented issues, I always ask about childhood. Were they loved well? Was there any abuse-sexual, physical, emotional? Did someone close to them die? Is there an aggressor now? As a counsellor, I then have a much better idea of where to start. We may fail to address the client's issues unless we ask those questions. It is a skill to do that while maintaining the counselling process safely.

The quality of our nurturing defines how our souls are formed. That formation will, in turn, define how well we are able to manage the vagaries of our lives as children and as adults. There are healthy life trajectories and unhealthy ones. I don't believe that a miserable life is a predetermined destiny for anyone, but I do believe it can be inevitable if the source of the misery is not attended to at some point.

Most people who get through an unhealthy upbringing have accepted it as normal at the time, despite the fact that they seem to be damaged in that process. The majority of my adult clients have childhood issues still playing out in them. The counselling process to unravel those issues can sometimes take years. I counsel young people too and it is my pleasure to see them before the damage they are sustaining becomes too embedded. I can often catch their problems in the bud and give them a healthy perspective on how to handle the stresses they are experiencing.

I am acutely aware of how my work with a young person can have much greater effect than if they come to their problems as an adult. It delights me when I have been the instigator of some really big differences for them. Sometimes my work changes a child's complete future by enabling them to defend themselves effectively and then discover their own potential. I revel in those times. However, all this can be more challenging if the issue is part of the basic mental foundations the client was born with. This is a deeper level of pathology.

34: Firmware Issues

The body, brain and mental software develop in the womb. Whilst birth is a major transition, with the greatest respect to delivering mothers, it is just an event in the building of the new human life. We know a lot about the body in utero. We know a lot less about the brain there. We know very little about the mental software at this stage beyond the reflexes we see at birth. The human baby is the least developed of all species in that it is highly dependent for a protracted period.

It is this feature which enables each generation to mutate and adapt its thinking processes during its early formative phases to the ever-changing environment in which it finds itself. The results are manifest in the extraordinary changes to society we have seen over the last few hundred years in our towns and cities, and in technology in the last few decades. Our mental capabilities are staggering.

In contrast, the physical body changes have not been significant over this time, other than larger physiques due to better nutrition. Paradoxically, health may now be in decline again as the excesses produced by our far too clever minds have become the new big problems in the shape of obesity, heart conditions, Type II Diabetes, addictions and more. There is a mismatch between our bodies which have changed very little over many thousands of years and our mental software which is developing at a frightening rate.

As in the rest of nature, all life does not develop perfectly. If mental abnormalities do occur in the very early stages, either in utero or perinatally, the depth of their impact can make them much harder to deal with in therapy. The emanating problems can often be complex. It can be impossible to define what exactly has gone wrong and when.

At the end of the day, all I can be interested in as a practitioner is how I can help this person get through life and how much progress they can realistically make. While it might help to know all the neuroscientific details of perinatal brain development, I can't wait for that research for me to make use of it. My client is in front of me and needs help now. I just need to focus on what I can see and sense in them. Above all, I need to understand them as living functioning people in their own particular worlds. That is the essence of my person-centred approach.

When I buy a computer or a printer, there is already some fixed software in it. That is called firmware. Whatever else is superimposed on that firmware, it won't change. In the same way, every human being has firmware imprinted from early development and has to progress through life with that.

As a counsellor, I have to work with whatever that is in my client. I find it useful to identify the line between their mutable software and their immutable firmware so that I can be realistic about prospects. It is not an analytical diagnosis I conduct. I simply find where my client's discomforts and limits are and work to help them progress the capabilities they do have at their own pace. The immutables make themselves apparent. I need to find these edges and work with them.

This concept of firmware is not restricted to emotional processing. My entire autonomic system, the software which runs my body systems - circulation, aspiration, digestive, immunity, etc.- is firmware too. The vast majority of how my thinking processes are organised and memories are stored is also firmware. While everything is running smoothly, I don't need to know about this.

However, when it goes wrong, I need to understand as much as I can about it. Clients can recognise the concept that there may be a differentiation between firmware and software within them and are often encouraged by the possibility that the software part of them can change. My job is to try and help them find which is which. If they can understand that, then those of us in the emotional healing profession need to as well.

As practitioners, we need to find consensus with each other about pathologies so we can develop our profession and help the sufferers we meet in our work. We need to investigate categories of ailment and develop a vocabulary for effective communication. The current diagnostic listings do not appear to be achieving well in this. Once we have achieved communicable meanings, we can construct ideas around them between us.

This cannot just be one person at a time. Ideas need be passed around and developed. That is the way we progress understanding. The converse it also true. If we cannot transmit our ideas clearly, we cannot progress. Too often, regrettably, the areas which psychology debates are often not the areas my clients are interested in. Research can be esoteric and niche rather than pragmatic. This is why I found myself creating a new form of therapy.

35: Resolving Stresses

In the same way that our bodies sustain attacks from physical impacts, from viruses and from malfunctions such as cancer, our psyches sustain emotional impacts when there are sudden changes and our emotional needs are not met. These attacks are not necessarily landmark events. Just as there is a myriad of small physical and biological attacks in a day for our bodies to deal with, so there is a myriad of small emotional impacts in a day for our psyches to deal with too.

We process most of these without noticing, but if some get stuck, they can build up and present abnormally, demanding greater attention and often needing external support to regain our balance.

Some people are less able to recover and maintain their emotional balance than others. A consistent inability to maintain balance is, by any reasonable definition, pathological. The resultant unhappiness can be due to a number of issues: biological hardware issues, less than resilient firmware, poor foundational software, early life challenges affecting the healthy formation of synapses in the brain, a significant trauma or being caught in a chronically oppressive emotional environment.

We are complex beings. I have nowhere near the capacity to understand myself fully, so I need to be able to listen to any messages which arise from within to discover what is going wrong out the myriad of other correctly operating functions. There are constant reports coming from our nervous systems updating our internal condition and telling us when something needs to be done to recover our life balance.

If I have damaged my leg, it will send a pain message to my brain focussed on that area and I should use that to guide some remedial action. If I can't identify and therefore process that message, the condition may get worse. It could even ultimately kill me, possibly through an infection. Similarly, if an emotionally related message is sent but not interpreted properly, I could fail to take corrective action and my condition may worsen. I become distressed or indeed a lot worse.

Continuing the analogy, as my body automatically takes action to rectify physical injury, the software of my being, my soul, automatically takes action to rectify emotional injury. Much may already have happened behind the scenes before I consciously take action. At least to begin with, this is not a conscious decision. It just happens.

I was knocked off my bike recently and sustained a few bruises. Nothing more, I am relieved to say. I did not decide how these would be healed or indeed in what order. My body just got on with it and all was well in a week or so. I did not break a limb so did not need any external assistance.

Similarly, if someone upsets me, I might go for a walk and take the dog as well. I'll usually feel a bit lighter when I get back. When I have had a good night's sleep, I'll feel better too. I may have not set out to analyse the whole thing. I have just given my soul space to get on with its healing work. It's a bit like a virus clean up in my computer. And if that internal process is insufficient because I have broken an emotional limb, to use a physical analogy, I will find a friend - or a counsellor - to help me resolve my remaining issues. The process will then start to become a more conscious one. But not everyone can do this easily.

Some people routinely struggle to process their own emotions. If that of itself is not enough of a trial, they will, as a consequence, also struggle to generate relationships with others to form the emotional contracts needed to relieve those excess emotions. They are doubly deprived of their routes to stress relief.

Further, a depression resulting from this deficit can often result in self-isolation. A triple problem. This inability to tap into the essential means of stress relief is unhealthy. It is a deeper pathology. The normal basic emotional mechanisms are not functioning properly and they are not happy.

So what is this pathology? Psychiatric criteria work with observable behaviours. While there is an institutional logic in this, a clearer and deeper understanding is needed to effect change for the individual client. Homo sapiens has evolved into an interdependent animal, both structurally and emotionally. If we are unable to relate well to others in either sphere, we are likely to experience imbalance and therefore distress.

Interpersonal emotional relationships are at the most sophisticated end of our capabilities and they will be the first to suffer in any personality malformation or duress. The Emotional Contract diagram illustrates the mechanism of stress resolution in healthy relationships. If emotional exchanges are impaired, then the individual will not achieve their healthy balance and will, as a result, suffer.

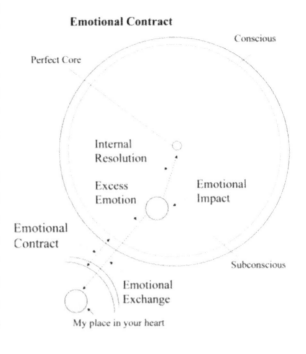

The currency of the Emotional Contract is empathy. We all need the gift of empathy to relate to others so we can mutually resolve externally those emotional impacts which we have been unable to digest internally.

I sought an accurate definition for the pathology which lacks this gift. In my last profession of engineering, we would define parameters to three decimal places. That way we got men to the moon and we can search the whole planet for information in seconds from our mobile phones. Psychology is far less precise.

Many would agree that the autistic spectrum would cover the concept of a lack of empathy, but it is used - or misused - to cover such a variety of features, that some people can become wedded to one or another set of manifestations. What is in my head for this word might be very different to what is in your head, or indeed your friend's head, so I am going to generally avoid it as a definition.

I find the concept of alexithymia useful as it appears to cover a deficiency in processing emotions internally with a resultant deficiency in engaging effectively with others. It was created to describe some extreme cases. It addresses a lack of empathy. It differs from the more conventional autistic concept by focussing on the immediately obvious feature, the inability to read emotions intuitively. It considers the internal deficiency first and then accepts that that will impact the emotional component of relationships, empathy. The following provides a valuable description which encompasses less alarming conditions:

'Alexithymia is a term to describe problems with feeling emotions. In Greek, it loosely translates to 'no words for emotion.' It is estimated that 1 in 10 people has alexithymia, but it is much more common in those with depression and in autistic people. 1 in 5 autistic people have alexithymia. People who have alexithymia may have trouble identifying, understanding and describing emotions. They may also struggle to show or feel emotions that are seen as socially appropriate, such as happiness on a joyous occasion.[1]

This simple definition enables me to go to the core of what really matters; how my client is feeling, how they are functioning and what general difficulties they may be experiencing. What a client is feeling is what counselling is about. Clients feel distressed when they come and are relieved when they leave. That is all that matters.

In amongst all the infinite variety of personality features to be found in any individual, empathy is the one which tells me the most. It is the key to the soul. It is the mechanism of emotional communication and therefore of emotional healing. In a profession which is dedicated to helping clients discover and secure their own emotional balance, an understanding of how empathy works is crucial. My whole aim is to help my client find peace within themselves.

In the chapter, Selfish Me, I described empathy as a Mirror Neuron function in which an observer spontaneously senses what another person is feeling. A focus on empathy provides the most effective emotional slice through a client's presented personality and can go to the heart of their problems. Whatever else a client is, if they are empathic, I can usually connect and help. If they are not, I will have difficulty in reaching them at this level and so will everyone else. The closer I can track my client's feelings, the more effective my work will be. Let me offer an example:

I was attending to one partner's issues in couples' counselling, when I noticed the other was becoming tearful. Counselling is about emotions and their management, so I stopped discourse with him to give her space. Before I could process her condition, tears were coming to my eyes. I have never actually cried in session and did not then, but she was left in no doubt that I was with her emotionally. We had connected at a level beyond words.

This was not a conscious process. It was a deep connection in which I felt what she felt before my cognitive processes even became engaged. This is intuitive empathy.

So how does this work in the context of emotional healing? If my client can manage their emotions, they can be happy. If they cannot, they are distressed and may visit me. If they are distressed in session and I actually feel that distress, they have connected to me as their emotional external hard drive. We are on the same wavelength. If I am also grounded at that time, then the client has found a route for an emotional discharge through me, much like an electrical current going to earth. That sharing provides a measure of relief for some aspect of their pain.

So, the next time they feel similarly distressed outside therapy, that memory is available, consciously or subconsciously, to help them find relief on their own. This is a primary function of basic counselling, usually known as Classical Person-Centred Counselling.

Empathy enables me to understand and connect with my client at a deeper level, addressing significant challenges effectively. It is by practicing as a Person-Centred counsellor that I can be with my client in how they feel rather than focussing on their behaviour as seen and categorised by others in diagnostic listings. External behavioural work such as CBT can be useful, but the best successes always come from the internal empathic function. This process is especially useful for young people whose brain hardware is still forming, so any good work early on in life can have a greater impact than if we waited until they became adults.

Addressing the concept of empathy is consistent with my Person-Centred practice which requires me to focus on my client and their feelings as they are. The founder of this modality, C.R. Rogers, cited three essential principal conditions for effective therapy. Empathy was one of them. If I want to help my client, I need to understand and tune into their most basic difficulties and help them grasp them too. I will need my empathic capabilities to do just that.

While alexithymia is often used to characterise extremes, I need to cover a spectrum from full emotional awareness to emotional unawareness. In order to avoid the confusion of multifarious interpretations of existing words, I have chosen to create a new word, 'dysempathic', to describe a spectrum characterised by poor sensory recognition of emotions in self and in others. The Greek prefix 'dys' infers an impaired function. The concept provides a description which, in its simplest form, identifies a lack of a sense of oneself and therefore of others without predetermining too many other features.

36: The Normal Curve

When I asked a teenage client what she wanted from counselling she replied, "To be less anxious." I suspected her reply, so asked in a different way. She then said she wanted to know how she felt. It was that basic. The 'anxious' script had come from a parent. She did not know what it meant. It soon became apparent that she was unable to sense even her body normally. There was a physical disability.

This was at the more extreme end of my practice. She was being assessed for autism at the time. Most cases are more nuanced, so it is useful to be able to identify a range of levels of pathology.

Like most other psychological features, empathy deficit can be viewed on a spectrum. We all have some internal emotional aberrations, often more in some areas than in others. Some may be mild and some not so mild. We are

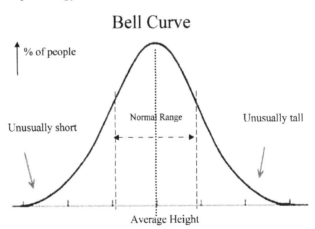

often more ready to identify these in others. So, it is important to gather a perspective on this particular feature in the light of what we might see as a healthy normality; one in which we can recognise and process most of our emotions and we can generally connect emotionally with others.

I find that normality in my own areas of life is usually straightforward to define and grasp with its various features manifesting within a reasonably recognisable range. It's what I am used to seeing. I walk through the town and I will notice people who are abnormally tall, short, fat or oddly dressed. The rest generally pass me by. Heights vary around an average, generally in line with the statistical Bell Curve, also called the Normal Distribution Curve.

This shape is applicable to variations across much of nature. Around 2/3 of us fall in the normal range shown. The remaining 1/3 are either abnormally tall or abnormally short. Beyond the more extreme height ranges, humans tend not to survive, so the graph is not too unrealistic of actual life.

Nature will always produce and replicate any feature which can survive and that includes all and any aspect of ourselves. I am fascinated by the creatures still being discovered in the ocean's depths. They are unconstrained by the force of gravity so their structures can be much more varied. Their shapes are bizarre to us terrestrial humans, but they survive and reproduce and have done so for millennia. The variations seem to be almost limitless. Natural rules seem to say that if they can exist, they probably will exist.

In the same way, some human behaviours can appear quite bizarre when viewed from a relatively normal construct in the middle section of the psychological Bell Curve.

Indeed, events on the world stage continue to shock us, despite the fact that the stories and their lead actors are simply displaying the enormous variety of nature's expressions. If we understood the pathologies at play here better, we might stop getting shocked into freeze mode and take sharper corrective action. By identifying these pathologies at an early stage, we can stop the destroyers from getting into their positions of power in the first place. The adage that 'If we don't see evil coming towards us, we may be travelling with it' resonates well here.

The dysempathic feature I have coined can appear in the autistic spectrum. While the autistic spectrum carries a host of behavioural features which may or may not arise in a particular case, dysempathy homes in on a particular aspect only, that of poor emotional processing. It avoids the challenge of identifying and negotiating a whole range of diagnostic labels. It infers a lifelong disorder indicating this simple criterion, regardless of any other features which may be identified, such as cognitive ability. It is of interest that if the heritability of autism spectrum disorder is approximately 80%, then this may apply to dysempathy also.[1] Family histories may offer clues here.

200

As a counsellor, I find it useful to identify empathy in my client in order to generate a healthy Emotional Contract with them. That enables me to make the healing process as effective as I can. The deeper the empathic connection I can make, the more powerful is the Emotional Contract and the more effective is the healing. I rely on these connections in my work.

The absence of empathic capacity in a client and therefore in the counselling relationship soon becomes apparent. Such people are likely to give cognitive answers to emotional questions. In England today, the word 'annoying' is used to cover a very broad spectrum of negative emotions. It's a head report and not a felt heart sensation. Part of our emotion sensitivity normally passes through our bodies.

Typically, a perceived awareness of fear triggers the adrenal glands to produce adrenalin to initiate the Fight - Flight response. We then sense the result in our bodies which amplifies the emotional response. Most people sense fear in the lower abdomen and peace in the area of the solar plexus.

For dysempathics, the message paths can be impaired so they struggle to identify their emotions, let alone their source. We need to interpret these inner messages well if we are to maintain our emotional balance. It can be useful to try and help clients connect the feelings they are detecting with sensations in parts of the body in order to invite some sensitivity. That can help expand their vocabulary and differentiate between their various emotions. That broader language enables them to express themselves more effectively to others who might help, like parents or counsellors.

If I can recognise this pathology, understand it and work with it, I can have reasonable expectations for my work. I recall my frustration with such clients before I appreciated this. While an awareness of this pathology in some form is a useful guide, it is still imperative that I remain interested in this specific person with all their other complexities so I can discover how I can help them within their particular condition. I start from there and let the client fill in the details. This recognition does not come with a treatment package, but it does help me understand what sort of challenge this is.

If I see these basic features and feel my client would be receptive to seeking help beyond the confidential one-to-one support I offer, I may invite them to do an 'online' test and perhaps see a doctor for a more formal assessment with a view to accessing further services. The online questionnaire 'aspergerstestsite.com' can be a useful start, especially if done by the client and not by a parent or partner. It may not reflect the dysempathic feature precisely, but could help them identify a more recognisable issue.

Dysempathic clients are the most in need of empathic connections but their poorly developed emotional recognition means that they are less able to take advantage of genuine relationships. The deficit will impair them from forming them.

A supervisee was struggling to understand her client's behaviour, most particularly in the context of her marriage breaking down. I suspected a lack of empathy somewhere in the mix. On prompting, the supervisee realised that the word 'love' or the lack of it had not appeared in any of her sessions, despite the fact that the declared issue of marital relationship.

The supervisee came to appreciate that her client did not seem to display much empathy. The idea of poor emotional recognition emerged and seemed to fit. It gave her a possible template to address her client's condition, not in the rigid terms of a defined pathology but reassessing her as someone who might struggle to process her own emotions. We need to understand our clients and this was a potentially useful insight.

Section 6
Aggression

37: Smart Pathology

We all have emotional needs to process. However, those who don't sense other peoples' emotions well can't form the essential bonding precursors which enable the creation of those Emotional Contracts needed to release surplus emotions in a healthy way.

Some people have an empathy deficit but they are still able to identify and negotiate others' emotions despite not feeling them viscerally. That gives them the same route empaths have for discharging their excess emotions but without the constraint of actually feeling the impact of their actions on others. Whether these people can be formally or conventionally classified as alexithymic or autistic is not material to my counselling work, but they do fit the basic definition of a 'dysfunction in emotional awareness'.

People who have the ability to read others' emotions while not feeling them intrinsically are potentially dangerous because they can manipulate others for their own purposes; and because they can, they often will. They can come into my world through my clients or indeed personally.

I need to be equipped to understand them myself and help my clients deal with them in their lives. They will not be inhibited about hurting us, so the level of pain they might inflict will be limited by their needs, not by ours. Our entreaties may not restrain them. The dysempathic model I have proposed provides a means of understanding and managing this.

British medical researcher, Dr Michael Mosley, ran a series called Trust Me I'm a Doctor which included a Mental Health Special. One of the articles helped me understand how an apparently normal person can function without a basic emotional response system. A patient had his adrenal glands removed for medical reasons and found his natural fear of riding on a roller coaster with his children had disappeared. He then elected to abseil from a very high industrial chimney. When he finally descended to the base, he was unperturbed. He recognised the danger but did not feel it. The mechanism for sensing the fear seemed to have been the release of the hormones, now missing, rather than the considered observation of the danger. His operation had removed that biological component. In this regard at least, he could know danger cognitively but could not feel it emotionally in the way he had before.[1]

The report did not suggest that the man became a threat to anyone, but it demonstrated a separation between felt and understood experiences. He became impervious to the emotive stimuli we would regard as essential, but remained apparently normal in other respects. Similarly, people recovering from serious brain operations may find they have lost intimate access to their own feelings and to others' feelings too. Many retain good cognitive functioning despite losing some emotional intelligence. Their memory of empathy and moral behaviour could constrain their actions in some degree.

If dysempathic people have been brought up in a morally guided environment, they will try and do the right thing. They will learn as best they can not to harm others. In the absence of sensing others' reactions, they learn morals and their moral behaviour usually yields positive outcomes. If they are not so educated in morals, they may not be perturbed about hurting others in getting what they need or even what they just want.

In the absence of the means of creating the all-important Emotional Contacts which empaths use to share their excess emotions by agreement, they may find people they can discharge their emotions upon by force. They can observe others' emotional reactions dispassionately and may find they can control them with no internal constraint. We may see them as trusted companions but they may see us as legitimate prey.

That cognitive recognition of others' emotions without feeling them internally allows them to behave and therefore present very differently to those who are simply unable to manage their own emotions well. They can learn to appear and behave apparently normally for the most part. But because they cannot relieve their emotions by agreement, they indulge in forcible Emotional Raids on anyone they have sufficient power over, coercing them into attending to their needs and accepting their excesses.

Such behaviour invites the term sociopathy: a pathology which affects their social group as opposed to themselves. Other more formal terms describing similar behaviours are Psychopathy, Antisocial Personality Disorder (DSM 5), Dissocial Personality Disorder (ICD 10) and Narcissistic Personality Disorder (DSM 5). All are described differently because they focus on the resultant behaviours which can vary

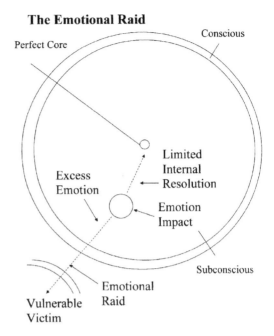

significantly. ICD 10 directly identifies an empathy void, referring to 'Callous unconcern for the feelings of others'. However, it also refers to a 'very low tolerance to frustration and a low threshold for discharge of aggression, including violence'.

Physical lack of control is not generally a feature I see my clients being subjected to. DSM 5 refers to the all-important feature of empathy as 'the lack of concern for feelings, needs or suffering of others.' None really spell out the most basic working feature deriving from dysempathy, the need to satisfy an emotional deficit combined with a deficiency in processing emotions internally.

This internal deficit and the relational empathy void, coupled with a cognitive observation of others' emotions, drives them to deposit their unwanted emotions onto vulnerable victims. It is the mechanism of this behaviour. Donald Black addresses Antisocial Personality Disorder in-depth in *Bad Boys, Bad Men*.[2] He focusses on the more overt behaviours as described in the pathology listings. He also seeks a treatment device for the condition, but regrettably, leaves me with little hope for that.

As a counsellor, I am not aware of any method I can use to 'treat' this condition. My focus is on my client who may be a victim of emotional aggression. My mission is not to cure this pathology, but to help my client

207

understand it so they can defend themselves against it. A far more feasible project.

The confusion I see in the psychological arena of attempting to define pathology on the basis of observed behaviour is all too apparent in the plethora of diagnoses offered in the various listings available. Amongst the pathologies discussed, I felt it particularly important to separate the useful term of sociopathy from the more alarming one of psychopathy. Xanthe Mallett says psychopaths are born and sociopaths are made.[3] Others disagree and say a psychopath is physically violent and a sociopath is not.

This debate typifies the lack of precision in definitions in the psychological world. I prefer to consider a sociopath as one who uses those they have influence over to discharge their excess emotions whereas the psychopath is one who gains pleasure from other people's suffering.

Lucy Letby was a neonatal nurse at Chester hospital in England. She was convicted of murdering seven babies and to have attempted to murder six others from summer 2015 to summer 2016. Her gratification from exercising immense power in the absence of valid empathy illustrates psychopathy well. The warning to us all is that she was able to present as normal for too long to those who controlled her destiny. The same pathology is evident in Vladimir Putin on an altogether different scale, but no-one got to stop him soon enough. He tells the Russian people he is caring for them but empathy is absent.

We need to understand the pathologies at play here if we are to protect ourselves from them. No field of study should avoid arguments about what features are or are not present. Rather, we should seek agreements on indisputable definitions all can subscribe to, accompanied by an acceptance of variations around them, all based on logically constructed investigations. Only then can we escape from the confusion that surrounds this and other topics and go on to develop a universal knowledge base across the discipline.

As a counsellor facing this sort of condition, I am only interested in basic tools to help my clients understand an oppressor better and to consider the potential permanence or otherwise of their condition. I don't want to confuse them. There is much debate about this pathology, but not yet in counselling circles. I decided that I needed a benchmark that worked for me at least. I find the term sociopathic fitted the features I see most. I would define sociopathy as:

> A consistent pathology in which a person harms others emotionally, apparently deliberately, but whose innate lack of empathy is such that they do not experience the pain they impose and are therefore not viscerally inhibited from their harmful actions.

While there are useful indicators which help discern this pathology, this definition avoids getting wrapped up in detailed behaviour types yielding multiple diagnoses. Accordingly, I will use the word sociopath in this book as a term for a type of person displaying certain destructive features, apparently driven by a lack of empathy. However, I avoid describing a particular individual as a sociopath and I discourage clients to do that for a number of reasons.

- Its definition is poorly established.
- The term is seen as pejorative and invites highly emotional arguments.
- For most people, including professionals, the word conjures up a caricature which is often inaccurate and therefore unhelpful for the real-life circumstance a client might be in. Most sociopaths are relatively invisible, hidden in plain in sight.
- Society struggles to come to terms with such a negative concept in its own backyard.
- We don't like to think of some sort of evil is embodied in the people we may have accepted into our lives and communities, despite evidence to the contrary.
- It implies a permanence which may or may not be there.
- Any sociopath involved will become defensive at the suggestion of sociopathy, even if directed at another.
- The counselling fraternity is generally unable to accommodate the concept yet.

Sociopathic people often portray themselves as good and respectable not obviously displaying their negative behaviour outside their victim circle. They generate convincing personal disguises, designed to appear normal and even community spirited. A former FBI Counterintelligence Agent, Joe Navarro, wrote a sobering article identifying many reasons why clergy, in particular the celibate Catholic priesthood, can be susceptible to performing predatory acts of paedophilia. He relates that to sociopathic behaviour.[4]

However, pointing a psychological finger can get us into a lot of trouble. I will not label anyone in the way the psychological diagnostic tools invite us to. Labels are only useful if they enable action such as treatment or, indeed, incarceration. I cop out a little here because incarceration is not my responsibility and sociopaths do not normally present voluntarily for help with their condition, so tend not to be clients.

It is far safer and more useful to identify sociopathic type behaviour which may or may not emanate from someone who could be assessed as a sociopath. I find the most frequently used colloquial term for this sort of behaviour is 'narcissistic', which tends to be expressed with some emotional baggage. I suggest to clients that 'narcissistic' can engender fear and hatred while 'sociopathy' invites understanding and defence strategies.

Despite the presented personas and the multiplicity of behaviours within the pathology, there are some features which are undeniable in the cold light of day against recognised criteria. Like addictions, these may only be aspects of a person's character, but prominent ones from the point of view of personal happiness of those around them and of social cohesion.

Many of us exhibit sociopathic behaviour from time to time, but only a small percentage of the population is so frequently destructive as to merit such a label. It is important to appreciate that this is a pathology and not a person. Grasping that concept is key to its management. Something is awry in the vast subconscious of the individual and has yielded a socially damaging disease.

While the depth of this disorder is substantial, it remains a disease in a person who might in most other respects be normal and would present as such. Indeed, they will go to great lengths to create and present a respectable persona. They will often be seen as effective in their working environments.

However, the vulnerable victim experiences another side completely, to the point where it becomes intolerable. If they are able to see through the presented persona enough to identify the pathology in their aggressor, they may come to conclude at a conscious level that it is they who are normal and it is the aggressor who is abnormal. From that revelation, they may decide their relationship is beyond their ability to change or even manage. They can then start to make decisions for their own safety and happiness and for others who are also close to them, maybe children.

An assessment like this gives clarity to the situation and is essential for addressing and understanding this issue. Life can be difficult in lots of ways. Both clients and professionals need to face the fact that this pathology exists and is afflicting many of our lives in very real ways. Clients are suffering from sociopathic attacks and professionals fail them when they ignore or choose to be ignorant of a prevalent pathology such as this.

38: My Revelation

I always respect a client's stories, not necessarily because I accept that they are true at the time, but because my client believes them and I need to walk with them, in session at least. Some of the stories I have heard seemed almost fantastic, but I always consider them afterwards and sometimes find myself drawn to them. It is that which has enabled me to first consider and then understand this pathology.

My own journey into it was originally a reluctant one. A client kindly gave me a book called *Confessions of a Sociopath*. It fitted an historic part my own life well and the current lives of some clients I was supporting. It provided an experiential canvas for a theoretical framework.

Amongst many other stories the author, M.E. Thomas, talks about the time that her parents, simply drove off and left her at the age of ten stranded at a country park. It was a significant distance home. They presumably got tired of waiting for her. The concept of sociopathy explains how this could be possible. The parents were clearly unable to sense how she might feel. She was resourceful and just hitchhiked home. She also related how her father had smashed a hole in the bathroom door in a fit of uncontrolled rage to get at her.

I offer some examples which someone who was unaware of the concept of empathy deficit might dismiss as being the improbable fantasy of a storyteller:

- A hospital consultant with a wife and young children wanted his new family and his parental family to get along. That included his brother's family. They had all cohabited for a year or so, but his wife became fearful of his brother who wanted to micromanage her, her family and most everything it seemed. When they eventually moved out, his obsession with extended family harmony persisted.

Finally, in couples counselling, when it was clear that his wife could not tolerate his brother, I suggested he might have to make a choice between living with his wife and young children or with his brother's family. Bizarrely, he chose his brother. An acrimonious divorce ensued with his behaviour becoming progressively more fantastic, lurching from offensive messages one day to visits for sex the next. He tried to use his elevated status in society to influence the social services, but his domestic violence record told a bigger story.

- A respectable businessman had tolerated his wife's habitual affairs over a long marriage. When his three children left home, he was an inconvenience to her, so she harassed him sufficiently that he came for counselling for his stress. During that time, she rallied the adult children around, took him to a mental hospital and had him sectioned. I have clients who have had psychotic episodes but I could see nothing mentally abnormal in his demeanour other than enormous anxiety over what was happening to him. I found him to be an empathic man who had successfully run businesses all his life and had supported his family responsibly. It was classic gaslighting. [1,2]

- A husband declared in couples counselling that he had married his blind disabled wife on a deal that he could take his anger out on her any time he wanted. While I have to be professional in my work, I found him deeply unpleasant. When she resisted, he threatened to leave her, taking her two healthy children and leaving her with the eldest who had severe behaviour problems.

- A young Iranian was ejected from his country by his father, a senior government figure because he would not desist from blogging concerns about the behaviour of the government. His father seems to have thought that having his son mock hanged in the state prison would make him conform, but he underestimated his son's zeal. When he was let out, he continued. His father had him deposited on the other side of the country's border without a passport. He became a refugee.

- A leader in a relatively developed country was insensitive to the complaints of some of his subjects, so he chose to bomb the area they lived in. The residents objected and found sympathisers abroad. So did he. The spat developed into a war involving world powers and many disparate terrorist groups. The war continued to escalate for over decades displacing over a million refugees, causing some ½ million deaths and many more casualties. Not a client, but a well-known figure.

- A 16-year-old fell for a school friend in Bedfordshire in 2012 and all seemed well until she disrupted his 18th birthday party with a tantrum. He seemed besotted with her but as her demands became greater, he was eventually persuaded by his family to leave her. However, she returned saying she was having his baby. She persuaded him to live with her in a nearby town and gradually cut off his contacts with friends and family for a period of 2 years. She physically abused him daily. She insisted he leave his job and escort her to college every day. The baby's arrival provided brief relief only and the isolating tactics returned. Soon there was another baby, with similar results. She controlled him almost completely, to the point where he was losing weight. She would have a kettle of boiling water constantly on the go to throw at him. She frequently stabbed at him with a kitchen knife. Police visits alerted by neighbours found him regularly denying domestic violence until he was eventually persuaded to tell the truth. He was taken to hospital, where he was declared so emaciated that he would die if it carried on. She was the first female in England to be convicted of domestic violence like this. The chilling aspect of this is that the victim did not appear to be abnormal in any obvious way. She had just been extremely skilled at manipulating him.[3]

Whatever the specifics of each situation, the common denominator is someone who is devoid of empathy but who has captured enough power to take extreme actions for their own ends, completely regardless of the consequences to others. Some aggressors fare better than others, but the victims always do badly, at least until they can understand the pathology.

Society has allowed these sociopaths to follow their own insensitive wishes to devastating effect, both on a micro-scale and a macro-scale. Too frequently, no-one believes what has happened because their actions are so outrageous, and bizarrely, the victim may deny their actions too. The results on the world stage are there for all to see, yet very few people are recognising the perpetrators as people with pathologies who should not be allowed any power at all.

Counsellors need to be there for the victims, equipped with this knowledge. A few decades ago, we didn't talk about cancer when it struck because there was no cure. Now we don't talk about this emotional disease, not only because there is no ready cure, but because there is no real recognition of it.

The lack of conversation ensures that ignorance prevails. There can be treatment for the victims of the sociopaths, but only if we are able to isolate the disease in order to discuss it without being overwhelmed by it. The key in this case is to identify the pathology with its destructive behaviour as being a separate entity from the persona which the aggressor presents. I have found myself being caught out sometimes by some of the personas I have been presented with.

A therapy approach known as Transactional Analysis, created by Eric Berne in the 1960s, tried to deal with the negative aspects of psychology by mechanistically analysing the human psyche and behaviour. However, the main theory is cognitively biased rather than emotionally sourced. Its focus is not on empathy, the presence of which is integral to my favoured modality of Person-Centred Counselling. It is the absence of empathy in a person which is key to the concept of dysempathy in general and to sociopathy in particular. The theory does however provide a valuable tool to model manipulative behaviour.

It describes emotional relationships as being between two of three positions, Adult, Parent or Child. In healthy adult relationships, both parties would be Adult. But if one party decides to dominate the other, it may assume a Parental controlling role, treating the other as an inferior Child. The aggressor's skill is in finding that vulnerability in their victim. If they can make the recipient respond impulsively like a child, they have achieved the control they seek. And this is not a response of people with learning difficulties. I have succumbed to this myself and have seen some highly intelligent clients fall for it too. The Child response is instinctively innate, ready to be tapped into by a clever aggressor. We can be surprised at our own vulnerabilities. Once that relationship has formed, the sociopathic aggressor will continue to reinforce it to establish long-term dominance over the empathic 'Child'.

As long as empaths either fail to recognise sociopathic behaviour or indeed refuse to, they will not only allow the sociopaths to destroy what is good in life, but they will even facilitate that by having families with them or elevating them into political office and corporate responsibility. Then the power corrupting demon kicks in to even greater effect. If we accept them and encourage their behaviour, we ensure their genes reappear in the next generation for the empaths to bring up, a bit like a cuckoo, and for the rest of us to suffer from. If we want peace in our time, we need to focus on the empathy element above all others as an essential primary ingredient for partnership and for leadership too.

That will help us make good decisions for our own happiness and for our societies. It is global. We humans have enough physical resources on the planet to keep ourselves alive and happy, but those without a conscience are extracting it from those who do. We need now to focus on enabling all people to be happy rather than allowing a few to be powerful and greedy by virtue of their pathology.

Edmund Burke is attested to have said 'All that is necessary for the triumph of evil is that good men do nothing.' Good men (and women) need to be aware of this pathology to support others, not least because one day they might be the victim. If it is important for us to know about this as citizens, we are certainly obliged to as therapists because some of our clients will inevitably be victims of it.

39: Neuroscience

The existence of destructive pathology is well established, even if it is poorly defined and researched in general, and studiously avoided in counselling training in particular. The discovery of Mirror Neurons which appear to be activated in an observer in sympathy with the similarly located active neurons in the doer provides an avenue of investigation. Neuroscientists believe they had found the apparatus of empathy, the value dysempathic people lack. The suggestion, therefore, was that sociopaths would have a deficit of these.

While there is little research on sociopaths, there has been some on psychopaths and that may shed some light on sociopathic behaviour. Shirley Fecteau found that mirror neurons in psychopaths were at least as responsive as those of empaths.[1] That challenged the idea that psychopaths we unaware of others emotions. Then Abigail Marsh did further work and found reduced amygdala responses in psychopaths: 'Neuroimaging research in both institutionalised and community samples implicates amygdala dysfunction in the aetiology of psychopathic traits. Reduced amygdala responsiveness may disrupt processing of fear-relevant stimuli like fearful facial expressions.' [2] I will try and explain.

The amygdala is part of the very basic animal limbic system which responds to sensory input prior to any cognitive processing. The conclusion being drawn is that our instinctive empathic responses are sourced in the basic limbic system rather than in the higher functioning areas where the mirror neuron feature has been observed. The mirror neuron response may therefore reflect a more processed recognition of the doer's feelings rather than the instantaneous raw experience provided by the limbic system.

That indicates that psychopaths can read others' emotions cognitively in the same way as one might dispassionately interpret an animal's emotions, but they are not viscerally affected by them from the more basic part of the brain. That allows them to use others' emotional indicators to work out how to manipulate them for their own purposes if they so wish without actually feeling their victim's pain. Predatory animals in the wild will do this too. They are not constrained by the suffering of their victims which would stop an empath in their tracks.

While the research was with people designated as psychopathic as opposed to sociopathic, there is insufficient differentiation of definitions between these categories to suggest the observed feature would not apply to what we would see as sociopaths. The sociopathic model seems similar to the psychopathic one. Interestingly, the widely used DSM 5 lists neither specifically, preferring the similar Antisocial Personality Disorder (ASP).

In the absence of a better definition, I regard the psychopath as a sociopath who exercises their aggression for gratification. The dysempathic feature of little or no intuitive empathy, combined with a working cognitive perception of others' emotions applies to both. For my counselling purposes, the basic approach is the same. The label is not so relevant.

40: Pathology Blindness

The primary difference between a simple lack of empathy as might appear in Asperger's Syndrome and sociopathy is that the sociopath is skilled to routinely discharge their excess emotions on others, however damaging that may be. Accordingly, they may not carry as much of the emotional excesses which trouble those who just lack empathy. Neither viscerally experience the emotions which enable mutual Emotional Contracts, so they don't intuitively feel other's suffering, regardless of whether they caused it or not. That insensitivity to other's emotions means that they have a poor picture of the emotional landscape around them. They are not aware that others may be thinking and, more to the point, feeling differently from them.

Without a perception of how others feel, sociopaths may think they are normal. They often appear to function competently in society and have most of their needs met by one means or another. The better a victim of sociopathic oppression understands this pathology, the better they will be able to manage it. That increased clarity of their emotional environment will help reduce their stress levels and release some mental space to start making informed decisions about the future. Their aggressor may seem to be specifically malicious, setting out to damage them. Their actions are effectively predatory.

However, a sociopath is normally unaware that they are doing anything much different from anyone else. They will not see themselves as being much different from anyone else. They are incapable of knowing what that difference might be.

I liken it to colour blindness. If I am colour blind and do not know that, and I stand next to a normally sighted person viewing a scene, we could both be forgiven for thinking we were seeing the same things. I will actually see less detail and will get less from the experience, but neither of us will have the ability to discover what we are seeing that is different. If we are not even aware of the concept of colour blindness, we could never know why.

In the same way, the sociopath will see their emotional world quite differently from the empath. Neither knows enough to understand that, let alone investigate it. Both parties may assume they are seeing, or rather feeling, the same emotional landscapes. The empaths will be continually baffled by the attitude of the sociopath and the sociopath will be equally baffled by the attitude of the empath. There is no language to join them. Neither know that, so both are perpetually frustrated.

The sociopath does not receive the emotional signals the victim might be sending to them and they wouldn't want to if they could. In their turn, the victim doesn't understand why their aggressor is not getting their message. The victim just wants them to close the emotional gap a bit. "Can you just see it my way for a change?"

The sociopath has a different agenda. Subconsciously and possibly consciously too, they rely on the victim's dependence on them and their need to pacify them. That gives them the control to continue discharging excess emotions onto the victim. Their method of stress resolution is parasitic. There is no benefit to the victim; only pain. Until the victim understands the mechanism of this pathology, they believe the aggressor is knowingly hurting them, but still carrying on. "How can they do that to me?" The word 'evil' springs to mind easily.

Just as a wild animal is unaffected by the feelings of its prey, the sociopath does not really sense how its prey feels either. If the victim can accept the sociopath is unable to empathise, they can defend themselves accordingly. Conversely, if they can't grasp that, they can't defend themselves.

We all learn behaviours to fit in with the communities we are part of because there will always be some gaps between our way of doing things and other people's. I have roles as a father, grandfather, counsellor, husband, etc and each play out a little differently in each community I am in at any one time.

Like us, the sociopath learns to play roles and looks like everyone else in order to get what they want and need. The difference is their lack of empathy in each of their roles. Empathy is crucial to healthy emotional exchange, essential for personal stress resolution and necessary for societal cohesion. Its absence in the aggressor is unhealthy for those close to them, so they masquerade to appear caring and normal like everyone else.

Their role playing does not derive from a generous urge to use different talents for others as the empath might, but a deceit to get what they want and need out of each situation, regardless of the consequences. The sociopath goes beyond simple role playing because they do not have a sound sense of self. Their roles are effectively different personas which can easily end up being in denial of each other. In psychological terms, their Configurations of Self are disconnected. They are not joined up to an honest, empathic core.

Sociopathic roles can be fractured and deceptive so they have to switch stories when the inconsistencies are discovered. It is these denials which do much of the damage. To the untrained and uninvolved eye in any one situation, they will behave much the same as the empath because they have developed the act well. Their acquaintances will be convinced by their stories, even though the victim feels very different because they are suffering.

In contrast, my own various roles are normally coherent. I can accept the existence of one while in another. When I am functioning one way because the role demands it, I remain anchored to my consistent Perfect Core and can easily envisage myself in one of my other roles and can even talk about them.

My counselling mission is to help my client discern any role abnormalities to identify a pathology, if indeed one does exist, and address their situation more knowledgably. Answering that pathology question is important. If a victim is to defend themselves from this behaviour, they need to address the clinical pathology operating within the other person rather than succumb to fearing and hating someone whom they see as becoming more and more destructive.

It is this concept of attributing the abuse to the pathology rather than the person which helped my old friend negotiate the enormous conflict between the extremes of love and hatred she felt every day for the husband she had lost. Victimised empaths need to see and understand this in order to protect themselves. Part of this understanding is that the aggressor may be suffering too.

Associate professor, Mike Koenigs researched behavioural abnormalities of people with brain lesions and other defects at the University of Wisconsin-Madison. While any particular subject he studies is not typically dysempathic or sociopathic per se, the behaviours he reports can tell us something about how an abnormal mind works in this area.

As part of a series shown in March 2018, the BBC interviewed one of Koenigs' patients, David, who in his 30s had lost part of his prefrontal cortex in an operation to remove a tumour from his brain. He had been in a loving relationship. He reported subsequently that he no longer felt what other people felt and his life seemed very empty. He resumed his work as an animal psychologist and his cognitive function seemed unaffected, but his relationship broke down. He felt he no longer loved his partner and she, of course, sensed that. She did keep a caring contact with him, but any weddings plans were ditched. There was no apparent malice in him, not least because he had, over his life, built in place a moral code which would provide warning of aberrant behaviour, even if the emotional experience was no longer there.

The fact that he had memory of his previous emotional life made his case particularly interesting for researchers like Koenigs and also for therapists who can process and use these ideas for their clients. David felt he knew how a serial killer would see the world, but he would not kill because he remembered how bad that would be, even if he could no longer sense that. He was, however, concerned that as the memory of his old life faded, that restraint might fade too.

Time would tell whether this experiential problem would enter another phase. The mechanism of viscerally experiencing emotions seemed to have been irrecoverably removed, but he was still capable of recognising others' emotions cognitively and being guided by them. What was striking about this tragic circumstance of someone losing their empathic function was not a malicious selfish pleasure seeker getting what he wanted at everyone else's expense, but a sad person who, for no reason of his own, had difficulty sensing himself intuitively and consequently of sensing others too.

He was definitely the sufferer and indeed could possibly become sociopathic in time. While there is no such thing as a typical anything in the psychological world because the human psyche is so complex, this case suggested that the lack of empathy was the external manifestation of a lack of access to internal feelings and this is where simply dysempathic candidates reside. Insofar as he talked about how he could imagine a serial killer would think, he may have fitted some sociopathic features, but the television programme did not give further detail on this.

This example is abnormal in the world of sociopathy, but illustrates someone who was unhappy in his new world as opposed to the image of one who might simply predate on others apparently maliciously and wantonly. He was presumably on a dysempathic spectrum but not clear quite where.

The need for such people to find external subjects to absorb their excess emotions is greater than for empaths because they struggle to process them internally. As a result, they can carry more unresolved issues. The extent to which dysempaths succeed in their internal and external emotion management will determine how much pain they retain. A truly 'successful' sociopath will manage to deposit most of their issues onto their nearest and not so dearest.

The victims who are dependent on a sociopath will take their suffering for them in a 'wind up' process. The sociopath goads them into a state of poorly controlled distress which satisfies their imperative to discharge their unwanted emotions on them. They seem to stimulate the victim's mirror neurons to match their own, thereby achieving their emotional download.

That parasitic need for their victims translates into obsessive control over them by whatever means necessary to keep them in place for the next emotional dump. This contrasts with empaths who seek emotional balance by agreement, and by virtue of that agreement, achieve emotional resolutions which are beneficial to all and which will stand the test of time. A much happier existence for all and the construct of a healthy society.

41: Upbringing

Dysempaths struggle to resolve their own stresses internally. If they are brought up well in a moral climate, they are likely to endeavour to abide by social rules and desist from depositing their excess emotions aggressively on others.

Some parents manage to get their children with empathy issues onto the right message. A bright teenager displaying obvious Asperger's features was brought to me. I felt she had the capacity to become manipulative and unpleasant, but a very caring family had nurtured a very likeable young lady with high moral principles. Indeed, she got upset when others did not adhere to those same principles. The nature component seemed to have been very much modified by the nurture component, even though her ability to sense the feelings of others was poor.

In contrast, some children from an early age, are permitted to be calculatingly aggressive and have embedded methods to persistently get their own way and dump their excess emotions in devious ways onto others. These young people may develop sociopathic features as they grow up and could merit the sociopath label as adults. I see young clients who readily fit this mould. I can have some difficulty in delivering that message to the parents.

A couple brought their two primary school-age children for therapy. The mother could not see the controlling aspect of the younger boy which was plain to me within a few minutes of our meeting. She focussed on the behaviour of the older girl who was simply reacting to her brother's manipulation. We got improvement in family relations, but even after many sessions there was no real resolution. I was unable to help the mother see her son's destructive tendencies, so focussed on helping the girl develop resilience within an unhealthy family script. The father was eventually getting the message, but this is one of those stories I didn't get to see to the end.

We can all appreciate that a child who is treated poorly will be less well balanced in life and therefore less successful and more troublesome than one treated intelligently and empathically. How that might turn out will also depend on the raw material, the firmware, that the child starts with. We are not all born equal.

Science seems to have identified a mechanism by which the features of even deep-seated disorders might be modified by a healthy and enlightened upbringing. Recent research into the psychological connotations of a phenomenon called epigenetics offers some neurological evidence about the shape of our developing personalities.

Many of our traits are not the result of single genes but complex combinations of multiple genes, so pathologies are not readily biologically trackable. Researchers including Caspi et al (2003) demonstrate that the effects of genes can be turned on and off by life events via biochemical mechanisms called alleles.[1] We may, for instance, inherit a propensity for high blood pressure. The way we are brought up and therefore behave may trigger that disease or leave it dormant. Just as blood pressure is about our hardware health, anxiety is about our software health. Our propensity to succumb to emotional stress can be altered by our upbringing too.

Some emotional disorders can be detected in infancy. The brain is still physically growing up to around five years old and the hard-wire connective synapses will continue to accumulate, develop and rationalise until the mid-twenties.

These features are the plasticity of the human brain which has enabled our species to mutate psychologically more extensively than any other. A wildebeest foal is good to go within minutes of being born. It needs to be. The human takes a few years. Humans have constructed systems of care to enable that. That far longer development period allows each individual to adapt more comprehensively to whatever environment it finds itself in. It enables a software evolution of potentially remarkable complexity and adaptability.

A brain may lack empathic skills which can leave its owner struggling in life. It is harder to maintain a good balance. The earlier in life that intelligent training and education which recognise the deficient thinking processes is applied, the more comprehensive use can be made of the brain's plasticity. Most parents are unlikely to know how this pathology works and an educated professional can be invaluable to help them get to grips with their distressed child.

As a child counsellor, I know that well directed parenting and effective talking therapies can change the course of a child's life path, and in the context of epigenetics, an element of personality too. I am also aware that meditation can make significant, and sometimes very significant, changes in a child.

The David Lynch Foundation has facilitated research into the effects of Transcendental Meditation (TM) on those with Autism Spectrum Disorder. It indicates that while meditation cannot claim to provide a cure for the causes of the various aspects of autism, per se, it can substantially reduce the concomitant stresses. That can enable better interactions with the world, which in turn, will work on the underlying deficits. One of the meditations I teach is similar to Transcendental Meditation. Indeed, TM was the first method I used. It does seem to deliver some remarkable results.[2]

I was presented with an eight-year-old with whom it was almost possible to have a conversation insofar as he would not only always change the subject, but offer such complete nonsense in reply that coherent discourse was all but impossible. He had some learning difficulties and it was difficult to see where these ended and the emotional problems started. He was frequently suspended from his fee-paying school. I felt his emotional age was around four years. He was hardly into Freud's ego stage, being unable to make a connection between his behaviour and the reactions of teachers and mother. However, as with many of my younger clients, I try everything I can and am sometimes surprised to get some very positive reports from the parents for my efforts. I may not be sure what I have done, but it has worked. I am encouraged that many of my peers in child counselling have similar experiences of therapy without obvious process. In this case, I taught him and his mother a meditation method. When they eventually got round to using it, there was a transformation and all within a few weeks. I could then sit happily with the child for the full counselling session, having a reasonable, rational discussion. Behaviour had improved immensely at home and at school. Mum looked so much better too. She attributed the change to the meditation they were doing together.

I have no idea where any line could be drawn between nature and nurture in this case, but I have no doubt that the meditation, more than anything else, altered the trajectory of his life. It had not been looking good at all for the weeks before they decided to give the meditation a try. There was now realistic hope of substantial normality.

42: The Blame Game

Because they have little experience of how others feel, sociopaths will normally assume everyone relieves their emotions like they do. Constant practice makes it second nature for them. If they can't control their own feelings and behaviours, others must be responsible so they blame them, and usually aggressively, which is how they dump their emotions on them. They don't see themselves responsible for the results of their emotional discharges on their victims. It's everyone else's fault.

Whilst this is a pathology for the rest of us, we need to keep a perspective on this. Most of us do some blaming from time to time. Hands up all those who have not at some time blamed someone for something which was blatantly not their fault. That occasional level of unreasonableness does not constitute sociopathy.

A great deal of the stresses we are subjected to come from our interactions with people who have been unreasonable with us, so we can argue that our stress is not always of our own making. But we will still need to resolve those stresses ourselves somehow, regardless of their origin. Some of them might touch the red buttons of previous hurts, so our responses may now become magnified out of proportion. We need to recognise when that is happening and curtail it. We have to find other ways of resolving our issues. If we don't, we simply generate another set of issues to resolve, usually involving those we have now offended. This is a lose-lose scenario. Most of us get that and deal with it, for most of the time at least.

If we can identify our true selves as a pure Perfect Core at the heart of our being, we can regard any unpleasant internal emotion as having been externally derived. If it's nasty, it may well have been dumped on us by someone else sometime in the past. Psychologists call this Introjection. The concept of blame is indeed valid here. I meet adult survivors of child abuse whose current

231

challenging behaviour can often be linked to that trauma. But the stress is now inside and whatever its original cause, it has now sadly become their responsibility to manage it, whether they like it or not.

My job entails helping clients control these occasional unpleasant blasts from the past better so they don't hurt others so readily. When that is not routinely managed, it becomes damaging to others in their community and starts to look like a pathology. There will come a point where they can no longer maintain the relationships they so much need. That becomes a crisis for all concerned.

By routinely assigning blame for their issues onto others, sociopaths justify what the rest of us would see as predatory actions. They will typically make absurd allegations of bad behaviour which continually leave their victims reeling, wondering what they have done to deserve this and how they are going to defend themselves from this apparently scheming attrition. They will be mystified as to why this is happening.

No-one has told the victim about this pathology and how their partner /brother/ mother/ boss, etc. could be a candidate for it. The aggressor may treat their victim as though they were someone else who had harmed them in the past, thereby justifying their actions. Psychodynamic adherents call this process Projection, but for me, that word fails to convey the enormous harm routinely done by this sort of attack. It seems to accept this behaviour as part of a normal life we just have to tolerate. It identifies pathological behaviour but declines to name it or its impact well.

I asked a client once what her earliest memory was. At a particularly mature 21 years old, she presented as robust, but the constantly fresh cut marks on her arms told a different story. Of the many abusive attacks she related, I recall a simple one. At 5 years old, her father had told her to sit on the landing till he got back. She was afraid of him. When he returned several hours later, he shouted at her for moving even though she was on the stair when the father got back. Only now did she understand the sociopathic psychology of her father's actions all those years ago. He needed to vent his anger on someone who would not cause him problems, so he fabricated a situation in which his own child would be forced to take his excess emotion. He was safe to do so because his child would not retaliate.

The child was dependent on an angry father and was carrying the hurt they experienced into his adult life. The father's inability to manage his own emotions or to feel his own child's emotions indicates dysempathy. His actions in depositing his excess emotions on another person, particularly his own child, indicate sociopathy. The girl was part of his circle of dependants whom he could abuse with impunity. It was not so much that one incident which caused the damage. It was the constant threat of this type of abuse which defined the child's upbringing and then impacted her life as an adult.

Unfortunately, this aggressive dumping is only good for today's emotional excesses. They will be back for another raid tomorrow and the wreckage will continue for as long as the aggressor has emotion to discharge and the victim is unable to resist that.

Their actions carry an interesting characteristic flag. Because the sociopath does not know empathy, they cannot learn about others' frames of reference even if they have lived with them for many years. Consequently, the misdeeds they accuse their victims of are normally untypical of the victim. They are usually the ones they have been accused of themselves. So when a client finds themselves being blamed for the sort of transgressions the aggressor displays, they can reasonably read that as sociopathic behaviour. It is a useful by-product of that observation that whatever an aggressor accuses us of reveals their own misdemeanours. If someone does that to us routinely, we know what their pathology is - and it's not ours. This routine Mirror Blaming is a good indicator of this pathology.

43: Manipulation

Sociopaths will cultivate anyone they can capture psychologically in order to deposit their emotional excesses by stealth rather than by empathic mutual agreement. They will need people who believe they are dependent on them and who will stay, even when they are attacked. This is normally family or work colleagues. Partners are primary victims for as long as they can be persuaded to stick around. Responsibility for children often anchors them in place.

Indeed, children are often also used as a means of manipulating the partner - or ex-partner if the family is fractured. In the days when societal forces bound parents together, the weaker partners often found themselves captured. The father earned the money and the wife's job was unpaid housekeeping and child-rearing, so she was dependent on him for the household money.

Nowadays in the western world, female independence makes separations more possible and therefore more prevalent. The victim often has the means to escape – at least in part. The predator goes on to seek new prey, which inevitably involves others. I see hitherto stable and happy marriages being predated upon with extraordinary power by a sociopathic suitor through an illicit affair. Very often, the children become involved as pawns in the game.

A client lost her husband to another woman, so the care of her two girls became shared across the two families. This became somewhat incestuous in that the children of both mothers not only shared the same school but the two mothers were active in it. It was a small rural community. The other mother seemed to spend significant time generating spurious problems for my client. She would insist that my client's children played the same sports as hers, despite their protests. It became accepted in the other house to openly denigrate my client. School letters were taken so my client was unaware of activities her girls might need to attend. That enabled the other mother to criticise my client for not attending important events, generating a malicious rumour on social media about her parental ineptitude. The objective seemed to be to demean my client to as wide an audience as possible for no apparent end other than to keep her suppressed so she could maintain control over the man she had stolen. It was about malice and power.

In my experience, it has usually been the husband who has been lured away by an offending female who is predating serially as she exhausts one victim after another. She seems to be using them as a means of discharging her accumulated stresses, asserting her power and creating a status for herself which she could not do by virtue of her own ability or her actual contributions to the community. The immediate victim, the new partner, may in turn fall in with her modus operandi and be irrationally aggressive towards his previous partner, possibly manipulating his own children in the process.

That way, the sociopath gets both him and his ex-partner inside their emotion discharge net. It is so bizarre as to defy belief until I see it unfolding in my clients' lives, week by week. We have to watch wildlife documentaries to see such callous behaviour in action in animals. It is well known that single male lions will slaughter a female's cubs in order to mate with her. There are many more gruesome lifecycles in the insect world like this. I learn a lot from conceptualising humans as animals with clothes on.

It can be hard for a victimised client to come to terms emotionally with the callous nature of this pathology, especially when it involves their own children. The sociopath's empathy void means that they sense little of what a child would be feeling, even their own child, so they are not perturbed by any harmful outcomes.

A father who had been drawn way from his own family into another, continually blamed his young son for all his developing ills, physical and emotional, using that as leverage to get him to meet his demands, some of which were designed to play the alimony system to the father's advantage. His ex-wife said that his behaviour had completely changed since the separation. She hardly recognised him now. The child was no longer in the empathy bubble inside his father's soul as it would be for most parents, so the father's own emotional balance was relatively unaffected by his child's distress. The mother found it impossible to believe that her ex-partner would not only put a child in harm's way, but their own child. She looked for any possibility other than this, including that it was all her own fault.

Sociopaths capitalise on this guilt and generate a perception of multiple failings in the victim, making them part of a whole belief system to be revisited at any time by them and, indeed, anyone else they could convince.

A client's husband regularly called her a slag, using a range of ever-changing justifications. He made use of her confessions of her troublesome earlier life to continually and repeatedly denigrate and control her. He consistently reminded her he had brought her out of the gutter, forgetting he was homeless when he moved into her house. The facts were irrelevant as long as the emotion behind the attack carried the moment for him. She had been captured by the images he kept portraying of himself and her for the last 20 years until his gambling debts forced them out of their home and it was time for a rethink.

Even when the results of the sociopath's maladjusted behaviour become apparent like this, they will always find ways of applying the blame to the victim, however absurd. Typically, the sociopath might arrive late for an important event and then blame the victim for not reminding them to leave earlier as they know they can be late for these things. The victim's dependency means they may have to accept that until such time as they can physically extricate themselves from the relationship.

The victim's inability to see regular bad behaviour as a pathology makes them more vulnerable to predation because they can't work out what is happening. Their baseline template is that of an empath. Sociopathic behaviour does not compute for them. They will ascribe the aggressor's behaviour to either a personality quirk or an aberration of their judgement of them. It is very difficult for an empath to conceptualise anyone as being unable to feel how they are feeling, especially when they have been living with that person for a long time or are dependent on them.

The sociopath makes use of this vulnerability by accusing the victim of intentions they do not have or deeds they have not done in order to provide an explanation for, or a distraction from, their own destructive behaviour. That leaves the victim feeling confused and guilty. The victim may either suspend belief in the obvious just to survive the day or have a massive argument with no logical resolution, other than allowing the aggressor to yet again vent their emotions on them.

This bullying can be systematic, scheming and relentless. Communications for child access arrangements can become more a device for dumping emotion than conveying information for the carers to organise activities. It can be more important to generate an argument than to get anything done, however essential.

The more important the topic of communication is to the victim, the more power the sociopath can exert on them and the more they can discharge their emotions. That is partly why social workers insist on third party communications when things get vicious between separated partners. That avoids the emotional attacks which can be so damaging.

The suspension of belief at this outrageous behaviour can last many years if there are other factors binding the relationship together. That is especially acute for mothers of young children partnered to sociopathic fathers. Any perceptive primary school headteacher will have observed this sort of conduct, not least because they need to avoid becoming a party in such toxic familial conflicts. The prevalence of this pathology makes it statistically inevitable in such a large community as a school.

There is a general belief that sociopathy is more a male disability, but the confusion on what the spectrum is and how it manifests itself, especially in this area of scheming aggression, leaves a question on how good the research is. I suspect that evolution has favoured the prevalence of an empathic mother caring for the offspring and a strong and possibly aggressive father defending the camp but, like any other gender biased feature, there is no simple divide.

It is often held that females are equally afflicted but their attacks are manipulative rather than physical. I have come across some appalling female behaviour indicating sociopathy and, as a counsellor, I have to be open to any narrative.

A most gentle man came to my practice fearing for the loss of his children three years after his foreign-born wife had been prevented from getting on a plane to her native country with the children in tow. She had convinced social services that she should keep their four young children in the family home and he should move out. Over the subsequent three years, the school observed ever more alarming symptoms. The mother had played the system so well that she was able to obtain free legal support on the grounds of domestic violence towards her and the children, despite the obvious fact that he did not even live with them. He was unable to access free legal support for himself and was nearing bankruptcy when I met him. All the many services involved were carried away with the horror of domestic violence, ostensibly from the father to his children and they could not risk being seen to be responsible for getting this case wrong. I supported him through counselling and into advocacy. At the final hearing, which he feared would end his parenthood, the judge saw that the obvious distress the children were suffering was from her and not him. The judge held the status quo for him. Not the ideal ending, but he was able to continue to see his children.

I find it is generally the female who complains of a sociopathic partner, but it is also the case that the cause of the original problem can sometimes be another female manipulating a male in the middle. I suspect there is no major gender bias. In any case, I always deal with each case as it presents.

An extensive study of psychiatric patients published by the American Psychiatric Association in 2005 indicated that 'correlations among the…gender variables and the psychopathy dimensions were minimal'.[1]

I have not seen equivalent data for sociopathy. A study published by PMC/US National Library of Medicine National Institutes of Health identified a difference between the male expression of the pathology and the female one. 'Women with ASPD present less violent antisocial behaviours and higher rates of aggressiveness and irritability.' Not a difference in prevalence but rather in behaviour type.[2]

44: Mechanisms

Like the rest of us, sociopaths want and need relationships with other human beings. Our species is social, and in the sense of needing relationships, sociopaths are too. The difference is that their lack of empathy means that they do not have the emotional language to contract fairly with others, so they have to obtain their emotional needs surreptitiously.

Their inability to be fluid in their relationships leaves them as impoverished emotionally as someone living on the street is impoverished financially. They just don't look it because they have learnt how to hide it. They seek out empathic people who may find them attractive for financial, employment, sexual or other reasons and some bonding may take place.

Whilst I regard empathy as crucial to safe and peaceful coexistence, we all carry many other features in our personalities which others would find desirable. A female may be attracted to a male who appears successful enough to support any children she may wish to have. He might seem very charming. A male may be attracted to a female for sexual gratification. He might think she is very beautiful. Whatever their intents, and they may not be conscious of them, the basic animal instincts are driving decisions. That is normal.

However, when someone enhances those features to convince another that they genuinely care for them when they don't, consciously or subconsciously they are grooming them. Grooming is not limited to older men soliciting young girls. It can be between any apparently, but not actually, consenting adults. When the bond is sufficiently formed in the empath, and having children creates enormous bonds, the sociopath is then more able to discharge their pent-up emotions in Emotional Raids. They will do that up to the point of alienating their victim and then they will try to reel their prey back in for another day.

This fishing process of reeling in and letting go is a typical sociopathic process used to gain the maximum emotional discharge while still retaining the victim. It sounds premeditated, but it is just the way it happens because the sociopath can't sense the damage they do until it threatens their own purposes.

They may withhold their emotions as long as they can initially to get their subject under control, releasing them onto their victim when they feel it's safe.

When they see they might be losing them again, they rein themselves in for a while and deliver what looks like care and kindnesses, often in the form of material gifts. Because we humans are always learning, the manifestation of this pattern is forever changing, so the victim struggles to keep pace with it all.

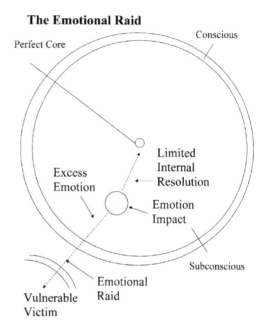

From the outside, we would see such actions as deliberate and unnecessary malice because we, as empaths, would have to be really 'evil' to do such things. "How could you do that to me?" But because the aggressors are not empathic, they cannot feel the extent of the hurt they are doing to us. They are often suffering themselves and believe everyone else is doing the same thing as they are in order to get what they need too. That does not make it right. It certainly does not make it healthy.

The answer for the victim is to understand the pathology, manage it and learn how to become a survivor, either within the relationship or by leaving it. The answer is not to offer more care to the aggressor, hoping that will reduce their aggression, any more than offering more money to a gambler will reduce their habit. There is no limit to the aggression. The victim must take control and define their own limits instead.

Typically, the aggressor will threaten divorce to coerce their partner into compliance. When the partner finally decides that divorce is a good course of action for them, the aggressor gets a shock. The bluff has backfired and usually terminally.

In principle, empaths go emotional fishing too to release their emotions, but because they intuitively sense and are affected by the other's feelings, they desist much sooner to avoid damage to them. That may significantly reduce the amount of emotion they can resolve on one occasion, but they still retain the goodwill of their partners or friends for another day and happiness resumes.

Holding back a little like this will minimise any pain caused and avoid loss of the all-important trust in the intimate relationships in which these exchanges can occur. That looks much more like

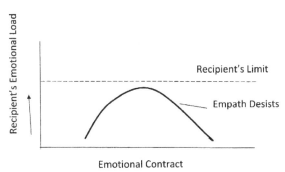

an emotional agreement with limits, the Emotional Contract. The Emotional Contract and Emotional Raid diagrams show firstly how an empathic person responds to the limits of someone in an Emotional Contract by desisting when they see their confidante is reaching their limit of endurance.

In contrast, the sociopath indulges in an Emotional Raid when they carry on well past their recipient's limit. Depending on how much power they can exercise over the victim, they

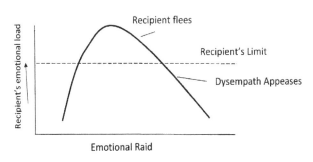

may then need to appease them to retain them for another day.

A further strategy of grooming involves acquaintances, but not for emotional discharge. They are not bonded enough to be retained. They use them to create sufficient insecurity around the actual victims to keep them in a place of vulnerability. They will typically generate rumours and beliefs about the victim, designed to support whatever construct they need in order to separate them from their support networks and retain them under their power.

A client found that the wife of her recently separated husband was using a communal website to spread demeaning scenarios. My client's girls had alternative weekends at the ex-partner's house. The other mother took it on herself to buy my client's children's clothes. Her blog inferred that my client was deficient in her parenting to that degree. If she could convince the surrounding group that my client was inadequate, she would be able to isolate her and control her more, thereby enhancing her own 'virtuousness' in order to disguise the exact opposite in herself. The victim then had to go through the humiliation of trying to unpick the rumour factory. From what I could tell, there was absolutely no material reason whatsoever for the other mother to attack in this way other than to groom their mutual acquaintances and exercise power over my client. I had no doubt about my client's parenting abilities.

This construct has all the hallmarks of a parasitic process. The aggressor sought to elevate themselves at the expense of the victim. However malicious this may appear to empaths, the sociopath is only trying to survive with their impaired emotional functions and may not realise that most people do something quite different with their emotional overloads.

The sociopath does not possess the equipment for effective internal stress resolution. Their view is that the strongest wins and the weakest lose. The weakest can be exploited by the strongest, so that is what the strongest do. There is a part of our animal psyche which drives that. There is no empathic brake on their actions.

This lack of moral and experiential awareness cannot be allowed to become mitigating circumstances for malicious acts any more than it would for a convicted criminal. We can see how unhealthy upbringing can lead to misdeeds, but we must deal with aggressors in accordance with societal rules. We all need to feel safe in our communities. So, while we may have some level of sympathy for those with unpleasant childhoods, we must still treat them according to their deeds and the risks they present to us. In the more extreme cases, that may include incarceration.

Treating this mindset as a destructive pathology is the key to identifying it and managing it competently. I had the privilege of meeting M.E. Thomas, the author of *Confessions of a Sociopath*. She thought she had just written an autobiography. I said her book was life-changing for me and for many others too because it wrapped evil up in a box and called it pathology. She then asked what evil was. I said that evil to me is that which diminishes me. Good is that which augments me.

A sociopath's actions are often so outlandish that many non-professionals might dismiss victims' reports as simply incredible. That leaves the victim unable to share their stories. They are too hard for their friends and relatives to believe. A seemingly trivial example a client related was of a wedding table placement of a motorbike for a guest whose brother had recently died in a bike accident. Possibly a regrettable coincidence, but also possibly power play. Attacks are usually more substantial and calculated:

A senior hospital practitioner was abusive emotionally and physically to his wife and used his status to mask that. His sister used a single unfortunate previous drinking incident as a means to fabricate stories of drunkenness about his wife at every opportunity, systematically destroying her reputation with no apparent reason than the exercise of malicious power. My client lost invaluable friendships and some of the rumours filtered into the legal case which was developing. She found it very difficult to maintain dignity amongst a community which was being fed salacious stories, some which she didn't even recognise, let alone defend. By the time she found out what they were, they had become part of the community folklore and beyond recall. When stories are delivered with emotion, they tend to stick.

When the truth seems dramatic, it can be hard for people to believe, so the victim struggles to counteract the effect of an aggressor's relentless stories. This scenario was obvious in Trump's Fake News claims to all those who were not carried away with them.

However, if we could all accept the existence of this pathology and understand a bit about how it works, we might avoid being drawn into slanderous stories designed to damage a victim. That way we will not become complicit in the sociopath's attacks. Our scepticism of the rumourmonger's malicious designs will clip their wings. We might even be able to come alongside the victim and help them.

Otherwise, we may allow and even support sociopaths advancing themselves at the expense of others to get themselves into high places in corporate, political and business societies. We need to stop them rising to power and perpetrating damage on large or even epic scales. There are always plenty examples on the world stage of this. Awareness is crucial.

45: Evolution

It helps to look at pathology from an evolutionary perspective. Placing it into a framework we can more readily understand will allow us to anticipate maladaptive behaviour a bit better. It is far more useful to regard it as an anthropological inevitability rather than an unpredictable evil. Better to accept the existence rather than continually be surprised and therefore unhinged by its consequences. It is a feature emanating from physically more violent eras, but it still persists in our psyches today. And if we care to admit it, violence in different guises is very much in evidence today. We just don't want to think about them.

In the ages of primitive tribal communities, adjacent groups would compete for limited resources especially during transient shortages. Some may have growing populations or just want to expand their territory. Either way, there would be competition at the boundaries. If these were not protected, the tribe's survival would be threatened because its resources would be taken by others. Scarce resources are about life and death, so territorial defence has to be that way too.

That meant that those tribes equipped with defenders prepared to eliminate competing neighbours would survive and those which did not, probably would not. They would become the victims and face extinction. Accordingly, the successfully surviving human species contained members whose lack of empathy would permit them to attack and kill. That would need to be a basic emotional driver, part of their visceral make-up.

The destruction genes therefore prevail, and they are in evidence today. We see this behaviour in chimpanzee troupes. They will kill to protect territory. We should remind ourselves that we are genetically very close to them. Because this feature is only part of the whole raft of features which define us as human at a personal level, this deadly pathology can easily be masked under all the remaining ones, subconsciously or deliberately, but usually skilfully.

On the basis that our biological evolution is vastly slower than our cognitive evolution, we could expect that this lethal feature would still exist in modern societies. They may profess harmony but not all their members are buying into that.

The development and use of reliable contraception to manage population growth and thereby reduce the need for conflict is less than a century old and has not fully entered the visceral part of our evolution. Our tormented world provides plenty of evidence on the macro scale for in-built aggression. Like the carried over defensive Fight-Flight response, this violence which was an asset at the time, however gruesome, now threatens civilised society.

If sociopaths successfully reproduce, this feature will persist down the generations. Romantic love is hormonally designed to overlook aberrant behaviour to ensure the perpetuation of our species, so this trait can be easily missed by a suitor. 'Love is blind' can have deep consequences. The drive for the perpetuation of the species will ultimately override individuals' judgements of other's personalities. Sociopaths develop skills at hiding their pathology, so they present as viable partners. It takes some time for the true nature of the underlying feature to become obvious to the empathic victim. They will want to establish a dependency before allowing their pathology to become apparent.

The sociopathic warrior may no longer be needed to physically defend his tribe in our developed civilisations, but the genes live on in him and continue to do the destruction, albeit in more psychological terms than physical ones. Their disguises may seem good enough to convince a partner they should start a family together. The sociopath will then have a little network of people on whom they can predate and their genes are handed down to the next generation to start all over again.

46: An Emotional Virus

In the same way as a carrier of a biological virus can spread it by infecting those who come into physical contact with them, a carrier of an emotional virus can infect those in emotional contact with them too. An emotional virus can come from a simple misunderstanding, especially amongst people who have in-built prejudices. Most of us carry these at some level. That can cause a lot of harm.

However, if those involved are basically emotionally healthy, recovery is likely and an honest, wholesome caring approach will resolve such harm. This sort of disruption occurs in families regularly. Mature parenting can remedy that. But if the pathology is persistent rather than passing, then a sickness prevails and the suffering continues. As it becomes chronic, further malaises evolve and the victims get unhappier. A web of lies may appear, hiding the aggressor's crimes and massively confusing the vulnerable, sometimes for a lifetime.

This emotional virus spreads its deadly destruction invisibly in just the same relentless way as a biological virus would. It is no less deadly than Coronavirus. It is not so much that it kills the body, which can have a merciful ending, but it cripples the soul and there is no ending. I use an adage which brings home the persistent presence of this threat. 'If we don't see evil coming towards us, we are probably travelling with it.' It is as insidious and prevalent as its biological counterparts, with the difference that we have not developed an antibiotic for it yet. We are unable, and worse unwilling, to develop an effective diagnosis.

The current 'head in the sand' attitude to this pathology ensures we will never address it. We walk alongside it and accept it to the point of voting people with it into political power. It is around all of us, most obviously afflicting those in disadvantaged situations, just as a biological virus would.

It affects all strata of society. It seems chance that some people get close enough to become infected while others avoid it. I find well educated empathic clients who have married apparently sociopathic partners. They often try to maintain the relationship for the children's sake until they are old enough to tolerate a family breakup. Many aggressors may appear successful in their careers even though their lives as a whole may be emotionally turbulent.

Our societies give significant credit to cognitive intelligence through our academic examination systems. Clever people can be elevated into high places quite quickly. But the intelligence which really matters to our own happiness and to that of those around us is emotional intelligence. That is reflected in maturity. We often don't measure that. Within any particular individual, emotional intelligence, mostly concerned with people and feelings, seems almost entirely independent of cognitive intelligence, mostly concerned with things and actions. Profession, affluence and status do not signify the ability to manage one's own emotions internally or to be empathic with others. Indeed, fast promotions ahead of maturity can lead to people exercising authority they cannot manage. If the new boss has sociopathic tendencies, a lot of damage can be done.

Influential sociopaths can wreak havoc in positions of power because they are skilled at convincing all around them that they have a genuine interest in the well-being of others when they do not. They will maintain their status by hurting and even destroying others at will. The old TV series Dallas displayed that well. The more recent BBC broadcast satire 'The Thick of It' showed nasty politics like this in play. Some of our TV soaps are built around conflict of which sociopathy inevitably forms a part. The English paedophile, Jimmy Savile, who was renowned for his charitable works fitted this pathology. The MeToo Movement, starting in the theatrical business, demonstrated chronic sexual predation by powerful males. That misogyny has been a fact of life for as long as anyone could remember. Sexual predation can be an element of sociopathic behaviour. It's about the power to express and deposit surplus emotion onto others with no regard to the consequences.

There are many ways in which empathic people can become subject to this pathology. Emotional stability does not seem to provide immunity. Some clients who are currently oppressed by a partner displaying this pathology have had relatively good upbringings. They are unfamiliar with this problem so have a level of trust of others, a naivety, which the sociopath can exploit to engage them in long-term relationships, often cemented in with dependent children. The problems often appear after a period of cohabitation and can increase as their partner's condition worsens over time.

It works the other way too. Children who grow up in families where any sort of pathology exists can become immune to its features, so the normal warning signals are muted by familiarity. Typically, a girl who is sexually abused in the home may very well walk into a sexually abusive adult relationship. She has gravitated to her perception of a remembered norm rather than to the healthy normality she was deprived of. People who have been subjected to even a relatively mild pathology in childhood may lack the emotional sensitivity to identify sociopathic behaviour easily and can easily fall into destructive relationships. And the range of damage can go well beyond the immediate contacts.

The sociopathic behaviour of some individuals in the financial sector who contributed to the 2008 financial crash spread their emotional disease well beyond their 'nears and dears' and out across the globe. The seismic result affected a colossal number of people, far more than the immediate victims of the mortgage scandal which triggered it. They suffered the consequences of severe financial insecurity, including lost livelihoods, lost homes and disrupted families. We didn't spot it coming and we could have done if we were conversant with the pathology. And over a decade later, little has moved on in this respect.

The devastation caused by just few people easily ran into millions of victims, most of whom never had direct knowledge of their oppressors. Despotic rulers are similarly guilty. The 20th century was full of this globally and the 21st is not looking a lot better so far. We are not recognising this pathology in the perpetrators.

Even as military conflicts rage on, we stand by and wring our hands, talking about bringing the culprits to justice. We could have stopped them at source with the right knowledge. It's the same disease as the one down the street and on the school playground albeit on a much bigger scale. And that is where it starts; in the family; in the home.

If we see sociopathy as a parasitic pathology which is incurable, the scene is set for chronic suffering for those within the power of the sociopath for as long as they remain in their emotional catchment. If the victims do not understand this pathology, they can be captured by their perceived dependence on the perpetrator and will have no way of escape. The perpetrator is exclusively self-seeking, usually highly skilled and unrestrained by the suffering of their victims. They will continuously strive to keep their victims in their place so that they can pursue their own ends, regardless of the damage they might do to all around them.

I liken sociopathy to an emotional Coronavirus taking hold, killing the souls of all it infects. But unlike its biological counterpart, the body lives on, continuing to suffer for the rest of their lives, which may indeed tragically end in death, but by suicide. The sociopath just carries on, oblivious to the carnage, spreading the virus.

The mechanism is not a physical virus but a well-rehearsed set of lies in which the perpetrator says they care for those around them, but cannot do so as they are unable to sense their victim's feelings. As one lie becomes exposed after another, the sociopath continually builds more fabrications to maintain the world they need to sustain their emotional requirements. The lies are covered by the charm they portray and they work because the victims are vulnerable. The aggressor seems unaffected by the damage they might cause.

They will continue their behaviour, making excuses and blaming others for their own misdemeanours. It's all about surviving the day, which may mean generating a new set of lies tomorrow. The sociopath is only concerned for their own preservation. As the lies get bigger, the damage they do gets bigger too. The smarter they are, the longer they can play the same game with the same set of victims and acquaintances. The less smart ones run out of credibility. Things fall apart and they have to find a new set of victims.

This pathology appears at a corporate level too.

Most Britons will be familiar with the story of the Hillsborough disaster of 1989 in which 96 supporters were crushed to death at a major football game in Britain, leaving a trail of physical and emotionally injured victims. Because a few individuals in the responsible authorities chose to lie rather than take blame, what could have been a manageable bereavement process was still unresolved 30 years later, with devastating connotations involving lots of people and massive legal costs. A few bad apples infected a whole barrel for a very long time. Affected relatives died before resolution was found.

This Emotional Coronavirus took hold and no-one knew how to stop it. It would be ill advised to suggest that any of the individuals involved were sociopaths per se, but we could describe the behaviour of some of the police as sociopathic insofar as they protected themselves in total disregard for the suffering of others. It demonstrated how organisations can behave sociopathically as well as individuals.

On the world stage too, political players in the richest economy in the world were amply displaying these features at the time of writing. Round the globe, we see the Syrian, Chinese, Russian and Myanmar governments blatantly denying what the rest of the world can see as incontrovertible atrocities.

Any organisation can be sociopathic when its constituents are and corruption always plays its part in this. The impacts of a few aggressors on whom many others depend like this can manifest just as powerfully at the micro end; in the family, the school and the workplace. However large the scale of the attack, the impact is always at a personal level and it all starts with individuals in their own communities.

47: Prevalence

The American psychiatrist, Harvey Cleckley, published *The Mask of Sanity* in 1941. It opened up the concept of a related feature, psychopathy. Robert D Hare then developed a checklist called PCL-R to help identify the pathology in individuals.

According to Professor Hare, psychopaths are impulsive - they lack empathy and remorse. They crave power and prestige and are extremely controlling. He described them as 'knowing the words but not the music'. 'They can learn to use ordinary words and to reproduce the pantomime of feeling but the feeling itself does not come to pass.'[1]

Despite his and Cleckley's work, the psychological fraternity has struggled to define this pathology well, possibly because their community like many others can harbour its own candidates. Some authors felt that the term psychopathy was too much associated with criminology and psychosis, which is indeed where the research started. In contrast, Kevin Dutton suggests an extended usage.

'Psychopathic behaviour…sounds very threatening and conjures up visions of serial killers. Indeed, serial killers are psychopathic, but many of those who would report as psychopathic are not in prisons but in our board rooms and law courts.'[2] In their book, *The Good Psychopath's Guide to Success*, Kevin Dutton and SAS veteran and author, Andy McNab, accept what most of us would consider a pathology for the macho lifestyle it represents, forgetting that if one person's success is another person's pain, society is the worse for it.

This psychology ignores the essential caring component of any healthy community and takes on the hallmarks of eugenics, affirming the right of the powerful to overcome the less powerful. It forgets that the reason any of us have confidence in our lives is because we had received sufficient love and care in childhood to enable us to function as we do in adulthood. It also forgets that we get old and start to need the kindness and unconditional love of others which cannot be bought or coerced. I can't support a culture which is able to destroy the very goodness which nurtures it.

Other experts who found the psychopathy 'alive and well' outside prison and mental hospital walls wanted to use a less emotive word which would allow rational discussion without frightening the horses. Sociopathy had already been around as an antisocial behaviour term and was adopted in some circles as being less pejorative than psychopathy. The DSM 5 shunned both and created its own; Antisocial Personality Disorder (ASPD).

In the second edition of *The Mask of Sanity* published in 1950, Cleckley derived 16 traits which have found common usage for identifying this type of pathology. Its prevalence is in the low percentages of the general population, but it does not take many bad apples to rot a whole barrel. Demographic pathology figures are vague, not least because not many people want to talk about, let alone confess to sociopathy.

I find that Antisocial Personality Disorder (ASPD) as defined in DSM 5 is reasonably close to the concepts I envisage. Research by the National Center for Biotechnology Information (NCBI) on ASPD indicates a prevalence of between 1–4% of the general population in North America.[3]

While this is a small number of individuals on average, the prevalence of ASPD points to around one child in every school classroom. That brings it into perspective and sometimes into our lives. So we will all meet it at some time and maybe early on in life. If parents and teachers are not aware of the research, they may decide this sort of thing could never happen in their backyard and so ignore it.

We all need to know more. It is from childhood that this pathology emanates and it is in childhood that it can be modified. We must be very careful not to stigmatise young people, not least because they are still developing their skills and personalities, but the problem does not just appear as they leave the school gates for the last time. It has been there, possibly incipiently since birth, and will appear as vindictive bullying, the control or not of which either cements it in for adulthood or modifies it into acceptable behaviour.

The only young person for whom I ever had grave concern for his own life had been oppressed by a school colleague for three years. It had gone well beyond bullying and into manipulation. Bullying can be seen as opportunistic attacks, however routine, which can often be combated by not reacting to the bully's goading. In this case, the child actively engaged my client to the point of persuading him to come on holiday with his family on two occasions. He was one of several young people in the class receiving counselling as a result of this child's manipulations. By the end of the third year at school, not only had the oppressor alienated his own classmates but most of the entire year. He could not find anyone to share a room with him on the annual school trip. Neither parents nor teachers had picked up on the seriousness of the attrition until it became a suicide issue for my client. This had begun for him when he first met the aggressor on starting high school and had fallen for the pathology, not least because it existed in his own family, so he had been conditioned to accepting it as a given in life.

However, it is important to note that while all sociopaths will bully, not all those who bully are, or will become, sociopaths. We must always resist bullies for their actions. It is only occasionally accurate to ascribe an embedded pathology, and even then, it is not usually useful to name it. We can manage it usually by intelligent responses.

The only time I professionally see someone with sociopathic tendencies is in couples counselling. They don't usually come of their own volition as the problem is always everyone else's and not theirs. More frequently, I meet their victims who do come along for individual counselling. Occasionally I see clients who are diagnosed with Borderline Personality Disorder or Emotionally Unstable Personality Disorder. They can present as empathic but their emotional instability means that they can behave sociopathically sometimes, so their pathology can be problematic for the therapist. They can turn on them unpredictably. The therapist can then become the victim. We all have vulnerabilities.

Sociopaths are frequently involved in relationship failures, sometimes serially because their lack of empathy manifests in a lack of motivation and indeed ability to care for their partners. The more the disruption, the wider the infection spreads. Anyone connected with a sociopath will be affected by their pathology in some degree. All the immediate family will suffer. Any extended family having an emotional relationship will be affected. It is all too easy to underestimate the dependency we have on each other and how easily we can get hurt. We can take our relationships for granted until they go pear-shaped. As Joni Mitchell said, "You don't know what you've lost till it's gone."

While the demographic prevalence of sociopaths may only be in the low percentages, the number of those who are emotionally tied into them is a different order of magnitude. All those close to them over a lifetime of attrition will be affected in some degree, usually family members and work colleagues, especially subordinates and indeed, all those who care for them.

The multiplier can be very big. Many ex-family members can get hurt too and they may continue to suffer in a very long aftermath, especially children who had grown up in such an unhealthy environment. The pain, confusion and disbelief surrounding that can make it very intense. It is unsurprising that I should see some of the victims of this pathology in my practice.

48: Recognition

Once I had formulated this sociopathic thinking process from my own experience and from my clients, it then became easy to spot the potential of it in clients' stories, so they could see it and understand it better too. I don't have to use the word. The following is a relatively mild but useful example.

A client was going through some particularly harsh financial trouble, essentially not of his own making. He was helping in the kitchen of a support centre along with other volunteers. One of them seemed to want to make trouble for him for no particular reason. He was a very genuine man, a real gentleman. He could not understand it. On this occasion, he arrived at the coffee station first and proceeded to make himself some toast. She arrived next and criticised him for not letting her go first. She turned to the man behind her and got him to agree that ladies should come first. My client was bewildered and just walked away leaving his toast to her. Not long afterwards, she accused him to his face in front of a member of staff of using racist language to her. That then became a bigger issue.

Firstly, I know this man would never do that. He was not born in Britain and believed he had been a victim of racism himself. He would never impose that on anyone else. Secondly, a witness of his supposed misdemeanour denied it took place. Thirdly, the race subject was taken seriously in the establishment. It involved him with higher management which he found particularly upsetting, not least because he needed them to get him through the next critical stage of his own survival campaign.

I found him more deeply distressed later that day than I had ever seen him, despite the fact that the journey he was already on was excruciating for him. To confuse him more, the previous day he had gone out of his way to help the woman deal with her own asylum application. When I explained that she was clearly displaying an embedded empathy deficit, he understood immediately and successfully. It took him a little while longer to come to terms with the fact that this pathology exists generally in our communities, albeit normally in a minority of us.

However, this community was a support centre, so we would expect to find more than the average number of pathologies there. She just needed to wind someone up to dump whatever emotions she was harbouring at the time. Because he was in a very stressful situation already, he would form a ready target for her. The fact that he had helped her would have made him more confused and the impact would be even higher for her.

In the grand scheme of things, this might seem trivial. But the big world is full of little people and their apparent trivia. And trivia to one person could push someone else over the edge. And for him, I knew the edge had been near before and could easily come again.

He was quite fragile. I had to explain to him that such people were predictably around and we need to be on our guard to identify them as potential oppressors, preferably before they identify us as potential victims. This event and my work with him on it proved invaluable. It enabled him to understand the far more insidious threat he was dealing with. He continually thanked me for the clarity I had given him. His whole demeanour changed from abject defeat to resolute defence.

Without exception, whatever else afflicts my clients, they come to me because they are anxious or depressed. I usually know nothing of my client to begin with, so the root problem could be anything. Most people are able to manage their ordinary life difficulties. It is when those difficulties become extraordinary and beyond their understanding that they arrive for counselling. Some will have internal issues such as trauma, Asperger's, dementia, gender dysphoria, bipolar, etc.

However, most are not psychologically abnormal in any other way than the duress they are suffering. If they have been bullied in some way in their lives, there is always a possibility that sociopathy has been a factor in that. That element may or may not be relevant to the therapy.

If it is, I need to know what I am doing even though I am not qualified to declare diagnoses formally for clients or indeed for any aggressor they may have. My person-centred approach precludes the need for diagnosis in the medical sense. There is little point in any diagnosis if it is not accompanied by an effective prescribed treatment. And in the world of psychology and psychiatry it is too often not. In contrast, I am primarily interested in who my client is and how they feel.

However, while I am focussing on the person they present and the problems they bring, it can be immensely helpful to recognise pathological features in their lives and how that may affect them. That may be a bereavement or an addiction. It may also be sociopathic oppression.

The counselling skill is being able to entertain the possibility of this pathology without necessarily declaring it. That way I maintain the person-centred approach which encourages client discovery. If I recognise some sociopathic features, I might suggest their aggressor lacks empathy.

They usually connect with that quite quickly. Some even arrive having read about this pathology, so their emotional journey may be shorter. The idea that it may be a permanent feature takes a little more consideration. If they do identify the condition as one that is not going to change anytime soon, the next step is the journey from head to heart. That may include grieving the loss of the person they thought they knew. They have just discovered that they did not really know them.

My counselling does not usually involve discussions on pathology per se because I use simple ideas and simple language. Adult clients' problems often emanate from a deficiency in emotional care in childhood. These clients may have been deprived of love in the same way that children in war-torn countries might be deprived of food. There was not enough to go around. It can be that basic and the results carry into adulthood. That emotional neglect can often create a vacuum in which further abuse can occur relatively undetected. A further issue for them. It can often be enough for them to come to terms with the fact that their parents simply weren't able to give them the love they needed for a whole variety of reasons.

Indeed, the concept of sociopathy does not normally appear unless it is a primary cause of current distress for which the client seeks some defensive devices. It is best to keep the approach simple. We are human and we all make mistakes. For reasons that we may never understand, mum or dad got caught up in something unhealthy and that made them unhappy. That, in turn, made us unhappy too. Although they did hurt us, they were struggling themselves and could not give us all we needed.

Very often, especially in the case of alcoholism, the adult child can recall the good times when the parent was caring, so they are able to ascribe their unhappiness to the addiction rather than to the person. That enables them to separate the doer from the deed, a process which had helped my jilted friend years beforehand. It defuses the blame, confusion and possibly hatred they may be harbouring for a parent who should have nurtured them but has actually damaged them.

Anyone who is being abused in any significant way would be likely to identify some of Cleckley's features in their oppressor. However, I rarely discuss the pathology in those terms. I don't normally need to. If I think that by giving behaviour a label may not help or could even do harm, I will not do so. I have to be particularly diligent that my client could be damaged by their subsequent use of controversial terminology.

Generally, I will normally only use the word if it is introduced by my client, although that has become more frequent recently. M.E. Thomas' book, amongst others, seems to have brought the idea into the public arena more. While clients might bring the word into the room, it is my experience which helps them consider whether the features are truly present and how that can help them understand their situation better.

49: Practical Psychology

Ongoing sociopathic behaviour often arrives in my practice with a client telling me that their partner can be really scheming and doesn't care how much they hurt them. The narrative I will use here for convenience is one of a male aggression on an empathic female partner, but the scenario could equally be female on male.

My client may complain that her partner just wants to dump all his emotions on her as often as he can. She tries to reason with him but gets nowhere. Because the emotional perpetrator is another human being, she assumes that he will feel like she does and will eventually gravitate to normal human behaviour. She gets upset that he does not see how much pain he is causing. She blames him and wants to punish him for his bad behaviour. She gets angry, but that doesn't achieve the required results. She may internalise her anger but that just fills her head. She tries to find a solution when there may not be one, or not a legal one anyway.

All this prevents her from enjoying her life. Her thinking space gets full of the negative thoughts, and the more she dwells on them, like ever deepening cart tracks, the harder it is for her to find a way out of them. She can become fixated in her Do Loops. It is corrosive. That makes her emotionally ill and can ultimately make her physically ill. Significant mental illness can follow obsessive worry, especially if there is a genetic disposition for that. Chronic Fatigue Syndrome, for instance, is a recognised physical condition frequently associated with extreme anxiety and depression.

If she sees that her partner's actions reveal a deep and consistent lack of empathy, the sociopathic model based on a concept of emotional deficit may help her understand him better. She might discover she can stop treating him as a normal emotionally healthy person when he is not and avoid wasting a lot of energy and life time because he is not going to get any better. If she believes he has a permanent pathology which means she can never appeal emotionally to him successfully, she can then treat that as one of nature's challenges.

She may come to see that this pathology is so destructive as to trump all the positive features she originally saw in him. This clinical approach categorises the problem more as a natural disease or disaster which she just has to deal with, rather than serial acts of malice designed by her partner to consciously cause her pain. She is no longer caught in the never-ending cycle of expecting him to behave normally and then being serially devastated by his aberrant behaviour.

This depersonalisation helps her understand that it is not the person but the pathology which is attacking her, albeit through the person. It reduces the anger which derives from that fear of not understanding him and what he will do next. She no longer has to view him in the empathic context she takes for granted in herself and in her friends. Recognising it as an emotional pathology which damages others just as a biological disease might, allows her to start addressing it more dispassionately.

It is easy to see the importance of a process which separates the force of some intangible evil power from the person of the perpetrator. It is the Channel Model at work, but in the negative this time. The evil power is not of the partner, but is working through him, coming from a subconscious in him which he did not himself create. It may have derived from abuse he has suffered as a child. The pathology could defeat any of his conscious deliberations in the same way that an addict is controlled by their maladjusted internal software.

It is like an aggressive dementia in which a close relative has been permanently changed by their illness. They can harm us emotionally if we continue to hold on to them as the person we once knew and loved, and who we believed loved and cared for us too. But impulsive reactions from us will only increase their aggression because their aggression comes from their fear. However, by managing our actions in the context of their pathology, we can control our own emotions better. That reduces the conflict and, as a result, their emotions too.

This is harder with sociopathy because we see an apparently fully functioning person in which there has been no obvious change that others might recognise and sympathise with as we might with dementia. It is the same person we always knew, but we are seeing them in a different light. We thought we knew them, but we now see their offending behaviour for what it is. We need to take stock for now and for the future. But the principles of a person being controlled by a pathology like dementia apply equally. We and they cannot change the behaviour. We can only manage it.

The sociopathy model has further benefits at the behavioural level. Accepting that the oppression is from a pathology which is afflicting the aggressor rather than from them as a normal healthy person, can help avoid rounds of tit for tat actions. In some types of community, that could ultimately escalate into acts of bloody revenge. Appreciating that the aggressor is ill but they don't understand that can help those affected deal with the illness first.

For the victim to descend into that same pathological behaviour provides no solution. Succumbing to impulsive emotion will only escalate the war to everyone's loss. The Christian process of forgiving helps avoid the emotional bloodbath, but that can be a struggle for the victim. Even for a religious victim that can often make little sense. I sympathise. Why should I 'give' anything to my aggressor? That is a particularly irksome thought when the pain is still ongoing. Victims will certainly not want to allow themselves to become vulnerable to the same attack again if they can help it, and an undiscerning forgiveness could lead to that.

Personally, I never blindly forgive per se, but I will always try and understand in the context of this model. That manages the emotion I am feeling. It is the other person's problem and I need to deal with it in that light.

The pathology model obviates the need to forgive the perpetrator. It says they are sick. A rabid dog will attack because it is sick and not because is it a dog. The disease is acting through the dog, so we have to deal with the dog, but in the light of the disease. Similarly, we need to deal with the aggressor in the light of their pathology. We will need a careful strategy which relies on a sound psychological construct.

That approach will reduce the emotional impact on the victim and enable them to either avoid the next attack if they can or manage it better if they can't. Notwithstanding my own methods, I have seen forgiveness working well in situations where the aggression is historic.

A sexual abuse victim was supporting a food bank when his attacker from childhood appeared in the queue. His choices were to run and hide or deal with it. He chose the latter and told the aggressor when he got to the front of the queue that he forgave him. The victim was no longer in danger and the aggressor was now the vulnerable party.

The power balance had changed and the forgiveness was an expression of that power. The victim was much relieved after this event. We are not told how the aggressor felt, but in this case, the victim of the past established that he could not be a victim in the future. Demolishing that fear was the crux of the resolution of the trauma. Not only would he not be attacked again from that source, he would feel more empowered to challenge any other attack in the future. The process he used does not imply that a blind act of forgiveness by rote is going to work at all times. It is circumstantial and dependent on a changed power balance. This was effective trauma resolution and it worked this time.

50: Deeper Psychology

It is always better to avoid the pathological detail if the empathy void idea works for a client. However, some more aware clients can find Cleckley's 16 features useful.[1]

1. Superficial charm and good intelligence
2. Absence of delusions and other signs of irrational thinking
3. Absence of nervousness or neurotic manifestations
4. Unreliability
5. Untruthfulness and insincerity
6. Lack of remorse and shame
7. Inadequately motivated antisocial behaviour
8. Poor judgment and failure to learn by experience
9. Pathologic egocentricity and incapacity for love
10. General poverty in major affective reactions
11. Specific loss of insight
12. Unresponsiveness in general interpersonal relations
13. Fantastic and uninviting behaviour with alcohol, sometimes without
14. Suicide threats rarely carried out
15. Sex life impersonal, trivial and poorly integrated
16. Failure to follow any life plan

The application of this listing has both benefits and challenges. If I hear my client talking about four of Cleckley's features when describing an oppressor, I might enquire about a further four. If my suspicions are correct, they are usually surprised that I should seem to know these additional features.

At that point, I may talk about the nature of the pathology, but not usually naming it. That could be just too startling. If I still sense it, I may offer the list but with no label on it. If they can correlate the behaviour of their oppressor with at least half of them, suddenly the whole scene can now make sense. The number of features they tick is not critical. It is rare for anyone to report all sixteen. Indeed, on the only occasion I recall when all were ticked, there was a question over the depth of the pathology. The important issue here is to open up the question as to whether the aggressor has a pathological lack of empathy and how permanent a feature it is.

A highly intelligent and empathic client navigated her way through a separation and divorce from a man who fitted enough features to qualify, but she could not come to terms with the concept of pathology, so we did not go there. It made her life harder in my view, but it was her journey and not mine and she made it in the end. As counselling concluded, she was specific about how my understanding, even without the explicit terminology, had been very helpful to her. The transition was managed well.

The appreciation of this phenomenon as an illness, and a potentially incurable one at that, can explain so much to a client very quickly. Some diagnoses are identifiable like physical ones in that their features come in clusters. The Cleckley list is one such. Whilst psychology is full of endless diagnoses with questionable purpose and limited cures, this pathology provides an understanding which can be of massive benefit to the victim.

Once a victim appreciates that their aggressor does not actually feel what they themselves would feel in similar circumstances, a whole raft of their relationship history seems to click into perspective. It is one thing to believe that my partner is deliberately manipulating and wrecking my life, knowing how much that really hurts me. "If I hurt someone like that, I would really feel bad about it, so I just could not do it. It is brutal." It is another thing to understand that they are manipulating and wrecking my life but are not emotionally aware of how this affects me, despite the fact that I keep telling them. I had expected them to see that but they cannot. They are behaving in this respect like a feral animal which is masquerading as a normal balanced human being.

They look normal and most people treat them as normal, but they don't have the equipment available to sense the hurt they are constantly causing.

They are socially impaired. "They hurt me. I feel it, but they don't feel it. They may never feel it. What next?" To quote a client: "He is not normal." Once a client understands how empathy works in them and then how an empathy void might work in their aggressor, they can review their aggressor's behaviour specifically and exclusively on that all-important parameter of dysempathy. If they see a consistent lack of empathy, they can get to grips with their aggressor's psychology and be in control, possibly for the first time ever.

That revelation can massively reduce the emotions they have carried. They have feared or hated someone whom they thought was deliberately making them miserable in the full knowledge of the hurt caused. They now realise it is an abnormality and have finally arrived at a place where they can construct a mental framework around the appalling conduct they are subjected to and start managing their own responses.

They will stop using emotional appeals to change their oppressor's behaviour and may start restricting communication to the structural issues only. That way they can resist their aggressor's emotion dumping better. Clients with sociopathic spouses change from trying to plead with them to being just pragmatic towards them. It does not solve the individual's pathology, but it provides some means of controlling its impact.

This revelation can break many years of suffering in silence, anguish and confusion, in which the victim believes that it's all their own fault, not least because the oppressor keeps telling them so.

In a short assessment session, a client told me how his relationship was failing and mentioned some features which seemed sociopathic to me. I offered him some of Cleckley's features, to which he responded enthusiastically. Within a few minutes, he declared that no-one had ever described his wife so well and that I had never even met her. This is not an unusual experience in my practice.

The incredible power of this pathology can trap the victim into silence by the knowledge that no-one would understand and accept their story. Once a sceptic of this, I now recognise the behaviour quickly. It is hard not to ascribe the word 'evil' to the process, but I just have to take a look at the daily news to realise that what I am seeing in my counselling room is a microcosm of what is happening on the worst parts of the world's stage every day. I cannot reasonably influence world events, but I can influence what appears in my work. The responsibility the counsellor takes in this work is enormous.

Such an emotive subject has to be dealt with delicately and sensitively or not at all. My client will only absorb what they are ready for and I have to accept that sometimes we don't get to a place of revelation. And maybe my assessment is wrong. However, if my client does correctly correlate their partner/child/parent/sibling/boss with the Cleckley list and is able to take on the weight of the concept, then they can embark on their emotional journey sooner.

To deny its existence, if true, is to disable the client's defence system. To fabricate its existence, if not true, is to endanger a struggling but survivable relationship. I meet this frequently in my couples work. It takes a great deal of discernment to enable the client to arrive at their own conclusions without prejudicing that journey.

A client expressed concern to me about a previous couple's counselling she had had. I find this often. Her husband had gambled the value of their home away and she was terrified as to what she would do with herself and her children. Because the counsellor was non-committal on this topic, she felt as though his addiction had been accepted and justified. It was seriously counterproductive for her. Whether addictive behaviour could be classified as sociopathic or not is not so relevant as a failure to face and flag an apparent pathology. I cannot know how justified my client's complaint was as I was not there, but this example serves to illustrate the problem of dealing with possible pathologies and the importance of getting this right.

How the counsellor uses some words and avoids others and how concepts are delivered is critical to safe therapy, especially when the client is still very dependent on their relationship with their partner. Any conclusions must be the client's. It is their choice and emotive terms can influence excessively. The counsellor must consider how this might play outside the counselling room and what is safe to articulate.

Couples counsellors will relate to this. The structure of the relationship they perceive may be a lot more obvious to them than to the partners, in particular a victimised partner, but all the counsellor can do is guide the discourse. If they simply state their stance, however correct, they may break something valuable irrevocably. The decisions must be the client's and the process to arrive at those decisions should, as much as possible, also be the client's.

The final result may not be what the counsellor would want to see, but it is not their life and not their choice to make. Their job is to create the climate for discovery. In individual counselling too, the counsellor may see their client as a victim of sociopathy, but they have to discover the nature of their oppressor for themselves. The counsellor must avoid becoming a third party in the relationship. The key concept to seek out is empathy or the lack of it. That usually works well.

The major issue clients seem to have is not so much in understanding the pathology cognitively, but in coming to grips with it emotionally. My client is always the victim. The oppressor may turn up sometimes in couples counselling but, as you can imagine, pathology tends to be avoided in that forum. I need them both to come to the next session if counselling is to continue and it would be difficult to discuss this item without seeming accusatory. My skill here is in recognising the pathology and conducting my sessions in that knowledge. Not an easy task, cognitively or emotionally.

51: The Truth Emerges

A partner or relative may not just be different at a fundamental level to the image my client had believed in, but a recognisable danger. Such a revelation is massive. To come to the realisation that they have been deceived all these years is an emotional challenge too. They have to leave that old image behind and take on a new concept which reflects current behaviour more realistically. It is not unusual, for instance, for me to help clients differentiate between the mother they have from the mother they had wanted to believe in. That can deliver enormous relief from oppression quite quickly.

Fiona Bruce presented a documentary called the *Parachute Murder Plot* on UK's ITV on 17/9/18. It illustrated how a wife struggled to come to terms with the real nature of her partner.

A 38-year-old British army sergeant, Emile Cilliers, appeared to have become bored with his wife as she approached the birth of their third child. He had had previous relationship failures and was a philanderer. His communications with another woman indicated that he had planned his wife's demise by April 2015. He was in deep gambling debt and the proceeds of her life insurance policy would resolve this. He tampered with the gas main in his home with a view to killing her. The fact that he would also be killing his two children seemed not to be an issue for him. They belonged to the same parachuting club. When the gassing attempt failed, he tampered with both her main and emergency parachutes immediately before her next flight. By strange fluke, when her chutes failed, she fell into a deeply ploughed field which reduced her injuries to the point where she could recover and live a manageable life. This behaviour displays classical sociopathy or some would argue in this case, psychopathy.

For my professional purposes, it is the same pathology type; an empathy void. It took three years to compile all the evidence, so his wife had plenty of time to absorb the facts. When she finally stood up in court, the case collapsed because she retracted her all-important evidence and tried to save him. She was unable to come to terms with the fact that the man she had loved, and to an extent still did, would try to kill her. Further evidence was eventually gathered later which did finally convict him.

Their relationship had been passionate and they had had many common interests. Not only during their relationship, but even in court afterwards when his intentions had become clear, she was simply unable to accept that there was a massive void in his character which made him an extremely dangerous person to be involved with. Such is the enormous holding power this pathology can have over its victims. A major feature of the pathology is manipulation.

While I don't have the details, it is very likely that he had influenced her to retract her statements. The pathology masquerades so effectively for the real thing. This was not a casual affair. She needed a stable man to support her in bringing up her children and she had not spotted the all-important fault in his personality, perhaps lost in the enjoyment of their shared sports. There must have been plenty of signals for her to pick up, but the report did not cover that.

Passionate love involves powerful hormones which seem to mask the inconvenient truth that our partner is not so perfect. It is these hormones which ensure the continuation of our species even when we have not actually found the partner of our dreams. We simply dream our ideal partner into what we have got and then fill in the gaps as best we can.

It is not so bizarre. We are told that normal vision does this too. We can't observe a scene in its entirety because of the blind spot or scotoma where the optic nerve leaves the eyeball. Our brains fill in the missing bits so we think we see a whole picture. The phrase 'love is blind' fits this analogy well.

If a partnership is based more on sexual drive than altruistic love, it can start to disintegrate after the honeymoon hormones have worn off. That powerful attraction can take between 18 months and 3 years to wane, depending on other circumstances like the advent of offspring. Views differ on this time period and research is poor in this area. The presence of dependent children may perpetuate the blindness.

It is a bit like two magnets snapping together. The force overcomes all others, but once they are bonded face to face, each is unable to see any other side than the immediate face. However, others will be able to see both in the round and the counsellor may be one of those people. I regularly observe this blindness between couples whose relationships are in trouble. If indeed my client is suffering from a sociopathic partner they may, with some help, be able to grasp a cognitive understanding of what is happening.

However, the all-important journey to the heart is the harder work. Because these relationships always have depth, there will be a bereavement process yet to come and that can take time too. Sometimes a shocking event such as the revelation of a long-standing clandestine affair may hit and the message gets through rather more quickly. Or it can come from focussing a little more on the blind spots.

A mature couple who had recently fallen in love came to me to resolve constant arguments. Both had three children from previous marriages and they felt they wanted to move in together. She had concerns for the way he treated his children and progressively her own as they spent more time together with their families. It seems he had wrested his children from his wife but now found them too much of a handful. He would repeatedly refer to his ten-year-old as a 'little prat'. He had had an unpleasant childhood himself but was unable to stand sufficiently far enough away to see which parts of himself were healthy and which were not. It was the focussing on this aspect of his behaviour which allowed her to balance her clearly powerful romantic love for him against her care for her own children. That enabled her to call a halt to the cohabitation plans. At no point was any pathology inferred, but my perception gave her space to see through the sexual passion and review the longer-term prognosis of their relationship.

Longer standing malfunctioning relationships can generate enormous emotions as conflict reaches the point at which counselling is sought. When a client has grasped enough of the empathy void concept to manage its impact on them, they may consider how to avoid emotions in any further contact they need to have with their aggressor. It can take some determination to limit communications to business only.

They will not be used to being rude and blanking their partner's emotional assaults. But emotional contact can derail the process of changing heart in the early days. Messaging and emails have been major modern assets in dealing with practical matters because they avoid vocal contact which can easily become controlling. Written correspondence gives the recipient time to sift the emotion out from any script and reply to the practical content only.

Emotional isolation from the aggressor provides the stress break needed to review their emotional landscape and make tough decisions. It's the same advice as for those being bullied. If you react emotionally, they have control over you. Avoiding reactions starves them of the emotive response they sought. They no longer control you.

It is important for counsellors, and indeed anyone in contact with this pathology to get this one right, and that includes parents and teachers. We need to know what can be changed and what cannot be changed. If the pathology is perceived as a firmware issue it is not going to go way. If it is the primary defect in the relationship, it is the nature of the person. It could derive from a multiplicity of physical and/or emotional disorders, but the bottom line is that the sociopath is someone who has not achieved Freud's superego state for some reason or another, but is intelligent enough to manipulate others to satisfy their own emotional needs and, to a great degree, their wants. Its actual pathological source is not relevant to the victim or the counsellor.

It may not be relevant to the aggressor either, but the nature of my profession is to attend exclusively to my client. That boundary is clear, effective and ethical. I cannot have concerns for an external person unless they are vulnerable, typically a child. If my client cares for themselves well, they will be more equipped to care for others they are responsible for. That will emotionally exclude anyone who is aggressive to them in any form as far as they can. The aggressor must find their own means of resolving their issues and that cannot involve me in my profession. I could not manage the inevitable conflicts of interests. I need to help my client recognise empathy deficit and manipulation, if indeed it does exist in this way, and help them to manage it.

52: Nature and Nurture Pathologies

Insofar as an emotional deficit can be perceived as a personality disorder, it won't normally change over life. I would describe that as a nature feature. If we conclude that we are emotionally tied to a Nature Sociopath, we need to accept that their personality is not going to improve a great deal and we can make our decisions on the basis of that revelation.

Do we find a way of managing them or do we quit before it gets worse and what are the consequences of that decision? A good understanding of how the emotional equations work is the key to this. How much is the aggressor insensitive to our feelings? How much do they find devious ways of dumping their surplus emotions on us? Can they be trained to change behaviour?

The 16 traits checklist will help us focus on this, but there is no definitive sum which will determine permanence or not. We just have to make a judgement based on our own experience in the context of a theoretical construct of this condition. We will be asking what our best life plan is going forward. Part of that will be to look around at other relationships and see how they compare to ours. We can't have theirs, but we can identify a new benchmark against which to assess ours.

A senior physician came to me suffering from his wife's disruptive behaviour. He was a very modest man and he started our dialogue with blaming himself. She was constantly linking aspects of his past into how she saw him failing her now. It became clear very quickly that she was the oppressor and he was guilt-ridden about not meeting her ever-increasing demands. They had three teenage girls. She kept threatening divorce of their 20-year-old marriage, but was shocked when he eventually chose to accept that. He managed to map her behaviour onto the theory, but struggled to get that at depth until true love fell his way, quite by accident.

He declared that he had had no idea what genuine caring love was until then. It was that and the threat of his wife destroying it, which enabled him to make the tough decisions much more easily. He had then moved from head to heart.

Reflection on his relationship from the start assured him that she was not going to improve anytime soon. That and revelations of her affairs affirmed his decision to leave her. The Cleckley list was never used with this client but it was hard not to suspect Nature Sociopathy.

The destructive features of this case seem fairly definitive, but we need to be aware that there are plenty of examples of sociopathic traits appearing occasionally in people who have not been given a personality disorder diagnosis.

I have related the story of a client who had been oppressed by another volunteer in the kitchen of a support centre. We had concluded that the aggression was sociopathic. He came later to me with a similar problem. The manager had been totally unreasonable to another volunteer and that had upset and disturbed him too.

However, my client's new understanding enabled him to deal with it calmly at the time. Later, the manager thanked him for the diplomacy he had exercised. It turned out that he had been under some stress and had been allowing his anger out onto his staff. His behaviour was temporary. Most of us will do this sort of thing from time to time. He displayed his empathy readily when he had recovered by appreciating the hurt he had caused and regretting it. This temporary lack of empathy did not qualify for the sociopathy label. The client readily understood the difference.

If we regard sociopathy as a personality disorder, it is permanent. However, I have come across people who appear to have been normal in the past, but seem to have developed some of Cleckley's features. I have also met people who have carried some Cleckley features in the past but who are empathic now. If the personality disorder type can be called Nature Sociopathy, this changeable condition could merit the title Nurture Sociopathy. It is learnt behaviour and learnt behaviour can be overwritten because the capacity for empathy exists. It's just been suppressed.

It is important to differentiate between the nature and nurture versions so we don't get carried away and label everyone who has offended us as sociopathic. I had the pleasure of spending some time with M.E.Thomas, author of best seller, *Confessions of a Sociopath*.

It was clear to me within a few minutes of meeting her that, despite a professorial diagnosis, she did not lack empathy and therefore was not sociopathic. Indeed, she talks in the book about loving and being loved by family and friends. This is not on Cleckley's list. Her book related some pretty horrific behaviour which she had learnt from her clearly sociopathic family, but she regretted that and had had some tough times dealing with it and changing it.

Indeed, the book title is a giveaway. Real sociopaths don't confess to anything. For me, empathy is the intuitive sign and she had enough of that in my view to qualify as reasonably neurotypical and fairly safe. Yet she had been diagnosed as having a 'prototypical psychopathic personality' in the 99% percentile of that cohort.

However, her data was self-assessment type. This does not work. The inherent deceit in sociopathy makes self-assessment a non-viable analysis method. Her guilt for her actions will have made her self-critical. Again, not a sociopathic trait. I got that she was focussed on that which made her different from others and I admired her for her courage in facing her own demons. I felt that her behaviour had in the past displayed some sociopath features, and some might still be around, but I would be happier to think of her now as an ex-Nurture Sociopath.

I have had sad experiences of people travelling in the other direction.

I met what appeared to be a fairly normal family for whom the father had concerns for his young daughter with inferences of autism. It was instantly clear to me that this was not the case. He was separated from the mother and about to get remarried. It was his new partner who concluded from the stress the girl was displaying that she must be on the autistic spectrum. She had no qualifications to support his diagnosis. What however transpired, when that episode was over and the now ex-wife came to me for counselling, was that the autistic candidate was not the child but almost certainly the new partner.

Further, she fitted a significant number of Cleckley's features. The relevance of this story here is that the father started to behave like his new wife, acquiring some of Cleckley's features himself. My client assured me that this was new. The interesting point was that he did it remarkably badly. Where the new wife's scheming was deeply insidious, he was clumsy and transparent in his machinations as a junior Nurture Sociopath.

This made it easier for my client to navigate her way round him once she had grasped the psychological theory and had gone through enough grieving for the man she once knew. She could now manage this new and disappointing person she had to deal within coparenting. It was as though he had become quickly and devastatingly infected with a psychological disease which had overtaken his very personality. As a sequel, my client visited a friend whose circumstances looked very similar to hers. That provided further confirmation to her of the model we had used.

This pathology can be more devastating when children are directly involved.

A 12-year-old was trying to continue her relationship with her father who had left for another woman. Over the space of a single year when he moved in with his new partner, his character appeared to mutate. His 20-year-old daughter quickly got the message and would have nothing more to do with him, but the younger one went through some really difficult times trying to hold on to the father she once knew but who was now rapidly being replaced by a not very intelligent, aggressive man with lots of problems they had never seen before. The father started blaming his daughter and his ex-wife in alarmingly expressive ways for all his woes, whether connected to them or not. It was hard for this young lady to manage the change in the father she once knew and loved dearly. The pathology has taken a menacing grip and the result was almost unrecognisable. My client told me about a friend who had been similarly afflicted and had also struggled with an apparently Nurture Sociopathic man. It seems the prevalence of this pathology exceeds the knowledge generally available amongst professionals to guide people through it.

More difficult cases to discern are those of addicts. Addictions take over our emotional reward system at deep levels and place the object of our addiction at the top of our priority list. That can soon swamp the needs of any of those people who would reside inside our empathy zone. It also subsumes our own genuine needs so we lose our emotional life balance too. It is not difficult to identify some of Cleckley's features in gamblers or alcoholics who have become adept at hiding their habits.

While their addictions prevail, and that can be for most of life, these features prevail too, and the victims of their behaviour still need to assess how long this condition could last for them and what they will do in the meantime. If and when the addictions are cleared, the features generally will clear, providing there is not an underlying Nature Sociopathy.

A client in her 40s had not done well in life, partly through her use of alcohol. She was the youngest of five children. Her brother had cerebral palsy and got the giant's share of the attention. Dad drank the wage and was aggressive in the house for most of the time. And then four cousins moved in. Unsurprisingly, her life was defined by attention seeking, which got her into a lot of trouble. A priest tried to sexually abuse her, but her lack of regular care meant she was unable to tell anyone about it. It just emphasised the love void in her emotional foundations. She was difficult to deal with most of the time, labelled as having a personality disorder. As she got clear of her addictions, I could see an empathic intelligent woman appearing. My client was clear that her mother had been doing her best and it was her father who was lacking empathy. He was insensitive to the family's feelings and damaged them by deprivation and by violence. In that sense, he behaved sociopathically, but I cannot know whether it was a nature or nurture type.

The device of destruction was the alcohol it seemed and the sheer family overload may have exacerbated any addiction if it had already existed. Love is an essential component of a healthy soul just as much as good diet is an essential component of a healthy body. Lack of either will result in unhappiness. This is what I saw in my client.

Insofar as an addiction may be treatable, abnormal behaviour can be normalised and the empathy function could return to good health. We can all indulge in some level of sociopathic behaviour as a malfunction of our normal lives.

I can recall times, but would rather not, when I suspended my empathy for my own purposes and hurt others in the process. It was usually when I was applying an employer's modus operandi of dubious integrity to an individual. It probably didn't tick a lot of the Cleckley features, but I am not proud of those times and I try and avoid repetitions. The fact that I feel remorse afterwards infers that I am empathic to those I have hurt so I am not any sort of a sociopath.

However, there are times when we actually suspend empathy for the good.

I had a minor operation recently. The surgeon visited me beforehand and seemed pleasant enough. Some hours later, I am an unconscious body on an operating table and he is cutting into it. He has withheld his immediate intuitive empathy which finds harm abhorrent in order to help me in the longer term. He saw me afterwards and was pleasant again.

I withhold expressions of empathy in my job too. Some stories I hear can be harrowing, but I have to restrain my instinctive empathic reactions for the sake of my client's well-being. I need to keep calm for them, even if I am drawn to feel otherwise. Like my surgeon, I need to be in control of my empathy switch, turning it off and on as needed. Empaths often use this switch to get the best out of our various talents in the service of their fellow human beings. Others can use it to their own advantage.

53: Collective Pathology

Organisations can behave sociopathically if some of their members are. Individuals supporting those sociopathic actions are morally responsible for them in some degree, even though they may not be naturally pathological themselves. It becomes difficult when they are coerced into behaving sociopathically in order to keep their status or even their job. Hare said in 2002, that 'Not all psychopaths are in prison. Some are in the boardroom.'[1] This must apply equally to sociopaths.

Malicious acts in an organisation can be the culmination of a series of relatively small acts by different people which, of themselves, may not seem so bad. The end product, however, can be devastating for some individuals.

Whilst I would often correctly defer to an organisational construct for making a tough decision about a subordinate, I would always endeavour to ensure my actions are fair and accountable within that context. Some people, however, will misuse their authority to exercise their own aggression. They enjoy the power of being the executioner instead of acting in as sensitive a way as possible to the individual on behalf of the organisation. The sensitive attitude can be harder to grasp, but is the only good one.

There are times in all organisations when corporate objectives clash with those of the individual and a manager behaves in an apparently callous way. They are persuaded in their role to isolate themselves from the subordinate's pain in order to exercise what they see as their duties. Firing people falls clearly into that category. Hard to do empathically. So often not done empathically! Legal systems intended to protect workers' rights can simply generate deceit to avoid infringing the law and that can make the process more complex and more painful.

Even if an English person resigns from their work, they can still claim under the law of Constructive Dismissal that they were treated unfairly, so have redress against their employer. The employer's defences against this can be highly sophisticated to evade liability. The deceit involved can be extremely damaging to the victim. I have helped colleagues and clients through such times, but when it came to me, it was still very stressful. The process is designed to make the pain of staying greater than the pain of leaving, while at the same time following a procedure which looks like it's fair in law.

Despite my ability to see what was happening, I was still faced with the same equation. The penalty for my getting this wrong was a significant working life change, so I clung to the ever-diminishing belief which had the most chance of yielding the best result. It was emotionally very painful because it affected my career not just the position. I flipped from one implausible explanation to another. Fellow sufferers have used the term 'emotional rape' for this experience. It felt like that. It is a powerful sign of an underlying deceit.

I tested the situation to breaking point and it broke. At least then I knew the truth. It was a salutary reminder of how challenging my clients' lives can be living each day in a deceitful environment in which those who have authority over them are living a lie to them. That is a long way from the empathic society we need to keep ourselves healthy. Mine was a brief encounter with this particular pathology. Some of my clients may have been living with this problem for years. The episode gave me a little more insight into their lives.

Sociopathy and psychopathy are the modus operandi of despotic regimes in which subjects can herd harmless fellow human beings and their children at gunpoint into death camps and then sleep at night. If the regimes leader is deified, then individuals will subsume their own conscience into it, disregarding reality. Blind faith in an external doctrine inevitably drowns internal empathy sooner or later.

The picture is by no means a simple one of pathology or not. Before we ever think of Cleckley's list, the sign that we might look for in someone is the presence or lack of empathy. Empathy is crucial in our ability to interact usefully to resolve each other's emotions. The existence of empathy also evidences our own intuitive ability to deal with the emotional impacts we sustain ourselves.

That is crucial to our own happiness. If we can manage our own emotions well, we can support others and that process of healing will potentially spread across our communities. If we cannot, we will need others to support us, even if we don't admit that.

In an ideal world, we will all be empathic. As we help those close to us and they help those close to them, the goodness spreads through all those who exercise it. We can see this in organisations which develop healthy ethics. Healthy empathy creates a peaceful society. Managed suspension of empathy enables us to withhold our emotions for the longer-term benefit of our fellow human beings. We then return to it for our normal functioning. Conversely, the pathological absence of empathy in just a few members can infect any community in a devastating way.

54: Global Pathology

Emotional attacks on the soul are just as prevalent as biological attacks on the body, but we have not come to grips with the implications of this yet, either as individuals or as nations. The medical world has not achieved the level of competence in psychological pathology as it has in physiological pathology. It is not therefore surprising that, despite the current 'mental health mantra', the general population at individual level still prefers to sideline psychological illness. It is easier to pretend it does not exist or at least, not in my backyard. It was like this with cancer a couple of generations ago until there was a breakthrough in treatment.

As a result, many of us as individuals suffer emotionally in silence. The problem becomes all too evident when it breaks out on the world stage. We still fail to recognise that many world events, both positive and negative, are precipitated by individuals, and those individuals grew up in families next door or around the corner and it was there that their personalities were formed. If the characters of those powerful people were malformed, disasters will ensue. It's that simple.

We wring our hands and talk of international court trials for war criminals while watching the atrocities from afar. The individual actors on these stages have become conditioned to seeing malicious behaviour and to accepting it as normal. It is the just a small step to participate in it. Nazi prison camp officers were educated in their childhoods into misaligned thinking when the ravages of post war poverty took their toll on the minds of the population.

Those brutal times conditioned the populace to accept misery and death, so it became easier for some of them to inflict misery and death on others. Many world atrocities emanate from conditioning to extreme hardships, out of which comes the promotion of a leader who promises the relief the populace sought, but then turns out to be unable to deliver it. They had become so accustomed to the hardships, that they accepted the voice which said that murdering other human beings en masse because they were a bit different would resolve all their problems. "Everyone around me is doing this, so it must be right."

Like the surgeon who switched out his empathy to cut my body open, they switched out theirs on the basis of an indoctrination they had absorbed, mostly in their younger years. But the switch got stuck, not least because the world they were in also got stuck. There was too much of it going on.

Whilst it is obvious that this sort of aggression harms others, it will also harm the perpetrators. Once they lose their ability to sense others feelings, there is no limit to the amount of havoc they can wreak at the individual level. History demonstrates that well. Pol Pot, Mao, Stalin, Darfur, Myanmar, Vietnam, Plantagenets, Assad, Putin... The list is endless.

Most of the major human catastrophes have been the culmination of years of incremental change under some form of duress. An initial moral benchmark was moved a bit at a time such that the populations were not too shocked at the next development. There comes a structural tipping point when people realise how bad things have become.

Very often it is then too late to stop the juggernaut of disaster. And this is why societies need defined and consistent morals and established laws to avoid their benchmark of good behaviour drifting incrementally into bad behaviour. Maladjusted individuals who are driving these changes need to be stopped from gaining power as early as possible. Otherwise, they will get into positions where they just keep moving the goalposts a little at a time so we don't notice.

Their only criterion is actually their own personal survival. They may have no genuine concept of others' well-being. Insofar as it is insensitive to others, their behaviour has become sociopathic in nature and it is the job of the empaths of this world who care for each other to recognise the pathology in their midst and put a stop to it in the same way they might discipline a disruptive child.

Whilst the empaths are seriously in the majority, they sometimes find it easier to be led by those who exude confidence in whatever dilemma prevails, so they vote for those who say they can fix everything. What they often miss is the reason these aspiring leaders are so confident may be because they are omitting people's feelings from their equations. Answers can come very easily if we ignore some of the limitations in the problems we are set.

I have woken up in the night sometimes with a Eureka solution to an intractable problem, only to find on sober analysis in the morning that I have missed out an essential constraint which wrecks the whole idea. We expect our leaders to be caring because we are, and how could anyone not be. Indeed, they have told us they care for us. We see them as so much cleverer than we are to be able to harness all this into clear-cut decisions. But they never were. They missed out the compassion bit. The solution became easy then. But not for long!

By the time the emotional fallout has arrived from the great decisions that were made in the name of the people, we empaths find it is all too late. Whenever a leader has created war, he has involved empathic people in a process which forces them into destructive behaviour. And that can be on epic scales as we have seen.

Once started, the initial damage caused by these events makes them all but impossible to stop. The time of writing this followed the centenary of the end of the First World War but was also looking at the war in Ukraine. The catastrophic carnage in the former war was as much to do with the pathology of a single person, Wilhelm II of Germany, albeit within an unhealthy hierarchical system.

Enough people around him allowed their moral benchmarks to drift into an unparalleled scene of utter carnage. The fact that it repeated itself twenty years later in World War II and now in Ukraine demonstrates how easy it is for the empaths to lose their grip yet again on those who behave in a sociopathic way. They were stubbornly blind to the now obvious deceit of a promise of better lives on which all this was sold. They failed to recognise the sociopaths.

The eugenic aspect of the Nazi regime, expressed through its Aryan ideology carried a hidden caveat in the context of this promise. It applied to the strong and powerful only. And even then, it spectacularly failed. Many became convinced that what was being done was the right thing for upright people. That sort of monstrous error is why we need to define morals and establish laws to make sure that the vulnerable are not trampled on while the sociopathic powerful sell them a vision which sounds good but may be unworkable for them.

The end aspiration must never justify the immoral means. Laws have to be crude at times because they are expressed in written words which can have serious limitations and they are always a bit behind the times. But well drafted legislation provides a safety net when empathy is under attack. This book aims to pull off the veil of deceit from the perpetrators by exposing the mechanics of a pathology which reliably destroys at the grass roots, sometimes on colossal scales.

While good law is essential, it can only be an ultimate backstop to healthy social functioning. If our behaviour always verged on the illegal, we would not be living happy lives. So there has to be a sound morality which pervades all society's members. Religion provided this, however imperfectly, in the past. Western Enlightenment arose, mainly to challenge a religion which was unable to accommodate burgeoning knowledge and which had its own corruptions too.

Unfortunately, it threw much of the spiritual baby out with the religious bathwater, so we lost some of the morality which was embedded in the old religion. Whilst many developed nations have laws which try and protect that all-important family environment which forms the foundation of all our lives, they are always limited in their ability to enforce from the outside. A healthy society is one in which the law is rarely invoked because its morals are doing the peace job, and its members are wise enough to discern pathology from promises.

References

Chapter 1: My Journey

1   Pybis et al. (2017) 'The comparative effectiveness and efficiency of cognitive behaviour therapy and generic counselling in the treatment of depression: evidence from the 2nd UK National Audit of psychological therapies', *BMC Psychiatry*, volume 17 article 215.
https://bmcpsychiatry.biomedcentral.com/articles/10.1186/s12888-017-1370-7

2   Duggan, C et al. (2014) 'The recording of adverse events from psychological treatments in clinical trials: evidence from a review of NIHR-funded trials', *National Center for Biotechnology Information*, 2014 Aug 27;15:335. doi: 10.1186/1745-6215-15-335.
https://www.ncbi.nlm.nih.gov/pubmed/25158932

3   Hill, A. et al. (2008). 'Counselling in primary care: a systematic review of the evidence', *National audit of Psychological Therapies 2013 RCPsychiatry*.
https://www.bacp.co.uk/media/1973/bacp-counselling-in-primary-care-systematic-review.pdf

4   Barkham, M. et al. (2021) 'Clinical and cost-effectiveness of person-centred experiential therapy vs. cognitive behavioural therapy for moderate and severe depression delivered in the English Improving Access to Psychological Therapies national programme: a pragmatic randomised non-inferiority trial', [PRaCTICED] *The Lancet Psychiatry*, 8 (6). pp. 487–499. ISSN 2215-0366, https://eprints.whiterose.ac.uk/172797/

5   Cooper, M. et al. (2021) 'Humanistic counselling plus pastoral care as usual versus pastoral care as usual for the treatment of psychological distress in adolescents in UK state schools (ETHOS): a randomised controlled trial', *Lancet Child Adolescent Health 2021*; 5: 178–89.

Chapter 5: The Evolution Mismatch
1   Roberts, A (2018). The Incredible Human Journey. *BBC4.*

Chapter 6: Circle Diagram1   Waite, D. (June 2015). 'Circle Diagram', *Therapy Today:BACP*, Lutterworth.

Chapter 8: Selfish Me
1   Rodrigues, S. (2009) 'Oxytocin receptor genetic variation relates to empathy and stress reactivity in humans', *National Academy of Sciences of the United States of America.*
https://www.ncbi.nlm.nih.gov/pmc/articles/PMC2795557/

Chapter 11 What is Trauma?
1   APA (2021) https://www.apa.org/topics/ptsd/index.aspx
2   APS (2021)
https://www.psychology.org.au/publications/tip_sheets/trauma/

Chapter 12: Processing Emotion
1   Fatal Familial Insomia (2016) *Genetic and Rare Diseases Information Center.*
https://rarediseases.info.nih.gov/diseases/6429/fatal-familial-insomnia
2   Walker, M. (2017) Why Do We Sleep, *Penguin.*

Chapter 13: Impact
1   Ogden, P. (2023) How Trauma Affects Body & Mind.
https://www.youtube.com/watch?v=5R3Bl-o1IjQ

Chapter 14: Healing Options
1   Rogers, C. R. (1951). Client Centred Therapy. *London: Constable and Robinson.*

Chapter 16: Project Client Recovery
1   *Integrative   counselling*   (2022)
https://www.counselling-directory.org.uk/integrative-herapy.html#whatistheaim ofintegrativecounselling

2   McManus, S. et al. (2016). Mental health and well-being in England: Adult Psychiatric Morbidity Survey 2014, *Leeds: The Mental Health Foundation NHS Digital.* http://digital.nhs.uk/catalogue/PUB21748.

3   Pybis, J. (2017) 'The comparative effectiveness and efficiency of cognitive behaviour therapy and generic counselling in the treatment of depression: evidence from the 2nd UK National Audit of psychological therapies', *BMC Psychiatry,* volume 17, Article number: 215 (2017). https://bmcpsychiatry.biomedcentral.com/articles/10.1186/s12888-017-1370-7

Chapter 18: Spiritual Research1 Brierley Consultancy (2016). Christianity in the UK. *Faith Survey.* https://faithsurvey.co.uk/uk-christianity.html

2   McSherry, W. (2010). Royal College of Nursing Spirituality Survey, *London: Royal College of Nursing.* https://journals.rcni.com/nursing-standard/understanding-spirituality-and-spiritual-care-in-nursing-aop-ns.2017.e10311

3   McSherry, W. (2009). The Challenges of Teaching Spirituality in Palliative Care, *Staffordshire University and the Shrewsbury and Telford Hospital NHSTrust.* nurselearning.s3.amazonaws.com/lecture_wilf_spirituality.ppt

Chapter 19: The Role of Religion

1   Church allowed abuse by priest for years (6 Jan 2002) *Boston Globe Media*   *Partner* https://www.bostonglobe.com/news/special-reports/2002/01/06/church-allowed-abuse-priest-for-years/cSHfGkTIrAT25qKGvBuDNM/story.html

Chapter 22: The Do Loop

1   Bhikkhu, T. translated (2006) Anapanasati Sutta: Mindfulness of Breathing   Access   to   Insight   *(BCBS   Edition).* https://www.accesstoinsight.org/tipitaka/mn/mn.118.than.html

Chapter 23: How It Works

   1   Waite, D. (2019) A Brief Introduction to Meditation, https://www.youtube.com/watch?v=IQ-yNzaimOA

   2   Waite, D. (2019) Meditation Can Transform Your Life—Mental Health, https://youtu.be/Uf5r6gT4lzw

3   Marsh, J. (2012) Do Mirror Neurons Give Us Empathy?, *The Greater Good Science Centre at the University of California, Berkeley*, https://greatergood.berkeley.edu/article/item/do_mirror_neurons_give_empathy

Chapter 24: Spiritual Depth

1   Waite, D. (Winter 2014). It's God's Job to do the Ripples, *Thresholds: BACP Lutterworth.*

2   Wax, R. (2013) Sane New World, *London: Hodder and Stoughton.*

3   Waite, D. Thresholds, (Spring 2016). The Sound of Silence. *Thresholds: BACP Lutterworth.*

Chapter 25: The Vedic Tradition

1   Swami Krishnananda (2020) The Mandukya Upanishad. *Divine Life Society*
https://www.swami-krishnananda.org/mand/mand_invoc.html

Chapter 31: The Malware

1   Brogaard, B. (2012) Sleep Driving and Sleep Killing. *Psychology Today.*
https://www.psychologytoday.com/gb/blog/the-superhuman-mind/201212/sleep-driving-and-sleep-killing
https://en.wikipedia.org/wiki/Homicidal_sleepwalking

2   Crime and Investigation (2019)
https://www.crimeandinvestigation.co.uk/article/she-killed-her-husband-but-sally-challen-might-be-the-real-victim

Chapter 32: Developmental Theory

1   Surviving Teenagers—*Skills for Life: Family Lives.*

Chapter 33: Pathology

1   Torjesen, I. (2016) 'Austerity cuts are eroding benefits of Sure Start children's centres' *BMJ,* 352, 19 January 2016.
https://doi.org/10.1136/bmj.i335

2   Treatment Advocacy Centre (September 2016) Serious Mental Illness Prevalence in Jails and Prisons.

http://www.treatmentadvocacycenter.org/evidence-and-research/learn-more-about/3695

3   Kaiser Permanente and the Centers for Disease Control and Prevention *(2014)*. The Adverse Childhood Events (ACE). *Injury Prevention & Control: Division of Violence Prevention*
https://web.archive.org/web/20151227092712/http://www.cdc.gov/violenceprevention/acestudy/index.html

Chapter 35: Resolving Stresses

1   Autistica   (2023).
https://www.autistica.org.uk/what-is-autism/anxiety-and-autism-hub/alexithymia#:~:text=What%20is%20Alexithymia%3F,depression%20and%20in%20autistic%20people.

Chapter 36: The Normal Curve

1   Bai, D. et al. (17/7/2019). 'Association of Genetic and Environmental Factors with Autism in a 5-Country Cohort', *JAMA Psychiatry,* 2019; 76(10):1035–1043.
https://jamanetwork.com/journals/jamapsychiatry/fullarticle/2737582

Chapter 37: Smart Pathology

1   Mosley, M. (22 November 2017). Trust Me I'm a Doctor, *Mental Health Special on BBC.*
2   Black, D. (1999) Bad Boys Bad Men, *Oxford University Press.*
3   Mallett, X. (2015) 'The difference between a psychopath and a sociopath',   *The*   *Independent.*
https://www.independent.co.uk/life-style/health-and-families/the-difference-between-a-psychopath-and-a-sociopath-10422016.html
4   Navarro, J. (2014). 'Why Predators Are Attracted to Careers in the Clergy', *Psychology Today.*
https://www.psychologytoday.com/gb/blog/spycatcher/201404/why-predators-are-attracted-careers-in-the-clergy

Chapter 38: My Revelation

1   Gaslighting (2023). https://www.relate.org.uk/get-help/gaslighting
2   (2023). https://en.wikipedia.org/wiki/Gaslighting

3   Skeel, A. Domestic abuse survivor was 'days from death'.
https://www.bbc.co.uk/news/uk-england-beds-bucks-herts-43799850,
https://en.wikipedia.org/wiki/Alex_Skeel

Chapter 39: Neuroscience
1   Fecteau, S. (2008) 'Psychopathy and the mirror neuron system:
Preliminary findings from a non-psychiatric sample', *Psychiatry Research*,
Volume 160, Issue 2, 15 August 2008, Pages 137–144.
2   Marsh, A. (2012) When psychopathy impairs moral judgments: neural
responses during judgments about causing fear *Soc Cogn Affect Neuroscience*.
v.9(1); 2014 Jan PMC3871724
https://www.ncbi.nlm.nih.gov/pmc/articles/PMC3871724/

Chapter 41: Upbringing
1   Caspi, A. (2003) 'Influence of life stress on depression: moderation by
a polymorphism in the 5-HTT gene', *National Centre for Biotechnology
Information.*
https://www.ncbi.nlm.nih.gov/pubmed/12869766
2   Autism, Meditation and Stress, a global webinar (2013). ***David Lynch
Foundation.***Tm-autism.org,
https://www.youtube.com/watch?v=M1mKDkmcpag

Chapter 43: Manipulation
1   Vitacco, M. J. et al. (2005) 'Testing a Four-Factor Model of
Psychopathy and Its Association With Ethnicity, Gender, Intelligence and
Violence', *National Center for Biotechnology Information.*
2   Alegria, A. (2013) 'Sex differences in Antisocial Personality Disorder:
results from the National Epidemiological Survey on Alcohol and Related
Condition', *National Center for Biotechnology Information.*

Chapter 47: Prevalence
1   Hill-Tout, J. (2004) The psychopaths in suits. *BBC News Online Wales*.
http://news.bbc.co.uk/1/hi/wales/3395443.stm
2   Dutton, K(2012) The Wisdom of Psychopaths, *Random House.*

3   Werner, K. (2015) 'Epidemiology, Comorbidity and Behavioural Genetics of Antisocial Personality Disorder and Psychopathy', *National Center for Biotechnology Information*
https://www.ncbi.nlm.nih.gov/pmc/articles/PMC4649950/

Chapter 50: Deeper Psychology
1   Cleckley, H. M. (1941) The Mask of Sanity: An Attempt to Clarify Some Issues about the So-Called Psychopathic Personality.
https://www.psychologytoday.com/gb/articles/201305/how-spot-sociopath

Chapter 53: Collective Pathology
1   Babiak, P. (2010) 'Corporate Psychopathy: Talking the Walk', *Wiley InterScience.* https://www.sakkyndig.com/psykologi/artvit/babiak2010.pdf

Index